Introduction to
GLOBAL SUSTAINABLE MANAGEMENT

Sara Miller McCune founded SAGE Publishing in 1965 to support the dissemination of usable knowledge and educate a global community. SAGE publishes more than 1000 journals and over 800 new books each year, spanning a wide range of subject areas. Our growing selection of library products includes archives, data, case studies and video. SAGE remains majority owned by our founder and after her lifetime will become owned by a charitable trust that secures the company's continued independence.

Los Angeles | London | New Delhi | Singapore | Washington DC | Melbourne

Colin Combe

Introduction to
GLOBAL SUSTAINABLE
MANAGEMENT

Los Angeles | London | New Delhi
Singapore | Washington DC | Melbourne

Los Angeles | London | New Delhi
Singapore | Washington DC | Melbourne

SAGE Publications Ltd
1 Oliver's Yard
55 City Road
London EC1Y 1SP

SAGE Publications Inc.
2455 Teller Road
Thousand Oaks, California 91320

SAGE Publications India Pvt Ltd
B 1/I 1 Mohan Cooperative Industrial Area
Mathura Road
New Delhi 110 044

SAGE Publications Asia-Pacific Pte Ltd
3 Church Street
#10-04 Samsung Hub
Singapore 049483

Editor: Ruth Stitt
Assistant editor: Jessica Moran
Digital content assistant: Mandy Gao
Production editor: Sarah Sewell
Copyeditor: Christine Bitten
Proofreader: Rosemary Morlin
Indexer: Caroline Eley
Marketing manager: Lucia Sweet
Cover design: Bhairvi Vyas
Typeset by: C&M Digitals (P) Ltd, Chennai, India
Printed in the UK

Library of Congress Control Number: 2021945337

British Library Cataloguing in Publication data

A catalogue record for this book is available from the British
Library

ISBN 978-1-5297-7174-9
ISBN 978-1-5297-7173-2 (pbk)

CONTENTS

CONTENTS

DETAILED CONTENTS

INTRODUCTION TO GLOBAL SUSTAINABLE MANAGEMENT

INTRODUCTION TO GLOBAL SUSTAINABLE MANAGEMENT

LIST OF FIGURES

LIST OF TABLES

ONLINE RESOURCES

Lecturers can visit **https://study.sagepub.com/combe** to access a range of online resources designed to support teaching. *Introduction to Global Sustainable Management* is accompanied by:

FOR LECTURERS

- A **Teaching Guide** containing case study teaching notes and model answers to questions in the book
- **PowerPoint decks** that can be adapted and edited to suit specific teaching needs
- **SAGE Business Cases** providing real-life examples from the global business environment

ACKNOWLEDGEMENTS

I am grateful to the many people who helped in the compilation of this book including colleagues from the Glasgow School for Business and Society at Glasgow Caledonian University (GCU). In particular, I thank Dr Niladri Palit and Angela Sutherland for their valuable contributions to case studies and Dr Alec Wersun, Dr Shariq Sheikh, Dr Vasilios Stouraitis and Lynn Lang for their collegiality and expertise in the delivery of sustainability teaching at GCU. The contributions to a case study by Hugo Pinto (University of Coimbra) and Carla Nogueira (University of Algarve) in Portugal are also greatly appreciated, as is the case study by Antonio Cecchi Fyfe from the University of Santiago in Chile. I have also benefited from the valuable guidance and feedback support of the editorial team at Sage including Ruth Stitt and Jessica Moran. Finally, personal acknowledgements go to Debbie, Richard and Ruby for their patience and understanding throughout the compilation of this work.

ABOUT THE AUTHOR

Dr Colin Combe is a senior lecturer in strategic management at Glasgow Caledonian University (GCU). He is academic lead for the MSc International Business Management programme and teaches modules in strategic management, sustainability, corporate social responsibility, entrepreneurship and innovation to a range of undergraduate and postgraduate courses. His research interests are in sustainable innovation strategies, innovation in the creative industries and e-commerce. Previously, he has worked as research consultant for the World Bank culminating in a report into business capacities in Eastern Europe. Colin has generated research income by representing GCU on the ERDF-funded INNOVATE project that focused on economic growth strategies for the knowledge-based and creative industries in the Atlantic Area of Europe. He has also been GCU principal investigator for the ERDF-funded HARVEST ATLANTIC project researching economic development of the maritime economy and lead partner for the 4H-CREATE project for the development of innovation in the creative industries. He is the author of two books on e-commerce and management.

PREFACE

The book provides a valuable introduction, explanation and discussion around key areas of sustainability management on a global basis. The content presents concepts, ideas, examples and theoretical perspectives on sustainability management that is of use to academics, students and practitioners. The book is of particular value to undergraduates and postgraduates who are new to the study of sustainability management. With this in mind, the content has been crafted and designed in a way that specifically appeals to those who are seeking an accessible and insightful introduction to the key management issues and functions around the concept of sustainability. Although the language of business is adopted, the narrative style is lucid and understandable with key concepts clearly explained and supported with examples and definitions. The book adopts a range of learning approaches including explanations, critical evaluation, case studies, text-based analysis, and follow up questions and tasks. The additional online material adds a further teaching resource that includes PowerPoint slides, and model answers to the questions and tasks.

The book comprises ten chapters and begins with an introduction to the concept of sustainability management followed by a theoretical treatment of the concept and the wider issues of sustainability, and stakeholder and sustainability value. The book goes on to cover the key aspects of management including strategic thinking, operations, and marketing in the context of sustainability. Underpinning much of the discussion throughout the book is the way that managers deal with challenges of aligning economic, social and environmental factors and this is given detailed treatment in the chapter on the Triple Bottom Line. The skills and competences required to drive forward the sustainability agenda are discussed from the perspectives of contributions made from government, business and education. The wider issues of ethics and corporate social responsibility are a key feature of efforts to advance sustainability practices across different business and industry sectors and is the subject of discussion and debate in the book. The way in which managers can influence the development of a positive organisational culture around sustainability is discussed using relevant theoretical frameworks. The book rounds off with a treatment of sustainability leadership which highlights some theoretical perspectives of leadership applied in different contexts.

The book has a distinctively international flavour with a series of mini and chapter case studies used to illustrate how the key concepts and ideas around sustainability management are applied in the real world. Cases have been specifically chosen to include all regions of the world and feature examples from advanced economies such as the USA, Japan and Germany, the newly emerging economic powerhouses of India and Brazil, emerging economies such as Chile and Turkey, as well as some nations with a specific interest in sustainability such as Costa Rica and the Maldives. Case studies in the chapter on leadership give examples of effective forms of leadership that have advanced the cause of sustainability and include key influencers from the world of business, science and politics. The international focus of the book, alongside the narrative style and examples, is designed to offer a truly multi-ethnic, diverse and global character to the work and to align to the attitudes, mindset and values of the modern student body. The content provides a valuable understanding of how to apply tools, techniques and management practices that help better understand how sustainability practices can be implemented in different industry sectors across the globe.

The issue of sustainability has become part of the national discussion in societies around the globe and this book provides a timely and valuable contribution to those seeking to better understand the role of management in pursuing the sustainability agenda with vigour and skill. This book is designed to enhance learning around the subject matter and improve understanding of the concept from an international perspective. Importantly, the content discusses management functions and related issues within a cultural and societal context to enhance its relevance to the wider community. At a time when the effects of climate change are becoming all too real for ordinary citizens around the world, this book provides knowledge, explanation and insight into how managers can shape and influence the development of sustainability practices around the world as a means of tackling some of the most pressing economic, social and environmental challenges of our times.

INTRODUCTION TO GLOBAL SUSTAINABLE MANAGEMENT

1

GLOBAL SUSTAINABLE MANAGEMENT: INTRODUCTION

LEARNING OUTCOMES

- Understand the concept of management and the functions of management.
- Appreciate the characteristics of sustainability management.
- Comprehend the context of global sustainability management when global business and sustainability interests intersect.
- Be able to critically evaluate sustainability management activities in different organisations.

INTRODUCTION

At the beginning of the third decade of the twenty-first century, humanity has been confronted by one of its most serious threats in the form of the Coronavirus pandemic. The sheer scale of death and disruption that the disease caused has been felt by communities on a truly global scale. No event in modern history has had such a devastating effect on lives, economic security and social cohesion. It has stretched healthcare resources to breaking point, led to high levels of unemployment, and transformed ordinary social lives in ways unimaginable only a few years previously. The pandemic has set challenges to governments, business and society that will be focused on recovery and, eventually, a return to normal life. The world has been subjected to a shock that has fundamentally altered the way in which people live their lives. And yet, even before the onset of the pandemic the world was under enormous stresses as the demand for resources to satisfy seemingly unending wants and needs of the ever-growing population placed the global eco-system under almost intolerable pressure. Population expansion has led to the rise of mega-cities, huge infrastructure programmes to service global demand for products and services, and unprecedented levels of social mobility as people migrate to places around the world that offer better opportunities and a more prosperous way of life.

The phenomenon of globalisation has been the catalyst for increasing economic growth not only in developed countries but also a raft of emerging economies such as Indonesia, Vietnam and Mexico. However, there have been significant costs associated with this growth that raises questions as to what the future of globalisation will look like. Martin et al. (2018) explain how globalisation is at a critical conjuncture. The emphasis on expanding production to meet global demand for products and services has depleted many of the world's resources to critical levels; fossil fuel use has raised carbon emissions to dangerous levels leading to increasing global temperatures; climate change has brought drought, fires and flooding that has devastated communities. At the political level there has been some progress in addressing these and other pressing problems such as climate justice, workers' rights and equality; however, so much more needs to be done. Although the United Nations Climate Change Conference in Glasgow in November 2021 addressed some important issues, progress on climate change at the policy level has been slow, demand for resources continues to rise, and there are large areas of the globe that remain marginalised from any benefit accrued by globalisation.

Alongside government and citizens, business plays a key role in driving the demand and supply of products and services, consuming huge amounts of resources whilst engaging in the on-going innovative processes that help deliver newer and better products and services. However, within this paradigm many organisations have started to address the issues of sustainability, climate change, workers' rights and many of the other factors associated with modern societies. In some ways, consumers are beginning to flex their market power by being more discerning about the types of products and services they buy, thereby forcing the hand of organisations to meet the expectations of consumers and other stakeholders. Where once, managers could largely ignore these issues, increasingly it is evident that companies are proactively including means of tackling them into their strategies. The key challenge is to maintain levels of growth, whilst simultaneously engaging in activities that do no harm to the environment, ensure sustainability in the use of resources, and maintain levels of social responsibility that demonstrate their commitment to ethical ways of doing business.

Traditionally, managers have concentrated on activities that improved internal efficiencies to become more productive and cost effective, or develop new products and services to expand demand or entice new customers; or access resources that could be transformed into attractive outputs. These and other activities such as marketing and customer service form the main areas of activities across a large number of commercial organisations. Management practice became specialised around many of these activities and some were focused on integrating them (Daft and Benson, 2016). In the modern era these still form the mainstay of activities in most commercial organisations. However, increasingly, the management role has extended to undertake these activities in ways that are sustainable. That is, sustainable activities do not deplete the world's resources to an extent that it places pressure on the very eco-system that we all rely on. The requirement for managers to adopt sustainable practices has now become a vital part of their skills and requires new ways of thinking about how they operate and apply their knowledge. This book focuses on sustainability management in a global context by introducing ideas and concepts around sustainability practices in many of the activities outlined above, such as operations and supply chain management, marketing, and strategy. The book also introduces the skills and competencies managers are required to deploy for sustainability, the leadership that champions and promotes sustainability management, and how managers can meet the challenge of operating a business in an ethical manner that demonstrates good corporate social responsibility whilst maintaining a competitive edge. First, it is necessary to define the key terms of management, sustainability management and, finally, global sustainability management.

MANAGEMENT

Management as a practice has a long history and is expressed in a multitude of ways and in many different contexts. Most of us apply management in some form during our private and professional lives such as in managing people, finances, work schedules, leisure time and so on. Such is the prevalence of management in ordinary lives that it has attracted the attention of celebrated academics such as Henry Mintzberg and Peter Drucker with both providing valuable insights into the theory and application of management in different settings. According to Mintzberg (1989) the key characteristics of management include:

- ensuring the efficient production of goods and services
- designing and maintaining the stability of organisational operations
- adapting the organisation, in a controlled way, to the changing environment
- ensuring that the organisation serves the ends of those persons who control it
- serving as the key information link between the organisation and its environment
- operating the organisation's status system.

Alternatively, Drucker (2001) presents five key tenets of management as being:

- making people's strengths effective and their weaknesses irrelevant
- enhancing the ability of people to contribute
- integrating people in a common venture by thinking through, setting and exemplifying the organisational objectives, values and goals

- enabling the enterprise and its members to grow and develop through training, developing and teaching
- ensuring everyone knows what needs to be accomplished, what they can expect of managers and what is expected of them.

Mintzberg's views on management are firmly set in the domain of the organisation, whereas Drucker emphasises the human element whereby management facilitates the coordination of skilled and knowledgeable people in order to achieve common goals. Both recognise the need for managers to carry out specific function to achieve those goals.

> **Definition: Management** is the organisation and coordination of activities to achieve stated aims and objectives.

FUNCTIONS OF MANAGERS

The main functions of managers can be identified as forecasting and planning, organising and coordinating, leading, and controlling as illustrated in Figure 1.1.

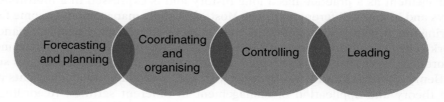

FIGURE 1.1 *Functions of management*

Forecasting and planning

Forecasting and planning is future oriented whereby assessments are made about factors that may impact on the business and then making contingency plans for them. Some factors are easily identified and planned for, such as increases in business rates or corporation tax; others prove to be more problematic or unexpected, such as the collapse in demand caused by Coronavirus. To manage all scenarios requires the coordination of effort, a clearly set out direction for the business, an ability to absorb negative impacts and a plan for taking the business forward. Forecasting and planning plays a key role in this process and managers have to be adept and astute enough to understand the environment in which their business operates and to make effective decisions based on the information and knowledge they acquire (Hanke and Wichearn, 2013). The more precise that information and knowledge is, the more managers are able to make effective decisions.

Planning requires managers to pinpoint and choose necessary goals and supporting actions for an organisation and largely determines its effectiveness. Both the forecasting and planning functions take place in a dynamic and changing environment where not all information and knowledge is available. Planning for the future is an integral part of management in all organisations and is, therefore, linked to forecasting in an effort to reduce the risks associated with decision-making. This is especially the case with large scale investments in infrastructure or technology whereby the risks and costs need to be matched with the likely benefits. For example, the proposed HS2 train line linking London with Manchester has to take into account factors such as increased environmental impacts, demand for rail travel set against that of other modes of transport, the benefits to business of increased transport connectivity, and the financial cost of construction and maintenance. Forecasting and planning help to inform decisions on projects of this magnitude that have significant social, economic and environmental implications.

Organising and coordinating

Organising as a management function is necessary to ensure that the correct type and quantity of resources are made available for the business to deliver products and/or services. This involves organising processes to support the activities of employees, financial requirements and the materials. Part of the organising function is the grouping of human resources into divisions or departments that align to specific types of tasks performed. This extends to formalising lines of authority, power and control that, ultimately, form the organisational structure. By organising a formal structure, managers are better able to coordinate resources that are deployed to achieve goals. Coordinating involves the manager working collaboratively with others to ensure business continuity and normally involves effective communication of information between employees and management. The achievement of stated aims and objectives of a business is often the result of effective coordination between different levels of management (functional, middle and executive) and employees whereby work activities and outcomes are aligned to the organisational resources and capabilities.

Leading

Leading is a function that requires managers to set the direction of the business, and devise and present a clear mission and vision that employees and other stakeholders can understand and support (Kotter, 1990). Leaders are given power and influence and need to use these to good effect when persuading others to follow their direction. Necessarily this requires good communications and negotiating skills, but very often leaders set an example by demonstrating a commitment and motivation to the business that sets the tone for others to follow. There is a distinction to be made between management and leadership with the former relating to functional types of activities to achieve set outcomes. Leadership, on the other hand, requires an element of management but is complemented by personal qualities such as charisma, interpersonal skills, analytical and critical skills, the ability to communicate ideas, and motivational skills. Essentially, leaders need to influence the behaviours of others in ways that align to their vision and aims. Effective leaders are able to achieve this without coercion but rather through persuasion and influence or by leading by example.

Controlling

Finally, the control function determines the link between activities carried out and a set plan. Different organisations have different levels of control depending on what the process of production is, the culture of the company (and the industry in which it operates), norms of behaviour, output levels, etc. For example, the civil service in the UK needs a high level of control because what they are engaged in is process driven with set outputs required at specific times such as in the case of pensions or welfare benefits. In other settings the control function may be more relaxed. In many of the creative industries there is no discernible hierarchy of authority and relationships are much more informal. Compare and contrast that with the army or police where a formal hierarchy and status underpins the high level of control. By undertaking control measures, managers can determine the extent to which the business is reaching set targets and goals and implement corrective action where necessary (Merchant, 1982). In many instances, the result of effective control is performance efficiency and effectiveness.

Mini case 1.1: Google, USA

Google is one of the world's biggest and high-profile technology companies with a brand recognised globally and a reputation for high performance. Driving that performance is management and the workforce. Traditionally, these two entities have been separated with the former issuing direction and instruction to the latter. At Google, the senior management wanted to find out what made good, effective management so that the role could be reconfigured to reflect the outcomes. To facilitate this process the company first reduced the level of power and authority that managers had over workers. Instead, the ethos switched to one where managers served the workforce and not the other way round. Rather than a culture based on reward for results, the emphasis was on unblocking barriers to effective communications and inspiring and motivating teams.

Project Oxygen was initiated to discover what made effective managers. Named because having better managers would be like a 'breath of fresh air', the project involved a series of interviews with workers and managers. The feedback from workers helped to identify the key characteristics of the best managers that included fair assessments of performance; helpful advocacy in meeting personal career objectives; efficiency in work and decision-making; treating team members equally and with respect; involving others in decision-making; and support for a work–life balance.

Managers at Google also provided insightful responses to interviews which led to the identification of eight common characteristics of the best managers. These included being a good coach; empowerment of the team and not micro-managing; expressing interest in the personal and professional lives of team members; being result oriented; being a good communicator; helping with career development; having a clear vision or strategy for the future; and possessing good technical skills that can be used to advise the team.

The results from Project Oxygen allowed the company to identify core behaviours of good managers and efforts were then made to introduce them into the management skillsets and mindsets. Although the project was a useful contribution to understanding what makes a good manager, one of the criticisms of the outcomes was that so many of the characteristics were already known. The project did not reveal many new insights beyond the context of the staff at Google. Perhaps the most important lesson from the project is that management comes in many different forms, styles and techniques. It is not useful to design a template for what makes a good manager as the environment, culture and requirements vary so markedly between different organisations operating in many different industry sectors.

Questions and task

1. What are the eight common characteristics of 'best managers' identified by managers at Google?
2. What parts of Project Oxygen specifically focused on human resource support?
3. Identify some limitations to the effectiveness of Project Oxygen.

SUSTAINABILITY MANAGEMENT

Often referred to as the three bottom lines, the key elements that managers have to consider are people, planet and profit. Very often the need to protect one of these compromises the ability to protect one or both of the others. For example, extracting and burning fossil fuel like coal and gas have long been known to be harmful to the environment, but has driven huge profits to companies adept at exploiting these resources. In other instances, stringent regulatory regimes, such as the fishing industry, have limited the exploitation of other resources leading to under employment and an inability of firms to make profits that contribute to job creation and economic security. Balancing these three bottom-line elements has always been a management challenge and makes sustainable management practice all the more important.

> **Definition: Sustainability management** is where business and sustainability intersect and where management practices impact on the future prospects of the Triple Bottom Line of people, planet and profit.

Sustainability management is where business and sustainability factors become entwined and refers to the ways and means by which businesses manage their impact on people, planet and profit. The key to effective sustainability management is that it should contribute to the delivery of products and services in a competitive manner without compromising the environment and the capacity of the planet to function as a habitable eco-system. Sustainability management means focusing efforts on reducing waste, accessing and using resources in a responsible manner, reducing plastic dependency in packaging, creating a safe and healthy workplace for workers, creating social as well as economic value, working with supply chain partners to reduce carbon emissions, building in sustainability messages in marketing communications, protecting the physical environment, educating consumers on sustainability issues and many more. In the modern business environment, managers need to engage effectively with a wide range of stakeholders to communicate the value of sustainability and to put into place the actions required to support it. Conversely, consumers and citizens have been vocal in communicating their needs around sustainability that managers need to listen to and act in ways that reflect their expectations.

Sustainability management requires a new way of thinking about the role of the firm in society. Whilst firms remain creators of wealth and deliver jobs and products and services that consumers demand, there is also a wider remit around protecting the environment and driving innovation in new and eco-friendly ways of doing business. In many ways, modern managers are the change agents that deliver solutions to some of the world's most pressing problems. Some managers are champions of the sustainability cause and become leaders in their field by effectively communicating the value of sustainable practices to others including board members, employees, suppliers, partners and others. The late Anita Roddick, founder of the *Body Shop* is one of the most widely cited managers who championed the cause of business ethics and sustainability. Increasingly, it is evident that managers are building sustainability investments and actions into their business strategy so that a long-term and meaningful commitment is made. The realisation that innovation around sustainable activities has a real impact on profits, market share and brand loyalty plays into the consciousness of managers every bit as much as the principle that it is the 'right thing to do'. The ethical imperative sits alongside the economic drivers in the motivation of some managers adopting sustainable practices. In fact, there are different levels in which managers engage with the concept of sustainability. In some instances, managers meet regulatory requirements regarding sustainable practice, in others there is a proactive aspect to incorporating new ways of doing business in a sustainable manner, and in some, such as apparel producers *Patagonia* or construction company *Skanska*, it features as a central plank of the company strategy for achieving competitive advantage. Whatever level managers choose to apply there is a range of key principles that sustainability managers must apply in organisations. These include:

- meeting minimal regulatory thresholds for identified sustainable practice
- developing new and sustainable initiatives, goals and strategies
- matching the competitive agenda with sustainability goals and strategic aims
- communicating the sustainability goals and strategies to stakeholders (both internal and external)
- ensuring that goals and strategic aims are met through transparent measurement and reporting
- using the learning and knowledge gained through experience of implementing sustainability practices to inform new and innovative ways of doing business in future.

In many organisations the application of some or all of these principles requires cultural change. Traditional practices may be challenged by sustainability commitments and that is something managers have to be able to overcome. Very often the most important task facing managers is to gain the 'buy-in' from workers who may be resistant to the changes needed to become a sustainable business. This, and other management challenges, feature in Chapters 5, 9 and 10.

There are numerous attributes and skills that sustainability managers require to be effective. Some align to traditional forms of management linked to ensuring operational efficiency of their organisations and the deployment of resources to achieve set targets for production, marketing output, human resource outputs and so on. Chapters 6 and 7 provide insights into the ways in which sustainable practices can be included in some added value activities in organisations. This book examines a range of key factors and activities where managers need to deploy specific skills and competencies to maintain competitiveness underpinned by sustainable practices. Consequently, a sustainable manager needs to exhibit and demonstrate a range of key characteristics to be effective. These are summarised in Figure 1.2 and include, but are not exclusive of:

- a values-based belief system in support of sustainability practices
- an understanding and compassion for human and environmental factors affecting the future viability of the planet
- an ability to effectively communicate a business sustainability ethos and principles
- an ability to work in partnership with key stakeholders
- an ability to persuade, influence and negotiate with key decision-makers to support sustainable practices.

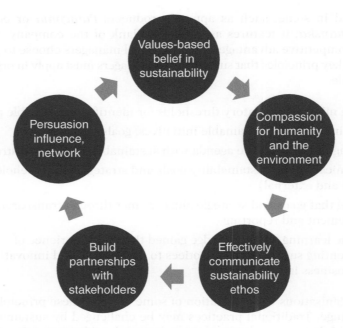

FIGURE 1.2 *Sustainability manager characteristics*

Sustainability management requires champions and leaders that support the ethos and principles of sustainability. Very often this is expressed in the core values they communicate to those around them and to the wider body of stakeholders. Managers have to possess a belief system that supports sustainable practices alongside one that supports the competitiveness of the organisation. Where these two imperatives conflict, managers need to strike a balance between them or find alternative solutions to accommodate both. This is perhaps the most challenging aspect of managing sustainability within a competitive environment and one that forms the basis of a wider discussion in Chapter 8. The effectiveness with which managers communicate and engage with stakeholders is key to building a culture of sustainability in organisations. In some cases, this will require negotiating skills with employees' representatives such as trade unions or specific workers' groups carrying out tasks where sustainability practices need to be introduced. These may prove to be delicate negotiations or acts of persuasion that transition working practices to those that align with sustainability practices. Externally, managers have to communicate the values of sustainability to suppliers, partners, trade bodies, NGOs, and even competitors as they try to influence new ways of thinking around sustainability issues across the industry in which they compete.

There is also a strategic aspect to sustainable management that requires long-term commitment to redirecting resources to support sustainability aims. This commitment may take many different forms but will almost certainly include a restructuring of the organisation to better align human resources to sustainable practices; a redefinition of existing skills and acquisition of new skills of human resources; the introduction of innovative processes to develop new and sustainable ways of operating and creating products and services; the redesign of marketing and promotional materials that better communicate the commitment to sustainable practices; and the development of strategic alliances with partner organisations that help to achieve competitive advantage in a sustainable manner that has economic as well as social value. Porter and Kramer (2007: 74–92) effectively articulate the link between competitive advantage and corporate social responsibility by stating that *'CSR can be much more than a cost, a constraint, or a charitable deed – it can be a potent source of innovation and competitive advantage'*. These are just some of many examples where the transition to sustainability can be achieved by managers incorporating the concept into their strategic thinking. This process forms much of the discussion in Chapter 3.

Mini case 1.2: Glengoyne Distillery, Scotland

The Scotch Whisky industry is a truly global operator with traditional markets in Europe, North America and Asia now being supplemented by growing demand in South America and Russia. Glengoyne Distillery is one of 128 licensed distilleries in Scotland and nestles in the picturesque countryside surrounding the village of Dumgoyne, north of Glasgow. This family-owned distillery was established in 1833 and subsequent generations of managers have been committed to producing the unique single malt whisky whilst ensuring that the precious environment from which it is made is protected and nurtured. Sustainable management has been a key feature of the organisation for many decades and has evolved as new knowledge, techniques and innovations develop. In particular, management have sought to find ways in which the raw material of water can be used in a responsible manner.

The distillery became the first in Scotland to trial new techniques in the surrounding wetlands with the aim of reducing waste and maximising the use of energy. The Glengoyne wetlands comprise 12 individual water cells that contain many thousands of types of plants. Sustainable use of the resource means that waste can be treated naturally and does not have to be transported to disposal sites elsewhere. Reed beds are used to filter effluence naturally and after a process of anaerobic fermentation the water is returned to the distillery river in pure form. The initiative has required managers to trade off short term gains (carbon emitting fuel processes that generate the same outcome is cheaper) against the long-term benefits of meeting expectations of consumers.

Glengoyne distillery is making investments in supporting the environment that they depend on in ways that are sustainable but also enhances the reputation of

(Continued)

the brand. Management at the distillery are aware of the changing nature of global demand that increasingly exhibits loyalty around not only traditional factors such as quality and distinctiveness, but also the manner in which products are produced and the environmental impacts they have. By being proactive in seeking innovative ways in which the distillery can demonstrate a commitment to supporting sustainable practices there are competitive as well as environmental benefits to be gained. Management at the organisation exhibits many of the characteristics of sustainable management including a values-based belief system in support of sustainability practices; promotion of sustainable principles to consumers, distributors and other stakeholders; an ability to work collaboratively with stakeholders (such as wildlife experts in the case of the wetlands initiative); and a commitment to support and protect the environment in which they depend.

Question and tasks

1. What are the main markets for Glengoyne whisky?
2. Identify two activities that the Glengoyne Distillery has introduced that support the sustainable use of resources.
3. Identify an example of sustainability management at the Glengoyne Distillery and explain how it creates value.

Beyond the skills and competencies of sustainability managers there are three other important traits that define their effectiveness. These are accountability, flexibility and authenticity. Sustainability managers need to be as transparent as possible in the ways in which they carry out their duties and report on the outcomes of the sustainable activities in their organisations. They may rely on external verification of their sustainability credentials by applying reporting measures recognised by the wider community or they may undertake their own internal reporting procedures and then submit it to independent review. One of the criticisms of modern managers who claim to operate a sustainable business is that they 'self-report' without any independent scrutiny of their claims. Managers need to be accountable for the actions they take to build trust and to uphold standards expected by stakeholders.

Sustainability managers have to satisfy a wide range of different stakeholders who have potentially conflicting aims and expectations. The ability to manage those tensions and operate a sustainable business is a major challenge for modern managers. They require flexibility in thinking and acting to balance the needs of different stakeholders, to find solutions to seemingly intractable problems, and to think creatively about new ways of supporting the sustainable and ethical business (Weiss, 2008). Sustainability managers need the flexibility in thinking to challenge and, sometimes, discard orthodox ways of running their business. Instead, they need to be open to new ideas, receptive to innovation, collaborative in working with others, and proactive in implementing change. These key attributes define the modern manager and are highly sought after by organisations around the world as very often they resonate with customers, suppliers, partners and other stakeholders. In essence, they are often a source of competitive advantage when used to redefine an organisation as a sustainable business.

Above all else, sustainability managers have to be authentic. They need to have a genuine interest and passion for supporting the ethos of sustainability that finds expression in the way they communicate, manage, and lead their organisations. This authenticity is evident in the way in which managers champion the cause of sustainability across their industry and beyond. In many ways, managers need to create a profile and reputation as a leading voice in the quest to transition business towards the principles of sustainability. As such they need to influence others, persuade decision-makers to support sustainability practices and demonstrate a long-term commitment to pursuing sustainable goals. The combination of accountability, flexibility and authenticity can provide the basis for effective sustainability management.

GLOBAL SUSTAINABILITY MANAGEMENT

Since the Industrial Revolution starting in the eighteenth century, there has been year on year increases in production of products and services to service demand by a global population that has similarly been increasing. By the twentieth century markets had opened up across the globe and the explosion in populations served only to fuel demand that placed increasing amounts of stress on the planet's resources (Levitt, 1983). Many of the productive processes required raw materials that depleted the resources without any prospect of replenishment. This is what makes those activities unsustainable as there will come a point when the resources run dry. One of the consequences of exponential rises in the use of resources is the environmental impact that this has. Sustainability has transitioned from a 'good thing to do' to being a business necessity. Kiesnere and Baumgartner (2019) argue that the sustainability of the economy and society cannot occur without the sustainability of organisations and that companies need to integrate sustainability into the core of their organisation. The importance of sustainability management has been introduced in this chapter, but it is necessary to consider this in a global context partly because sustainability is a truly global issue but also because many modern companies operate in global markets or source from global suppliers.

> **Definition: Global sustainability management** is where global business and sustainability intersect and where managers in business that operate internationally undertake practices that impact on the future prospects of the Triple Bottom Line of people, planet and profit.

Global managers operate in organisations that have a global reach in terms of products and services and/or a global presence in the international trading arena. Global managers are responsible for managing groups of workers and overseeing operations across multiple international locations and usually involves dealing with staff, suppliers, partners and other stakeholders with diverse cultural characteristics, customs, and means of undertaking business. Bartlett and Ghoshal (1992) identify three strategic capabilities that companies need to compete effectively in global markets, namely, global-scale efficiency, local responsiveness, and the ability to leverage learning worldwide. Global-scale efficiency refers to the economies of scale that accrue to companies operating in global markets such that their average costs of production decrease. Local responsiveness is how effective companies are at serving the needs of customers in international markets. The learning process that companies experience provides invaluable knowledge that can be used to inform better decision-making in future. To affect advantage, it is necessary for groups of managers to integrate their assets, resources and people in a coordinated manner. Thus, the authors emphasise that no one single manager can affect this advantage so there needs to be a coordinated effort by groups of managers. Bartlett and Ghoshal identify three types of managers that fulfil the needs of a global business. These are:

- the global business manager who builds worldwide efficiency and competitiveness by identifying opportunities and risks and linking activities and capabilities on a global scale
- the country manager who builds knowledge of local markets, and acquires and deploys local resources and capabilities
- the functional specialist manager who transfers knowledge and expertise from one business unit to another across the globe by exploiting the learning around innovation, ideas and best practice.

Global managers need to possess a series of attributes to fulfil these obligations regardless of what type they fit into. These include being able to scan the environment for opportunities; to embrace diversity and the opportunities and challenges that cultural differences present; thrive in a rapidly changing environment; manage complexity and deploy an entrepreneurial mindset. The mindset of global managers should also feature a number of key attributes or characteristics. Rhinesmith (1992) lists them as constantly seeking context; viewing life as a balance of contradictions; focusing on process; valuing diversity and teamwork; seeing change as an opportunity; and striving for openness to the unexpected. These attributes and characteristics need to be contextualised around sustainability for managers to be considered global sustainable managers. Global sustainability managers apply these attributes and characteristics within a business ethos of sustainability across all the activities of the organisation. Figure 1.3 highlights some examples of sustainability activities in companies.

FIGURE 1.3 *Examples of sustainability activities in companies*

Global sustainability management involves developing and delivering low environmental impacts across all activities such as accessing sustainable materials, reducing waste and carbon emissions, protecting workers' rights, and promoting sustainability in promotional and marketing materials. One of the most important aspects of global sustainability management is developing, managing and implementing a sustainable supply chain strategy that features traceability of materials and reports on them in a transparent manner. For example, some furniture suppliers only source timber from regulated and accredited sources that are licensed to exploit specially grown wood in forests in West Africa. Each fallen timber is registered and tracked using RFID technology so that the material can be tracked from forest to customer. This allows control and sustainability of the logging operations and facilitates the replenishment of trees. Companies who demonstrate this traceability and transparency earn the trust of customers and, ultimately, help to protect the forests from illegal logging. As a guiding principle, global sustainable managers need to be proactive in engaging with suppliers by producing independently verified audits that help to drive ethical standards across supply chains. Organisations that are most proactive in supporting sustainability invariably build it into their structures whereby systems and processes are created to ensure traceability; reporting and compliance with standards are the remit of a departmental head.

Mini case 1.3: Dutch tulips, Netherlands

The Netherlands is famous for its flower growing and in particular the iconic tulip flower that is exported all over the world. The industry has been criticised in the past for its excessive use of pesticides to ensure high quality products are available. This has affected the reputation of the sector leading many bio-scientific organisations to collaborate on finding ways to adopt a more sustainable approach to production. Part of this process has relied on the vision of managers to bring together the necessary skills and experience of scientists to create the means of producing tulips faster and in a more sustainable manner. A consortium comprising three Dutch companies has been collaborating to deliver on this strategic aim since 2017. Scientists at BaseClear, Generade and Dummen Orange have been able to identify the DNA sequence of the tulip genome. The characteristics of a tulip emerge from DNA that is revealed by the tulip genome. This knowledge facilitates advanced breeding giving not only valued characteristics of the flower but also making them resistant to common diseases thereby reducing the need for plant protection products such as pesticides. It is now possible for growers to produce tulips faster and more sustainably than ever before.

Collaboration is evident across the tulip producing industry in the Netherlands including the formation of the Dutch Flower Group (DFG) comprising 33 member companies across the whole floral supply chain. Although the companies are independently managed, they all benefit from knowledge sharing leading to higher standards and better quality of product and service. The management of DFG has sustainability at the core of their efforts as they seek to introduce corporate social responsibility more prominently into their activities. Management have devised three key pillars supporting this effort including transparent and fair trade, sustainable deployment of employees, and a volume of at least 90% of sustainably purchased products. The DFG is a signatory to the United Nations Sustainable Development Goals and this guides many of their initiatives including carbon emission reductions, reduced waste and energy-efficient buildings.

Progress through collaboration has been evident across the supply chain of the industry but more needs to be done to reach ambitious targets. The industry is still grappling with different regulations related to the use of substances that are either banned in the EU or banned in the Netherlands or both. Companies have to comply with legal frameworks or risk damage to reputation. Managers across the sector have to collaborate to find solutions to some persistent problems facing production. This involves monitoring the use of chemicals, making plant protection information from experts available to growers, and working together to influence policy. Managers across the tulip (and other plants and flowers) industry in the Netherlands have seen the benefits of a proactive and collaborative approach to sustainability to protect the future of their industry and the welfare of flora across the region.

Questions and task

1. What UN SDGs link to the initiatives of DFG?
2. What are the barriers to effective sustainable practices of DFG?
3. Identify the key areas of sustainability that support corporate social responsibility at DFG.

It is important to understand the complexities and challenges posed by introducing sustainable practices. Business is not a community of homogenous organisations operating with similar practices. The experience of managers in companies situated in developed countries will be very different to their counterparts in emerging economies. That poses a number of challenges not just for business managers but also regulators, suppliers, consumers and other stakeholders. Differences in economic activity, access to materials, financial differentials, customs and practices mean that the issue of sustainability may be significantly more advanced in one part of the world as compared to another. This often presents dilemmas for managers of Western companies who seek to introduce sustainability practices across their portfolio of business around the globe. What works in a developed country may pose specific threats to business continuity in another. For example, in some countries, such as the Netherlands, the practice of recycling is firmly embedded in the consciousness of citizens and business follows suit. However, in other countries this is a relatively new concept with little 'buy-in' from citizens or the business community. To align such countries with the practice of others more used to practising recycling requires not just new processes to be put in place but also a significant cultural change at societal level. In some countries, such as Chile (copper and iron ore) and Ukraine (coal) the main source of income derives from extractive industries and to impose limitations on those would prove inordinately punitive to the economic security of those countries.

Consumers also play a role in maintaining practices that lack sustainability such as fast fashion products from low cost factories in Bangladesh or Indonesia, or furniture made from endangered species of trees such as the acacia from Mozambique. Very often communities in emerging economies rely on foreign direct investment as their source of income whether it is Nike factories in Cambodia or Volkswagen in Mexico. Workers in emerging economies are predominantly involved in the production of global brands rather than being the consumers of them. This state of affairs presents some ethical challenges for corporations who exploit cheap labour, lax regulatory regimes, and compliant governments. The necessary pursuit of competitive advantage has traditionally been the primary motivator for such companies, but this, in itself, is now unsustainable. Even large and powerful corporations need to align economic performance with sustainable practices or risk being alienated from the core beliefs of a significant swathe of consumers. Again, there is no uniformity in the timing and manner of scale to which companies transition to sustainable practices but there is a distinct trend towards incorporating some of the principles into management practice such as reducing waste, recycling or procuring eco-friendly supplies. In many ways, it could be argued, that large and financially robust companies are best placed to reallocate resources towards this transition. Small and medium sized companies have to invest a relatively higher proportion of their revenue to support sustainability practices. This accounts for the lag in adopting sustainable practices by SMEs compared to larger organisations.

Global sustainability managers have to effectively deal with a range of economic, social, cultural and environmental factors when designing sustainable strategies and implementing them in vastly different areas of the globe. In some instances, the alignment of sustainability practices with common local practice may prove impossible and lead companies to reassess their commitment to that region or even their commitment to being a sustainable business. Alongside addressing cultural challenges in the external environment, global sustainable managers may face some resistance to change internally. Research by Cameron and Quinn (2006) highlighted the existence of tools, techniques and strategies for implementing change in organisations. Akins et al. (2013) point to organisational culture determining the necessary organisational adaptability and flexibility required to support change in a competitive environment. If this is true of competitive environments then it is also relevant to the changes required to support sustainability. As global sustainable management gathers momentum it is clear that influencing the development of organisational culture is one of the key determinants of how successful companies will be in the transition to sustainability. Global sustainability management and organisational culture is explored in more detail in Chapter 9.

Global sustainability managers have to engage with support mechanisms to take forward their sustainability ambitions. The growing awareness of the importance of sustainability on protecting the planet and its environment has created numerous support agencies across different industries and attracted the attention of Non-Government Organisations (NGOs), charities, social enterprises and others. One of the most high profile initiatives is the United Nations Sustainable Development Goals that has been the catalyst for greater assessment and accountability among the business community regarding how they support sustainable practices. It is useful to highlight the purpose of the initiative and how global sustainable managers can support it. The UN SDGs present an opportunity to drive change in business by facilitating checks on their impact on society. The initiative is a set of goals that governments are expected to adopt. Signatories to the SDGs then encourage citizens and business to undertake appropriate actions to support them. There are 17 SDGs covering diverse global issues such as health, education, hunger, equality, consumption, environment, economic growth and others. Business is expected to make a meaningful contribution to helping governments achieve the goals and that is where global sustainability managers have to deliver on stated aims and objectives. For companies that sign up to the SDGs there is a need to transition from traditional ways of doing business to one where sustainability is at the core of their activities. The reputational capital, goodwill and resultant brand loyalty links the strategy for sustainability to economic growth as well as supporting ethical, responsible and environmentally friendly ways of doing business. The SDGs also highlight potential sources of competitive advantage. The range of challenges that address the world's most pressing problems presents opportunities for global sustainability managers to channel efforts into innovation, creativity and new means of doing business centred on the identified areas of need. There are economic and societal benefits to be gained. Both government and business signatories are interested in monitoring and assessing the impact of the SDGs and the outcomes inform the development of strategies to further positive outcomes in future.

CASE STUDY

Finlays, UK

The impact on the environment in the production of goods and services varies markedly between different industry sectors. The extractive industries, such as oil, gas and coal, exact relatively high costs in terms of the environmental costs of accessing, exploiting and using the products. In agri-business (agriculture conducted for commercial purposes), the use of pesticides and other chemicals similarly exhibits high costs to the environment. The production of rubber, tea, coffee and other products has generated huge wealth for producers, but the whole of society has to absorb the environmental costs (this is called negative externalities in economics). The counter argument is that products such as rubber provide huge benefits to society in the form of a multitude of products and processes that rely on the material. Industries such as tea, coffee and rubber create employment, very often in emerging or low-income economies.

Amid growing awareness by consumers of the environmental costs, these industries have had to become more proactive in dealing with environmental issues. For example, the production of natural rubber consumes large volumes of water and energy and requires the use of numerous chemicals to deliver the end-product. Waste and the discharge of pollutants into rivers and other dumping sites are not uncommon across the industry. The coffee industry requires land to cultivate the crop and the expansion of markets has led to deforestation in key growing areas such as Central America. Millions of acres of forest have been cleared for this purpose with potentially devasting impacts on biodiversity and wildlife species. Workers' rights have also been the focus of attention. In a briefing paper by Banjeri and Willoughby (2019), the tea growing region of Assam in India was identified as one where workers have been denied a basic living wage and decent living conditions. Many rely on government ration cards issued to those living under the poverty line. The paper provided evidence that pointed to 95% of the value of tea sold being the preserve of tea brands or supermarkets with the remaining 5% used to cover workers' wages. Companies that operate in these industries are under increasing pressure to address these and other environmental and human issues with some taking a more proactive approach.

Finlays is part of the global conglomerate Swire Group and has been active for over 200 years in producing, packing and supplying tea, coffee and botanicals to global markets. The company is also involved in producing timber, rubber, flowers and crops. Operating in North and South America, Europe, Africa, the Middle East and Asia, the company is a truly global player with around 24,000 employees and an annual sales value of over half a billion dollars in 2018 (*Finlays Sustainability Report*, 2018). The management at the company became acutely aware of the changing consumer attitudes to environmental issues, especially those that impact the physical environment of land and sea. It became clear that those companies whose products derived from exploiting land resources would need to demonstrate high standards of protecting the environment to maintain the confidence of consumers. Also, the company relies on the long-term viability of the landscape where their suppliers operate so there is a strategic aspect to business continuity that also motivated change along with a greater emphasis on workers' rights. The company was issued with a law suit in 2019 from a group of former workers in a subsidiary tea company in Kenya claiming that they were not provided with a safe working environment and that this had left them with health problems in retirement.

The company has been active in building a 'sustainability' programme with a strategy of incorporating the concept into its core values. This has involved managing the process of change across the organisation's global supply chain. The company assigned a Global Sustainability Manager to oversee this process and report results to the Head of Sustainability. The role requires not only passion and commitment to the sustainability cause, but a series of skills and attributes that can offer the type of leadership to take the strategy forward. This includes an ability to drive low impact initiatives with a focus on environmental compliance, understanding needs assessment, auditing and reporting; an understanding of international labour laws and processes for resolution of non-compliances; stakeholder engagement skills and relationship building skills with suppliers; and the ability to work in diverse cultures with an understanding of the differences in international business environments.

The sustainability initiative of Finlays reveals a number of key decision-making factors and motivations for implementing the strategy. First, the company were able to determine a shift in the values of customers that required a response. This links to retaining brand loyalty by reflecting the values of consumers. This is just one of several aspects of the strategy that impact on the pursuit of competitive advantage alongside the drive to demonstrate good corporate responsibility. Thus, the business and ethical aspects of the strategy form a mutually beneficial synergy. Whilst some of the actions that underpin the strategy can be applied relatively quickly and at low cost, such as reporting processes, others require long-term investments. For example, changing the relationship with suppliers to incorporate sustainability into their working practices may take time, negotiation, new sources of materials, and rescheduling of activities. Even though the motivation for undertaking the change to sustainable practices may be laudable, at the strategic level the investment still needs to be fully justified economically as well as ethically. In the case of Finlays the company benefits from the differentiation that sustainable practices deliver in terms of brand loyalty, reputational capital and goodwill of stakeholders.

INTRODUCTION TO GLOBAL SUSTAINABLE MANAGEMENT

To continue to benefit from the differentiation that sustainability brings, Finlays have to embed the initiatives into their sustainability strategy. To that end the management identified six key objectives set around the Triple Bottom Line criteria of people, planet and profit. The 'Sustainable Future' strategy launched in 2018 supports the long-term commitment to the six objectives with targets set for each to the year 2022. The six elements that form the strategic objectives are set out in Figure 1.4.

Integrated Landscapes set a target of protecting and enhancing 100k hectares of natural forest by 2022. This initiative aims to balance competing demands for land use linked to human activity, the environment and biodiversity. Key areas of concern include deforestation, climate change impacts, depletion of natural resources, economic and food security for local communities, tackling poverty, and sustainable development of industry. Finlays are proactive in developing tools and concepts designed to address these issues including partnerships with interested parties such as the South West Mau Forest Reserve in Kenya where they engage local farmers in best practices for livestock management. The 60,000 hectare area is a vital water catchment region and requires careful management of forests to ensure the sustainable use of resources and the protection of biodiversity. The company has also worked

FIGURE 1.4 *Finlays' Sustainable Future strategic objectives to 2022*

Source: Finlays Sustainability Report (2018)

with the Stawisha Mau Charitable Trust and the Initiative for Sustainable Landscapes to protect and rehabilitate forests. Finlays' management has developed the concept of integrated landscapes to contribute to the protection and viability of the landscape for the benefit of local communities and the environment while continuing to exploit it as a business asset in a sustainable manner.

Land Stewardship aims to reduce agro-chemical use by 50% by 2022. The strategic aim of land stewardship is closely linked to integrated landscapes where the company seeks to strike a balance between commercial exploitation of the land and the protection and sustainability of the land. Effective land management is the key to achieving this aim with the company investing in good agricultural practices (SANS) and sharing knowledge and expertise across their supply chains. In particular, the company is committed to reducing the use of agri-chemicals by placing more emphasis on practices that deliver better farm resilience, soil quality and yields. As a form of oversight into the effectiveness of these practices, the company has acquired a number of accreditations including those of Fairtrade and the Rainforest Alliance. These have been particularly important to demonstrate their sustainability credentials in tea and coffee growing countries such as Sri Lanka and Nicaragua respectively.

Our People has as a target an increase in the participation of women in management at all levels by 30% by 2022. Finlays operate a number of initiatives to underpin equality, fairness, opportunity and safety for their employees. Gender equality and opportunity is one aspect of this strategic aim that requires commitment and communication.

The company offers training and career development opportunities including the Management training and Entrepreneurship training schemes that are particularly aimed at increasing the number of women operating at management level or developing their own businesses. Very often this requires a significant cultural shift in attitudes in parts of the world where traditionally women have only played a maternal role in the family or worked in low skilled occupations. To manage this change requires effective communications skills, understanding of cultural norms and respect for traditional hierarchical structures in tribes and local communities. What appears to be a laudable ambition from a Western perspective may be viewed as a threat to traditional customs and practices that have characterised community cultures in Africa and Asia for many centuries. Clearly, the cultural shift needs to be managed with a high degree of sensitivity.

Low Impact Operations aims to reduce year on year the environmental impact of operations. Finlays are committed to better understanding their global footprint and the impact their operations have on people and the planet. The main products of tea, coffee and rubber have traditionally exacted a heavy price from the environment with high levels of land cultivation, demand on water resources, and the use of chemicals in the production process. These have been areas of great concern to the company as it pursues more sustainable means of production and distribution. Key aims are to reduce resource consumption and waste production, invest in technologies that help to reduce the carbon emissions on products and services, and to participate in the circular economy whereby waste and pollution is designed out of the system. Finlays has implemented a series of changes to support this initiative including transforming tea waste into biogas or compost, introducing a zero waste to landfill policy in the UK, recycling and waste segregation on tea plantations in Sri Lanka and Argentina, and developing new, innovative and sustainable packaging materials for their products.

Empowered Communities aims to ensure a positive impact in communities in which the company operates. This strategic aim means supporting actions that bring positive changes to communities where Finlays operate. Typical initiatives include training in best practices in land management and resource use, skills development, managing changing livelihoods, and supporting health and wellbeing. This has involved investments in water rehabilitation that ensures safe water for farming and domestic use. Finlays also provides economic security for a large number of people. The company employs around 24,000 people globally and consistently generates hundreds of millions of dollars in economic value.

Sustainable Supplies aims to have 100% traceable, transparent supply to internationally accepted standards by 2022. Finlays have built long-term relationships along the supply chains of all their products thereby creating a global network of stakeholders. Increasingly, the partnerships with local, small scale farmers or cooperatives of growers of tea and coffee has proved vital to the ambition of the company to demonstrate to their consumers the source of their products and their sustainability credentials. The company's aim to have all their products traceable and transparent by 2022 is a key component in their sustainability plans and will become the standard for building consumer confidence in future.

This case has revealed some of the challenges that global firms face when addressing the issue of sustainability and developing a strategy that balances the commercial ambitions with the principles that underpin the protection of the environment and human rights. The extractive industries and agriculture have been open to criticism for the disproportionately negative impact that their activities have had on both those elements thereby making the commitment to sustainability all the more prescient in the twenty-first century. Finlays operate across many industrial sectors where sustainability has become a key strategic issue and have been proactive in designing and implementing plans to achieve stated sustainability goals by 2022. In future, it will be possible to match the outcomes to set targets to determine how successful their global sustainability management has been in achieving their goals.

Questions and tasks

1. What is the main role and responsibilities of the Global Sustainability manager at Finlays?

2. What initiatives have Finlays introduced to support gender equality at the organisation?

3. Identify examples of what Finlay's management implement to support the Integrated Landscapes goal.

4. Research the CO_2 emissions data linked to the production of coffee, tea and rubber. What does the data reveal?

SUMMARY

The opening chapter has set out the background to the rise of sustainability as a concept in the consciousness of consumers, managers, suppliers, government and other stakeholders. To put global sustainable management in context the chapter started with definitions of management, key characteristics and a summary of the key functions of managers. The concept of management was then extended to offer explanations as to what constitutes sustainability management. Here, the functions of managers were extended to that of examining the business activities and sustainable practices in each. These practices can be part of the strategies implemented by firms depending on the level of commitment to sustainability exhibited by managers. Key principles of sustainable management were presented alongside some of the skills and attributes, most importantly accountability, flexibility and authenticity.

The chapter also gave attention to the context in which the book is compiled, namely, global sustainability management. This section put in context the rise of globalisation and global management by identifying the exponential increase in demand for products and services to service the huge explosion in the global population growth, especially throughout the twentieth century and beyond. The discussion called on theory from Bartlett and Ghoshal (1992) in identifying three key types of managers evident in driving forward global business. The chapter discussed the mindset of global sustainability managers and the attributes and characteristics that underpin good practice. However, the chapter also focused on the tensions that inevitably arise when implementing global sustainability management practices where economic and/or social and cultural factors present significant challenges to making the necessary changes when incorporating sustainability into traditional ways of doing business. Here, the discussion included the support mechanisms in place to encourage commitment to sustainable practices including the United Nations Sustainable Development Goals.

This introductory chapter has set the scene for the discussions around key aspects of global sustainability management in the forthcoming chapters. The concept of global sustainable management has attracted the attention of business leaders, consumers, suppliers, NGOs, government and many others. The issue of sustainability has become part of the global citizen narrative and has a high profile in reporting from media outlets around the world. Academics have also shown a great deal of interest in the concept and the next chapter uses some of the theoretical outputs to offer a better understanding of some key concepts and ideas around global sustainability management.

REVIEW QUESTION AND TASKS

1. What are the four main functions of managers?
2. Define a global sustainability manager.
3. List six key challenges facing global sustainability managers.
4. Research and list the 17 United Nations Sustainable Development Goals.

FURTHER READING

Molthan-Hill, P. (2017) *The Business Student's Guide to Sustainable Management: Principles and Practice* (2nd edn). Abingdon: Routledge.

This book is a useful contribution to both students and tutors with a broad range of sustainability issues discussed in a clear and precise manner by different authors. Each chapter has a suggested seminar structure that tutors can apply in class.

Rendtorff, J.D. (2019) *Philosophy of Management and Sustainability: Rethinking Business Ethics and Social Responsibility in Sustainable Development*. Bingley: Emerald Publishing.

This book brings together the disciplines of philosophy, business management and sustainability to enhance the understanding of the UN Sustainable Development Goals (SDGs). The book features key themes that explore the transition from CSR and business ethics to the SDGs, the philosophy of management and ethical economy of sustainability, and responsible management of sustainability.

Sroufe, R. (2018) *Integrated Management: How Sustainability Creates Value for Any Business*. Bingley: Emerald Publishing.

This book addresses the issue of what individuals, functions, organisations, value chains and cities can do to integrate and align sustainability. The discussion focuses on integrated management and strategic sustainable development as a means of enabling enterprise value propositions that include environmental, social and governance goals as measures of performance.

2

GLOBAL SUSTAINABLE MANAGEMENT THEORY

LEARNING OUTCOMES

- Appreciate the nature of theory as an academic practice.
- Understand the concept of sustainability management theory.
- Comprehend the different theoretical models used in the context of sustainability management.
- Assess the value of different theories and their use in understanding sustainability management.

INTRODUCTION

There are many different definitions of theory but most are variations around the theme of a set of principles around which the practice of an activity is based. Theoretical perspectives are developed to help us understand the world around us and the phenomena that comprise that world. The complexity and dynamic nature of the world means that the same phenomena can be viewed in different ways depending on the perspective. For example, differences in language, culture, climate, education, history and tradition are just some of the many factors that inform perspectives on different phenomena. Theory helps to create a construct or set of parameters within which a particular phenomenon or area of study can be investigated and analysed in more detail to elicit a greater understanding.

All academic subjects have evolved over time as knowledge on the subject matter is increased. Each has its own body of knowledge and theoretical models or frameworks around which that knowledge has been generated. Some theories are transferable across different disciplines whilst others are designed for a specific purpose within a specific discipline or area of investigation. Management theory is relatively new compared to that of the arts or sciences. Management only emerged as a recognised academic discipline in the mid-eighteenth century thanks largely to the development of the Industrial Revolution that spawned a number of studies into how best to manage resources in a mass production setting. Although management as a practice has been around for many centuries, for the purposes of this chapter the discussion focuses on the development of theory from this period.

> **Definition: Theory** is a set of principles designed to help explain a group of facts or phenomena.

Many transformational innovations and scientific breakthroughs start with the development of academic theory. The development of the World Wide Web interlinking computers and creating the internet (Sir Tim Berners-Lee at the European Organization for Nuclear Research – CERN), DNA fingerprinting (Sir Alec Jeffreys at the University of Leicester) and the development of the concept of microcredit and microfinance for the poor (Professor Muhammad Yunus at Chittagong University in Bangladesh) are a few examples. Academic enquiry through research is the foundation of knowledge that drives innovation and the myriad practical applications that deliver added value to the wider community. Academic research and the development of theory adds to the stock of global knowledge by providing a valuable source of concepts, ideas, methods, techniques and innovations across a wide range of disciplines.

This chapter offers a chronological account of the evolution of management thinking around the concept of sustainability. A common theme throughout the chapter is the critical analysis of the relevance of each of the theoretical perspectives to modern global sustainability managers. To aid this analysis, examples of the different perspectives in different organisational settings and timeframes are used.

SUSTAINABLE MANAGEMENT THEORY

It is clear that sustainability management requires a theoretical treatment that extends beyond that of traditional management theories. This is due to the lack of cognisance towards quality of life parameters and the understated impact of the natural world in the theoretical underpinning of academic outputs in management. Latterly, we have seen attempts to incorporate 'green' issues into existing theories and there has been a significant trend towards producing better informed discourse around sustainability management issues. Nevertheless, there remains much to explore and discover around sustainability management, thereby making the development of theory a work in progress. Given the complexity and range of factors that comprise sustainability management, it is likely that the formulation of theory will depend on an amalgamation of existing and new theoretical perspectives to offer new insights and understandings. For the purposes of this chapter the theoretical contributions feature stakeholder theory, stakeholder mapping, paradox theory, Balanced Scorecard and the sustainability value framework. These are illustrated in Figure 2.1 linked to the era in which they were first developed.

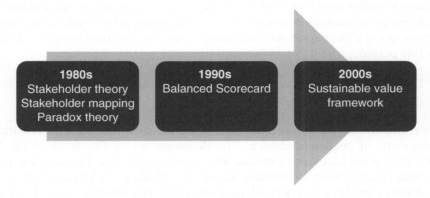

FIGURE 2.1 *Theoretical contributions for sustainability management*

STAKEHOLDER THEORY

Perhaps one of the most applied theoretical frameworks in the social sciences is Stakeholder Theory. This approach has been the means by which academics and practitioners have explored social and environmental phenomena in many different settings and contexts and has featured as part of research into sustainability management (Montiel and Delgado-Ceballos, 2014). To understand the theory, it is necessary to start with a definition of what a stakeholder is. This is no easy task as there are a multitude of different perspectives evident within the literature. Laplume et al. (2008) provide a valuable critical review of the development of stakeholder theory reaching as far back as the late nineteenth century. Gilbert and Rasche (2008) point to the lack of consensus around a definition as the consequence of the theory emerging from an 'amalgamation of eclectic narratives', meaning that the concept of the 'stakeholder' transcends business to feature in other disciplines too. Much depends on the purpose to which stakeholder theory is applied but for the purposes of this discussion it remains in the confines of the business world. Ian Mitroff's *Stakeholders of the Organizational Mind* (1983) provided a conceptual framework based on the idea that organisations should serve the needs of stakeholders and not just shareholders. The work proved to be a catalyst for increased attention on the development of stakeholder theory and the search for a definition.

One of the most cited definitions of a stakeholder is that provided by Freeman (1984) who perceived it as 'any group or individual who can affect, or is affected by, the achievement of the organization's objectives' (1984: 6). For the purposes of this section it is relevant to link stakeholder theory to sustainability management and for this we can call on the definition by Starik and Kanashiro (2013) and the framework design developed around that link. The authors define sustainability management as the formulation, implementation and evaluation of both environmental and socioeconomic sustainability-related decisions and actions.

There have been numerous different versions of stakeholder theory proposed ranging from the normative, where the discussion focuses on the purpose of business and the moral obligations therein (Freeman and Gilbert, 1988; Reed, 1999), to the instrumental, where contributions to achieving corporate goals form the basis of the discussion (Berman et al., 1999; Mathur et al., 2008). Also, the identification of key stakeholders forms the basis of the descriptive approach to understanding stakeholder theory (Sangle and Ram Babu, 2007; Wallis, 2006). However, for the purposes of explanation, this section sets out the integrative stakeholder theory where all three of these versions feature as linked factors (Freeman, 1999; Freeman et al., 2010). The guiding principle of the integrative approach of stakeholder theory posits that there is a mutual interest between managers and stakeholders rather than one based on trade-offs. Trade-offs refer to the preferences of managers for stakeholders who exhibit characteristics that enhance the position of management. The integrating approach views business success as being dependent on stakeholder inputs and, therefore, there is a mutual interest in stakeholder welfare. Consequently, the proponents of the integrative approach argue that stakeholder theory aims to create value for all stakeholders. Critics, such as Jensen (2002) argue that trade-offs will always exist but others, such as Horisch et al. (2014) counter by emphasising that in the context of sustainability management, managers are proactive in seeking the means to overcome trade-offs and that stakeholder interests should not be part of a trade-off (favouring one stakeholder group over another). This approach aims to integrate interests and forms the basis of identifying similarities and dissimilarities between stakeholder theory and sustainability management. Figure 2.2 summarises the similarities.

The first, and perhaps most fundamental issue, is that of the purpose of business. This philosophical debate has been on-going since the inception of business practices. To further the understanding of the integrated approach, the purpose of business is deemed to be broader than that of maximising short-term shareholder value by including the creation of social and environmental value. This broader perspective allows many more factors to be taken into consideration beyond those of economic value. Other key similarities stem from this principle including that of separation fallacy whereby ethics and business activity cannot be set apart but rather have a mutual symbiotic relationship (both benefit from working together). These mutual benefits are enhanced by sustainability management where proactive approaches to integration are evident.

A further link to this concept is that of opposition to residual corporate social responsibility where managers are required to integrate responsible leadership and management practices into their core business. This principle rejects notions of compensating or philanthropy (the redistribution of value based on altruism

FIGURE 2.2 *Similarities between (integrative) stakeholder theory and sustainability management*

Source: Adapted from Horisch et al. (2014)

or market intervention) in favour of elevating the responsibility of management to implement and demonstrate responsible business practices. This principle fits into the perspective on profit-making where the emphasis is placed on finding synergies and mutual benefits between different stakeholder interests. Thus, making profits is deemed an acceptable aim if the core practices that support it are grounded in mutuality. The link to strategic management is also important whereby the short-term operations of a business are complemented by a long-term perspective. Finally, many of the issues that form the integrated approach are neither simple nor easily arranged. Complexity forms a challenge to meeting the requirements of the integrated approach and the multitude of issues surrounding sustainability management adds to the scale of the challenge for managers. The environment in which these factors play out is constantly changing, difficult to control and complex in its construction.

There are a number of dissimilarities between stakeholder theory and sustainability management that are worthy of note. First, it is clear that sustainability management has a more direct link between societal, economic and environmental goals as these form the fundamental building blocks of the concept. The latter factor of the environment particularly differentiates the two by emphasising that business operates within ecological systems. Also, whereas stakeholder theory accommodates practices that enhance stakeholder interactions, sustainability

INTRODUCTION TO GLOBAL SUSTAINABLE MANAGEMENT

management requires business to be constantly proactive in contributing to sustainable development.

STAKEHOLDER MAPPING

Following on from stakeholder theory is the application of the stakeholder map as a basis for analysis. Undertaking stakeholder analysis helps to identify the key stakeholders, their interests, and how they affect or are affected by any organisational activity. Mitchell et al. (1997) and Bryson (2004) provide useful contributions to the techniques and tools for stakeholder mapping. The analysis helps inform managers in the planning process around how these interests are to be addressed. Stakeholder analysis also helps managers understand the aims and roles of different stakeholders which helps to determine the best way to engage with them. In many instances, the success of an organisation (or a stated aim of an organisation) may depend on how well managers and other internal stakeholders communicate with external stakeholders to manage tensions, conflicts or competing interests with a view to finding solutions. In some cases, identified stakeholders may even become involved in organisational activities to ensure mutual understanding and benefit. Stakeholder mapping is a tool for analysing the likely interests and actions of stakeholders. Key to producing effective analysis is gaining an insight into stakeholder expectations and their ability to enforce them.

> **Definition:** A **stakeholder map** is a process and a tool that catagorises identified stakeholder groups based on the level of interest they represent and the power and influence they possess.

Managers analysing a stakeholder map need to determine the ability of each identified stakeholder (or stakeholder group) to enforce their expectations; whether or not they have the means to do so; and the likely impact of stakeholder expectations on the organisation's ability to achieve stated aims. This can be expressed in a power/interest matrix as illustrated in Figure 2.3. The framework links stakeholders to the power they have and their level of interest in the organisational activity they affect or are affected by. The matrix is demarcated into quadrants that reflect the type of relationship managers need to establish with stakeholders.

Stakeholders with little interest in the activities of the organisation and with low levels of power or influence are allocated to quadrant A and would require little or no engagement effort by managers. Stakeholders in quadrant B do exhibit interest in the organisation's activities but have low levels of power or influence. This group needs to be kept informed of what the organisation intends to do and how it may affect the stakeholders. This approach maintains good communications with the stakeholder group and may be considered the socially responsible

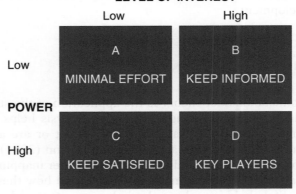

FIGURE 2.3 *Stakeholder map*

thing to do. The other two stakeholder quadrants exhibit characteristics that require a much more proactive and engaging response from organisations. Stakeholders in quadrant D have a high level of interest and a suitable level of power and influence to make a difference. Consequently, this stakeholder group requires managers to initiate and maintain close contact, and perhaps engage in negotiation, persuasion and, in some instances, collaboration. Stakeholders in quadrant D are already established and methods of managing the challenges they present will be well understood. Stakeholders in quadrant C present a different, and possibly more challenging one. These stakeholders have a high level of power and influence but a relatively low level of interest. Managers need to ensure that this group remains satisfied to prevent them from exercising their power and moving towards quadrant D. Normally a stakeholder mapping exercise comprises four key requirements:

1. Identify the stakeholder groups, organisations or individuals.
2. Analyse the stakeholder perspectives and issues.
3. Map the relationships to specific objectives and other stakeholders.
4. Prioritise stakeholder importance and related issues.

Identifying stakeholder groups is a subjective process but can achieve a high degree of accuracy through involving others in compiling the list. It is also important to identify both current stakeholders and future ones. Experience of existing stakeholders and possible new ones will help towards achieving completeness. For example, changes to industry regulations may initiate the creation of new groups of stakeholders to monitor and ensure compliance. Emerging markets, new technologies or evolving customer needs may be other catalysts for new stakeholder groups to emerge. A version of Lozano et al.'s (2015) typology of commonly identified stakeholders for corporations is set out in Table 2.1.

TABLE 2.1 *Typology of stakeholders in corporations*

	Primary	Secondary
SOCIAL	Shareholders	Government
	Investors	Regulators
	Employees	Civil institutions
	Managers	Citizens
	Customers	Pressure groups
	Suppliers	Media
	Business partners	Academic institutions
	Unions	Trade bodies
	Local communities	Competitors
NON-SOCIAL	Natural environment	
	Future generations	

Managers need to be future oriented in their thinking when considering the list of stakeholders and their appropriate position within the stakeholder map. Managers also have to be inclusive in their selection and not be bounded by race, gender, geography or perceived power. A common mistake in developing a stakeholder map is to automatically assign high power and interest to those with authority such as local or regional councils or government agencies. In many instances the most vocal and proactive stakeholders emerge from those without formal power but who seek to have their views heard.

Analysing stakeholder groups is a skill that is based partly on the ability to apply effective tools and techniques, and partly through experience. Analysis requires objectivity around evaluating the contribution that each stakeholder group can make to understanding the key issues and how engaged they are in the process of finding solutions. Determining their level of influence (and where that influence is exercised) and involvement are other important factors in the analytical process. Once the identification and analysis of stakeholders is complete the mapping can proceed based on the design that was set out in Figure 2.3. This will help identify where each stakeholder group resides in the power/interest matrix after they have been evaluated using the same criteria and then compared to each other.

The final requirement is to prioritise the stakeholders' importance and related issues. It will become clear through analysis that each stakeholder group will exhibit their own level of power and interest and that there will be differences in the extent to which they engage with issues. Consequently, managers need to take a pragmatic view of which stakeholder group merits their attention, resources and proactive engagement. By prioritising stakeholders, managers can achieve a better understanding of how the issues are perceived by priority stakeholders and the extent to which the organisation has engaged with them. The case study at the end of this chapter shows how a stakeholder map can be applied in the context of Ibá, the association that represents the Brazilian tree planting industry.

PARADOX THEORY AND SUSTAINABILITY

The concept of paradox as a part of the human experience has been a staple of philosophical debate since ancient times. Referring to the presence of simultaneous opposites, the concept has traditionally been linked to ideas of contradiction, irony or oxymoron. In the context of organisational studies, Quinn and Rohrbaugh (1983) refer to the paradoxical nature of organisational effectiveness. Later, Quinn (1988) produced a guide for managers on how to consider paradoxes and competing demands of organisations. As the concept gained momentum, academics provided insights by developing paradox theories around different contexts such as just-in-time manufacturing (Eisenhardt and Westcott, 1988) and management studies (Morgan, 1996). Subsequently, paradox theory has been used by academics to analyse many different organisational phenomena such as Tushman and O'Reilly (1996) on the tensions of exploitation and exploration in organisations, the dichotomy of stability and change (Farjoun, 2010) or the paradox of control and collaboration (Sundaramurthy and Lewis, 2003).

It is increasingly evident that the performance evaluation of companies around the world is being judged on sustainability criteria as much as economic factors. This creates challenges for managers as they seek to meet or exceed the expectations of different stakeholders, some of whom may hold conflicting views as to what constitutes good performance. Evaluating sustainability is fraught with difficulty as it encompasses social, economic, and environmental factors (the Triple Bottom Line) thereby increasing the complexity of the measures used to determine performance. Nevertheless, managers are required to deliver on this as the importance of sustainability has grown significantly since the turn of the millennium. These challenges have been met at different levels and at different speeds by companies around the world, making any comparison problematic. In many cases, the actions to support sustainability by companies have not matched the rhetoric. In some instances, the issue of sustainability has been used for promotional and public relations advantages more than being the catalyst for real change. In other cases, companies have adopted the concept of sustainability and included it into their long-term strategic aims and matched the plans with real and decisive action. Part of the reason for the wide discrepancies in 'sustainability' performance has been the different ways in which managers deal with the paradox of seeking competitive advantage and shareholder value (economic) with that of social and environmental concerns. Smith and Lewis (2011) contend that a paradox approach 'presumes that tensions are integral to complex systems and that sustainability depends on attending to contradictory yet interwoven demands simultaneously'. Ozanne et al. (2016) identified the main tensions evident in managing the Triple Bottom Line as set out in Figure 2.4.

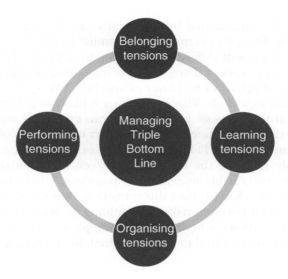

FIGURE 2.4 *Tensions at the intersection of managing the Triple Bottom Line*

Source: Adapted from Ozanne et al. (2016)

Belonging tensions

Tensions arise when managers try to accommodate or appease stakeholders and relate to how they identify with each stakeholder group. Stakeholders will have certain expectations relating to the identity of managers in the relationships they develop with them. In some cases, as managers pursue Triple Bottom Line outcomes, these identities will align to the most favoured of the social, economic or environmental elements of the Triple Bottom Line. This presents the challenge of how they manage the other identities that diverge from their favoured one. Belonging tensions can be evident both at the individual and group (or organisational) level. Inevitably, the divergence creates tensions as managers attempt to control competing stakeholder objectives. Belonging tensions are evident when managers seek self-expression and group affiliation simultaneously. In business, as in life, being all things to all people all the time rarely works.

Learning tensions

Tensions can emerge as organisations transition between traditional and new processes and practices. These can develop anywhere along the value chain of an organisation and often require new values, beliefs and attitudes to change. All organisations need to adapt and to manage change to ensure they remain competitive and that their processes and ways of doing business remain relevant and are conducive to achieving stated aims. Within this change process managers need to take the learning gained from previous experiences and use it to initiate improvements. This process may create conflict internally, require new skills and aptitudes, and present different challenges to workers in different parts of the organisation. New ways of doing business may diminish the influence or relevance of one set of activities in favour of another. New types of activities may emerge that require new skills. This state of flux is likely to generate tensions that stem from the learning process. Learning tensions emerge as organisations transition between existing and new activities as part of a process of innovation and change (Smith and Lewis, 2011). In the context of sustainable management this process inevitably refers to the transition between unsustainable management practices to more sustainable management practices. Often, managers need to balance the approach taken to effect this transition. Hahn et al. (2017) assert that an over-emphasis on innovation risks undermining the widespread dissemination of sustainable innovations, whereas an over-emphasis on incremental change risks limiting the scale required to meet sustainability challenges.

Organising tensions

The design of organisations can create tensions linked to structures, processes, lines of authority and span of control. Different groups of specialist workers may vie with each other to influence the development of a structure or set of processes that are conducive to their aims and objectives. This can create a form of internal competition for accessing the resources and decision-making capabilities that can lead to tensions. This dynamic is fluid, open to change and often politically motivated. Managers need to create a structure and process that best fits the organisational aims and not be swayed by the lobbying or influence of any particular group. In the final analysis, there is likely to be unequal divisions of resources and influence and the tensions that this gives rise to require careful management.

Performing tensions

Managers will often be confronted with competing strategic aims and objectives that create tensions. In particular, it is evident that strategic aims linked to Triple Bottom Line factors have the potential for being mutually exclusive. For example, organisations that are performance oriented with strong shareholder influence and power may struggle to incorporate performance ambitions linked to sustainability practices. This tension is explored later in Chapter 4 - but it is worth noting here that tensions will arise when there are trade-offs required or where a binary choice between the choice of aims has to be made. In many cases a compromise is possible that alleviates the tensions. However, these dynamic situations play out differently and with different levels of intensity in different organisations. Consequently, managers have to determine the appropriate response to these tensions in the specific context in which they emerge.

A dynamic approach to paradox theory

By adopting a paradox theory approach it is possible to address the tensions from a perspective of both/and rather than either/or decisions (O'Driscoll, 2008). Key to the effectiveness of the paradox approach is to frame tensions as situations that managers can address as they emerge. Hahn et al. (2017) define a paradox theory on corporate sustainability as one that 'accommodates interrelated yet conflicting economic, environmental, and social concerns with the objective of achieving superior business contributions to sustainable development'. Thus, a business-only case seeks to align environmental and social aspects with financial performance, whereas, a paradox approach creates strategies that accept tensions in the quest for achieving sustainable goals. This approach can prove informative to global business managers as they seek to better understand the complexities inherent in dealing with contradictory and interrelated elements of the environment at one and the same time. Indeed, it can be seen that the success of managers in dealing with this reality is dependent on the extent to which they can manage all the demands that this complexity entails through splitting a paradox and synthesising responses as opposed to trading off one against another.

A dynamic theoretical framework developed by Smith and Lewis (2011) provides a basis for applying paradox theory to help managers contextualise the tensions around environmental issues of scarcity, plurality and change. The framework is developed on the assumption that organisational tensions become evident when these three environmental factors combine to reveal the contradictory nature of the tensions. Scarcity refers to the limitations on resources available to organisations; plurality is the level of uncertainty aligned to the conditions in which managers set strategies to achieve organisational goals; and change refers to the dynamic environment that requires organisations to adapt and evolve to meet the challenges that present.

The concept of splitting a paradox and synthesising responses is one that provides a basis for managing competing and contradictory tensions. Splitting a paradox allows a more detailed examination of the value that derives from that element and offers managers the latitude to develop the type of organisational goals that align to the most important of the identified paradoxical objectives. However, rather than a stand-alone, one-off action, Smith and Lewis argue that this should form a cyclical process through synthesis with new priorities emerging after each cycle. The framework presents the long-term prospect of the emergence of a 'dynamic equilibrium' involving what the authors describe as 'purposeful iterations between alternatives in order to ensure simultaneous attention to them over time' (Smith and Lewis, 2011: 392). This process creates a 'virtuous cycle' of understanding tensions and creating resolutions to those tensions over time. Importantly, in the context of sustainability, paradox theory presents a framework for managers to better understand how to deal with the competing and contradictory demands of the 'Triple Bottom Line', that is, managing people, planet and profit. The value of this theory is the dynamic, rather than static, nature of the framework which offers a more realistic reflection of the environment in which these tensions and changes take place.

Mini case 2.1: Walmart, USA

Founded in 1962 by Sam Walton, Walmart is an American multinational retail corporation that operates over 10,000 supermarkets and grocery stores across 27 different countries, often under different brand names. It is one of the most profitable and successful retail companies in the world but has not been without its critics for its policies and actions linked to a wide range of issues including racial and gender discrimination, anti-competitive practices, exerting excessive pressure on suppliers, environmental practices and employee rights. To address these issues and maintain their position as a global leader in retailing, the company has had to address a fundamental paradox – how to maintain growth and profitability whilst ensuring the highest standards of behaviour in support of environmental and social responsibility.

In 2018 the company released their Global Responsibility Report that focused on their commitment to meeting consumer expectations of low prices and eliminating abuses in the supply chain and employee rights. The company has committed to working with industry experts, Non-Governmental Organisations (NGOs), and suppliers to improve internal and external relationships by 2025. Other issues are linked to the environment, with the company having previously been one of America's biggest users of electricity by any privately owned organisation in the country (Epstein, 2009). To meet the stated aims linked to global responsibility the company has introduced more sustainability actions such as reducing solid waste by 25%; reducing energy use in stores by 30%; improving the efficiency of their large fleet of distribution vehicles; and introducing more sustainable food items including more organic foods. These and other actions to support employee relations represent some of the measurable actions the company has taken to address areas of concern. Critics argue that the actions implemented are piecemeal and limited in scale but others view the developments as a serious and long-term commitment to meeting the challenges of economic prosperity with sustainable practice at the company.

Question and tasks

1. Download the latest Walmart environment, social and governance report and assess the company's performance against set targets.
2. Identify the profitability of Walmart in the years since the publication of the 2018 Global Responsibility Report. Is there evidence to suggest that Walmart have been able to grow the business, achieve increasing profits whilst meeting environmental, social and governance targets?

BALANCED SCORECARD AND SUSTAINABILITY

The Balanced Scorecard (BSC) is a framework devised by Robert Kaplan and David Norton in 1992 to implement and manage strategy by creating linkages between strategic aims and objectives and measuring key initiatives and targets. The BSC is essentially a business management tool that can be applied in many different contexts. What makes the BSC a useful tool is that it extends analysis of business performance beyond simply financial measures, such as income or profit, to include other organisational functions. This more 'balanced' approach incorporates other perspectives such as internal processes, customers and organisational capacity. These factors, alongside finance, are identified and linked to strategic priorities and related measures, targets and initiatives. The framework, as illustrated in Figure 2.5, provides the basis for managers to consider how strategic objectives can be measured so that initiatives can be implemented to drive these objectives.

Strategic objectives transform strategy from a concept to a set of actions. The BSC has been adopted by many managers operating across a wide range of industry sectors as it provides the basis for understanding causal relationships between the four perspectives. For example, an increase in the organisational capacity initiates changes in business processes that have an impact on customer loyalty or the attraction of new customers. This scenario can result in improved financial performance.

FIGURE 2.5 *The Balanced Scorecard*

Although Kaplan and Norton (1992) devised a useful generic framework, they did not specifically focus on environmental or sustainability issues. Epstein and Wisner (2001) attempt to integrate environmental issues into the BSC of the corporate entity Bristol Myers Squibb – a global biopharmaceutical company. The authors provide some insight into how the BSC can be applied in the narrowly defined field entitled Health and Safety and Environment within the organisation with environmental factors featuring in the internal process perspective. The others include finance, customers and learning and growth perspectives. The main criticism of this example is that there is no evidence of integration between the different perspectives. That is Health and Safety and Environment is a shared service unit within the organisation and not integrated with the business units they serve. This lack of integration limits the effectiveness of the BSC approach. As Zingales and Hockerts (2002) highlight, the work by Nilsson (2001) advanced that of the Bristol Myers Squibb case by more closely aligning the perspectives of the BSC as well as delivering an insight into how it supports a specific environmental initiative within Telia Nara Linkoping (Telia NL), a business unit of Swedish telecommunications company Telia AB.

Mini case 2.2: Telia NL, Sweden

The application of the BSC at Telia NL (a business unit of Telia Nara Linkoping) was reliant on managers identifying the causes and effects of initiatives that linked to environmental performance. The performance indicators had to be mapped and recorded as part of the business unit scorecard. The specific project that Nilsson (2001) identified was the so-called Virtual Meetings Project (VM). The project followed an initiative by the company to reduce foreign travel by extending the use of video conferencing facilities. The aim was to derive twin benefits of environmental value by reducing carbon emissions linked to international air travel, and economic value by capitalising on the expertise and knowledge sharing using communications technologies that could be sold to their clients. The initiative first involved Talia NL developing the technology internally before promoting and marketing the 'product' to a range of clients around the globe. The initiative was designed to demonstrate an ability to maintain the economic development of the business alongside that of environmental benefits. This aligns to the Triple Bottom Line aims of matching the requirements of people, profit and planet.

To implement the VM project, Talia NL designed a three-stage approach consisting, first, of identifying strategic objectives and indicators linked to drivers and barriers to the use of virtual meetings. This was followed by another stage whereby the objectives were refined and prioritised and others added. The third stage involved the process of transferring the indicators to the strategic objectives and integrating them into the existing Balanced Scorecards at Telia NL. After applying the Balanced Scorecard the key findings that emerged from the strategic objective of gaining economic and environmental benefits from the use of virtual conferences were that it had the potential to reduce costs (by reducing travel) and increasing the motivation of staff (through training and awareness of the use of virtual conferencing technology). Both have positive environmental effects as the value of this way of undertaking business using technology reduces the environmental impact of the company activities. However, it can also be noted that the case lends emphasis for the need to have champions of the environmental cause embedded in the process of determining strategic objectives and attendant indicators.

It can be seen that many of the initial attempts to include the environmental perspective into the BSC were welcomed by those who believed it was a step change in recognising the importance of the issue in strategic thinking within organisations. Thus, in this context, the environmental perspective formed a new addition to the original BSC format as illustrated in Figure 2.6. This extended BSC not only featured the perspectives of finance, internal processes, learning and growth and customers, but also the environmental perspective that included factors such as carbon footprint, waste management and social impact. The key issue facing managers was how best to integrate the environmental perspective into the BSC for their organisations.

FIGURE 2.6   *The Balanced Scorecard with the environmental perspective*

Figge et al. (2002) presented three possibilities. First, there is the option of merging the environmental perspective into the existing four perspectives of finance, customers, internal processes, and learning and growth. The second possibility is to add an additional perspective that accommodates the environmental element, which would be consistent with the theory presented by Kaplan and Norton (1992) whereby new (or renamed) perspectives can be added. This is justified when the strategy of the organisation includes non-market oriented aspects such as environmental aims. The third possibility is to generate an environmental oriented BSC. It is not intended that this be a stand-alone and separate entity from the conventional BSC, but rather one that integrates environmental factors into each of the other four perspectives. Thus, the environmental perspective becomes a key feature and point of reference when considering the other perspectives. As Johnson (1998) noted, a separate environmental BSC helps create links between certain types of environmental performance and the strategic and financial objectives of an organisation.

Mini case 2.3: Iberdrola, Spain

Iberdrola is a Spanish multinational electric company based in Bilbao and employs around 35,000 people across many countries spanning four continents. This global energy company has a strong commitment to renewables, especially wind power, and has operations centres in Toledo (Spain), Portland (USA) and Glasgow (Scotland). The company monitors and controls activities that support their commitment to sustainability, producing an annual sustainability scorecard to reflect the performance against set targets around energy sustainability and business sustainability. These are illustrated in Figure 2.7.

The business element of the strategy includes competitiveness by providing energy supply at lowest possible prices, the use of technologies to improve efficiencies and lower costs, and to diversify the portfolio of types of energy supply. The security of energy supply is underpinned by investments in technologies that promote energy efficiency, high quality service and the use of local and renewable primary energy sources.

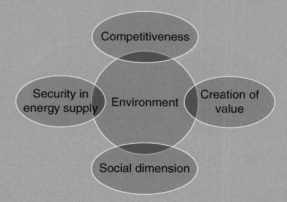

FIGURE 2.7   *Iberdrola model for a sustainable company in the energy sector*

Source: Iberdrola Sustainability Scorecard (2020)

INTRODUCTION TO GLOBAL SUSTAINABLE MANAGEMENT

The reliability and availability of energy supplies is the core function of the business. However, a central focus of this part of the Iberdrola strategy is the environment and the sustainable use of resources that underpins the company's commitment to protecting it. The focus of investment is on developing efficient production and the efficient use of energy leading to lower emissions and more effective waste and water management processes. The company also includes a commitment to biodiversity protection as part of the environmental strategy. There is also a distinct social dimension to the strategy that features respect for human rights and improvements in the standard of living for people in those areas where the company operates.

Question and tasks

1. Research and discuss an example of an activity that supports the sustainable use of resources at Iberdrola.
2. What are the main areas of activity that support the social dimension of the sustainability scorecard of Iberdrola?
3. Give two examples of biodiversity protection that feature as part of the sustainability scorecard of Iberdrola.

It should be noted that simply adding an additional perspective to accommodate the environmental factor has not been without its critics. In particular, Jones (2011) argues that the usefulness of this approach is limited if the detail of what constitutes the environmental perspective is missing or how the other perspectives may be affected. In many instances, it can be seen that attempts to apply the BSC by integrating the environmental perspective have been blighted by excessive lists of wide-ranging possible environmental factors being included. The main criticisms of this approach are, first, that rather than integrating, the environmental perspective is seen in isolation from the others. Second, it also fails to highlight those factors that inform thinking and drive, and enable the environmental impact. Although it can derive an outcome, it does so to guide managers as to what to do next to capitalise on it. Third, the hallmark of the conventional BSC – the cause and effect aspect – is lost thereby making the environmental strategy unclear. That is, it does not elaborate on how the organisation's knowledge and skills play out in the strategy for addressing environmental impact. The issue of 'impact' reflects the consequences of the actions undertaken by organisations to address environmental challenges but is often missing.

SUSTAINABLE INVESTING AND ENVIRONMENT, SOCIAL AND GOVERNANCE (ESG) INVESTING

In the context of investing, there is a distinction to be made between sustainability investing and environmental, social and governance (ESG) investing.

Sustainability investing has a longer history than ESG and accounts for the greater understanding among stakeholders of its meaning. Sustainable investment is a values-based approach to identifying different types of funds that feature both financial returns and non-financial outcomes. Essentially, sustainable investment caters for those who take a broader world view and seek to align their investments with non-financial values that better reflect their ethical, social and environmental values. These non-financial elements are additions to the traditional financial returns more commonly associated with investments. In some instances, they reflect the specific social and environmental issues most pertinent to the investor. Typical examples include seeking investments in ethical projects such as water resource infrastructure, healthcare provision, educational programmes, disease mitigation or eradication, micro and small business development, or environmental protection. In other cases, investors will deliberately avoid supporting specific activities that are counter to their ethics such as tobacco, weaponry, animal testing, gambling or non-sustainable industries such as oil and gas or mining.

Environmental, social and governance (ESG) refers to the integration of risk factors into the investment process. This approach supports managers in risk analysis around long-term and sustainable returns on investment. Figure 2.8 illustrates how these key elements are inter-dependent.

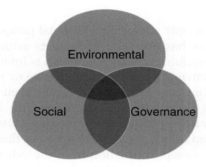

FIGURE 2.8 *Environmental, Social and Governance framework*

The environmental element includes a wide range of criteria, most commonly waste, carbon emissions, energy usage and other resource requirements. The social criteria typically include workforce issues such as diversity and pay equality, gender equality, reputation, and engagement with stakeholders. The governance element features internal processes, accountability, transparency and the procedures and controls in place that help the company comply with legal requirements as well as meeting organisational ethical standards.

The distinction between ESG and sustainable investing is that the former remains relevant to all types of investor whereas the latter is focused on those with distinctive preferences towards investments that are geared towards sustainable activities. ESG provides the basis around which managers can have a more holistic view of performance as it combines financial returns and those based on actions designed to support environmental, social and governance factors. Examples may include the level of diversity in the workforce, gender equality performance, waste management, energy use, carbon emissions linked to activities, or the practices of supply chain partners. Fund managers can make better informed decisions when factoring in these types of risk factors and can help detect issues to be addressed by companies for improving long-term performance. Inertia by companies could lead to fund managers directing investments away from non-responsive companies towards those with a more proactive strategy towards ESG factors.

Throughout the 2000s there has been a significant rise in ESG and for many organisations it has become an integral part of the reporting process. Quite apart from the social and environmental benefits linked to ESG, there are a number of important performance-enhancing aspects to it as well. In particular, the potential it has for increasing profits based on the value created around building strong relationships with consumers leading to brand loyalty. Effective relationships with workers also filters through to stronger performance based on high levels of motivation and 'buy-in' to the strategies of the companies around sustainability actions. These improve productivity and, increasingly, act as a magnet to talent as career-oriented workers search for roles within companies that exhibit similar values around sustainability as themselves. Performance can also be enhanced through strong and targeted ESG initiatives that reduce costs and improve efficiencies. Here, the use of materials, resources and the management of waste can all contribute to added value. In particular, the use of water resources and energy consumption are two key factors that have potential for innovative means of reducing costs. Innovation can also deliver higher returns on investment when funds are allocated to long-term sustainability projects and infrastructure. This is one of the key competitive drivers across a wide range of industries and has had the effect of delivering added value to the activities that support sustainability actions.

There are some notable limitations associated with ESG. In the first instance, it is not always easy to measure ESG criteria, especially ones that relate to social factors where criteria around culture, behavioural norms and customs may be interpreted differently. These interpretations and follow-up findings do not always translate directly to improved performance. Also, the level of commitment to ESG by investors remains relatively opaque and hard to monitor. Signatories to the ESG exhibit a broad range of behaviours along the spectrum between proactively and positively supporting investments linked to ESG criteria and those who remain focused on delivering the highest financial returns. Another limitation is the range of different metrics used to measure ESG criteria. This has led to a lack of precision in the ratings and inconsistency in the key performance indicators (KPIs) used to measure them. Combined, these issues undermine efforts to incorporate ESG into investment analysis. Nevertheless, there are evident efforts to address these criticisms. For example, in the US in 2020 the Securities and Exchange Commission (SEC) committed to making ESG disclosures more standardised and ratings more consistent. It is expected that companies will make similar efforts to provide relevant and accurate data.

SUSTAINABLE VALUE FRAMEWORK THEORY

Strategies for addressing the paradox of simultaneously driving sustainability and shareholder value forms the basis of the development of the Sustainable Value Framework theory devised by Hart and Milstein (2003). They argue that sustainable development in a global context is multifaceted in the same way that shareholder value emerges from multiple performance drivers. Sustainability and shareholder value can be viewed as a three-step approach as illustrated in Figure 2.9. Step 1 of the frame is diagnostic in nature as managers in organisations assess the extent to which the organisation is involved in sustainability actions and if it represents a discernible and meaningful commitment. Step 2 is the assessment of opportunities identified by managers for exploring innovation and value-creating activities that support sustainability. Step 3 is the implementation of sustainability actions around identified projects and business experiments that inform decisions regarding the ones that deliver the most value.

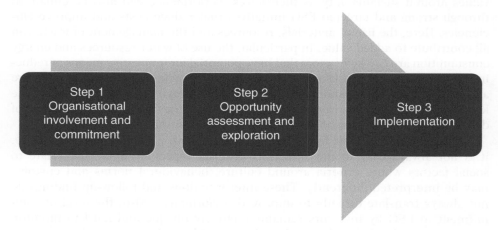

FIGURE 2.9   *Three step model of sustainable value*

Hart and Milstein developed the Sustainable Value Framework to address the challenge of creating shareholder value and, simultaneously, meet some of the most pressing global sustainability challenges facing society. Figure 2.10 illustrates the Sustainable Value Framework. The Sustainable Value Framework is a valuable means of showing how managers can develop strategies that address global sustainable challenges whilst simultaneously driving shareholder value. Often considered a paradox, this approach highlights how a 'win-win' can be created through sustainable value.

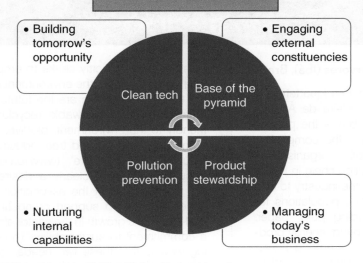

FIGURE 2.10 *Sustainability Value Framework*

The four elements to the framework consist of:

- Pollution prevention: by minimising waste and emissions. Practices that support this have the potential to reduce risk and costs that can lead to enhanced shareholder and sustainability value.

- Product stewardship: through stakeholder engagement and the management of the full life cycle of products, organisations can improve sustainability and raise their reputational capital.

- Clean technology: by developing and deploying new and innovative clean technologies that increase efficiency and reduce carbon emissions.

- Base of the pyramid: co-creation of new businesses to meet the unmet needs of the poor and underserved to create new growth trajectories and address social needs.

The challenge facing global managers is to determine what sustainability value goals to pursue and how to manage the realisation of the benefits that potentially accrue from the effective actions and practices that support them. Hart (2005) suggests that organisations begin the process by compiling a sustainability value portfolio that can reveal where the organisation stands in relation to each element of the framework. This understanding allows managers to redeploy resources and knowledge as part of a strategy to address gaps and create sustainable value.

CASE STUDY

Indústria Brasileira de Árvores (Ibá), Brazil

Established in 2014 and headquartered in Brasiília, the Indústria Brasileira de Árvores (Brazilian Tree Industry) (Ibá) is the primary association that represents the companies, associate partners and other organisations in the planted tree production chain in Brazil. The association supports the industry to add value by exploiting the tree populations for industrial purposes including pulp, paper, wood panels, laminate flooring, energy products, packaging, and biomass, among others. In 2020 Ibá comprised 48 companies and 10 state associations. Investors and trade unions across all sectors of the planted tree production chain are also represented. The mission of the association is:

> to strive to make the sector more competitive, bringing member companies into line with the highest standards of science, technology and environmental responsibility throughout the entire forest production chain, in the search for innovative solutions for the Brazilian and global markets. (www.iba.org/eng/about-us)

The work of the association spans many different areas of interest and necessarily includes a range of different stakeholders such as government, environmental organisations, academic institutions, consumers and the media. Exploitation of the forests of Brazil is a highly sensitive issue and has led to clashes and tensions between conservationists and environmental groups and those seeking to use the forest for industrial purposes. The vision of Ibá clearly recognises these tensions and explicitly seeks to emphasise their commitment to the environment by stating that 'Planted trees are the future of raw materials that are renewable, recyclable and friendly to the environment, biodiversity and human life. The planted tree industry is the industry of the future' (www.iba.org/eng/about-us). There is clearly a desire within the management of the association to balance the need to support competitiveness and economic growth in the sector alongside a commitment to sustainability. The prevailing view is that these two needs can work together within the principle that forests are a perennial social and environmental resource which provide vital inputs to a sustainable and economically successful business. To achieve this the association supports industry innovation that delivers technologies that support sustainable exploitation and regeneration of the forests as natural assets. Part of this commitment also involves engaging with all appropriate stakeholders.

It is important for managers at Ibá to identify the key stakeholders or stakeholder groups and determine the strategy for engaging and communicating with each group. This helps to develop an understanding of the main interests of each group so that appropriate action can be taken to meet expectations, engage effectively or respond to challenges they present. Importantly, the stakeholder analysis provides the basis of developing strategies for delivering on the needs and expectations of different stakeholder groups and informs them of the ways in which they can contribute to the various projects and plans designed to balance the support of planted tree production activities whilst supporting conservation, environmental sustainability and economic growth. Ibá undertakes stakeholder analysis to identify the interests of all stakeholders who could be affected, or can affect, planted tree production activities and management plans. It also helps to identify potential conflicts between different stakeholder groups and provides the basis of developing relationships between the association and different stakeholder groups. The analysis also helps to identify those groups who require closer engagement to encourage participation in the different stages of planning as part of the planted tree production chain activities. This will support efforts to better understand the effectiveness of plans and lessen any negative impacts. The development and use of a stakeholder map helps Ibá undertake stakeholder analysis that better informs decision-making. First, however, it is necessary to follow a process of stakeholder engagement as illustrated in Figure 2.11.

Understand stakeholder engagement

In the first instance the association needs to understand stakeholder engagement requirements by determining the extent to which engagement with different stakeholders needs to be achieved. This understanding will be developed over time as the key factors determining the extent of engagement becomes known. It is also a dynamic factor that has to be updated and kept relevant as the influence of different stakeholders changes over time. For example, ownership of forest assets is subject to change, urban development into forested areas creates new neighbours to tree planting companies; new regulations create different forms of industry oversight; or environmental groups may acquire greater influence under different governments.

Building knowledge of this dynamic environment is an important step in the process of effective stakeholder engagement. The time and effort afforded to each stakeholder is another important feature of understanding stakeholder engagement. Some stakeholders, such as regulators, local authorities or legislators may wield significant power and influence and, therefore, Ibá needs to engage much more closely with these groups to support policy compliance and business continuity for their members.

Identify relevant stakeholders

It is vital that Ibá identify and list all the relevant stakeholder groups that have an interest in, or who can affect, the activities of planted tree production chain companies. This list forms the basis of analysis around what

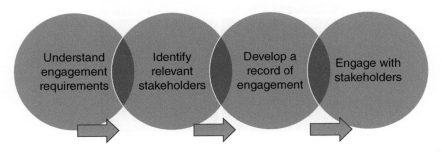

FIGURE 2.11 *Stakeholder engagement process*

influence or power each possess and how each group should be engaged. This process supports the strategic planning and development in the industry as it ensures stakeholder views are considered (and, in some instances, acted upon). There are a wide range of different stakeholders relevant to the work of the association and Figure 2.12 provides a stakeholder map for some of the most prominent ones.

Starting with recreational users of forests, it can be seen that they wield relatively little power and their level of interest does not extend much beyond their ability to carry out pursuits such as walking, cycling, camping and exploring the forest flora and fauna. The association do not perceive this group as influential but their activities need to be taken into account and, therefore, the level of engagement is minimal. Other groups require a more proactive engagement due to the fact that their activities are likely to have some level of impact on the forest environment or they may have influence on other more powerful and interested groups. This group of stakeholders may affect the operations of the companies that work the forests or present challenges to be managed. Here, the wider citizenship (especially those in close proximity to forests) can wield some level of influence; the media can present, inform, educate and influence thinking around planted tree production activities; trade unions can influence workers' rights and welfare in the sector; farming operations may impact the environment and operations of companies; and the tourist industry may have objectives that conflict with the interests of the companies in the sector. Although the level of interest by this group is necessarily high, their power to influence is variable, as is their likely impact. Nevertheless, this stakeholder group need to be kept informed of the plans and activities of the companies and their views taken seriously.

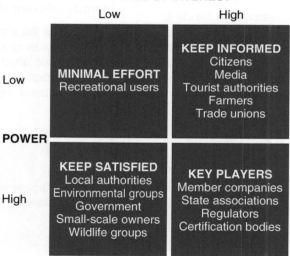

FIGURE 2.12   *Stakeholder map for Ibá*

There are a number of stakeholders who require active engagement at a high level to reflect their power. Although their level of interest may be narrowly defined to the remit they have, this group has the potential to use power to impact the aims and objectives of Ibá and the companies they represent. Government and local authorities will restrict their influence to those areas that directly affect their own stakeholders. Environmental and wildlife protection groups will pursue their agenda vigorously and hold companies to account for the environmental impact of their activities; and small-scale owners of forest land will also protect their interest either through lobbying or gaining the support of influential authorities. This group needs close engagement to keep them satisfied and this process is likely to be on-going and subject to change depending on how they perceive the response from the industry to their expectations, needs and concerns.

The most powerful and influential group that take a close interest in the activities of the sector include the regulatory and certification bodies who license the rights to exploit the forest assets. For Ibá the companies they represent and the state associations they have as partners are also considered key players whose interests they are formed to serve. It is vital for the association that they meet the expectations of these key players in the stakeholder map. The association needs to dedicate its time and effort to supporting their strategy for delivering added value to their members as well as to helping them demonstrate their compliance to regulations and the criteria that underpin awards of certifications to operate. These represent stakeholders that have prioritised engagement status.

The final two elements of the engagement process include compiling and maintaining a record of stakeholder engagement that helps the association monitor and review relationships going forward, and the actual strategies for engagement that pertain to each stakeholder group depending on their position within the stakeholder map.

Questions and task

1. What are the main aims and objectives of the organisation Ibá?

2. Why are environmental groups not considered 'key players' in the Ibá stakeholder map?

3. Identify three types of stakeholder engagement activities that Ibá could undertake to maintain appropriate levels of communication with different stakeholder groups.

SUMMARY

This chapter has provided a definition of theory and explained the purpose and value of theory for helping to better understand phenomena and issues in general, and sustainability management in particular. The discussion provided an overview of the development and application of theoretical perspectives and frameworks linked to sustainability management. Some key chosen perspectives and frameworks were chosen to help explain how theory can be applied effectively in this context. Starting with stakeholder theory the chapter provided an overview of key issues including the purpose of business and what constitutes a stakeholder. This discussion led on to the presentation of a stakeholder map whereby different categories of stakeholders are identified and analysed according to their relative power and interest around key issues of sustainability and business.

In many cases, it can be seen that the competing expectations of stakeholders creates paradoxes that business managers have to contend with when devising strategies. The work on paradox theory offered an insight into some of the conflicting pressures on management and the organisational tensions that arise as part of managing sustainability such as achieving economic growth whilst simultaneously meeting environmental protection targets. The discussion was extended to incorporate the dynamic approach to corporate sustainability that is designed to accommodate interrelated but conflicting economic, environmental and social concerns. The Balanced Scorecard tool was also presented as a means of explaining how managers can implement and manage strategy by creating linkages between strategic aims and objectives, and measuring key initiatives and targets. The discussion was extended to include a critique of the advantages and challenges presented by including the environmental aspect alongside traditional criteria of internal processes, customers, organisational capacity and finance. The work continued by introducing the concept of sustainable investment and a framework for environmental, social and governance discourse that broaden the analysis beyond that of narrowly defined financial data. The chapter discussion was rounded off with a presentation of the Sustainable Value Framework where the focus of attention lay principally on the means by which shareholder value can be created simultaneously with meeting sustainability challenges.

REVIEW QUESTIONS AND TASKS

1. Define what theory is and explain its purpose.
2. What is a stakeholder map designed to achieve?
3. Identify three possible paradoxes linked to the Triple Bottom Line of economic, environmental and social factors.
4. What are the main criticisms of incorporating an environmental aspect to the traditional balanced scorecard?

FURTHER READING

Harrison, J.S., Barney, J.B., Freeman, R.E. and Phillips, R.A. (2019) *The Cambridge Handbook of Stakeholder Theory*. Cambridge: Cambridge University Press.

This book brings together the key influential thinkers in stakeholder theory and stakeholder mapping. The book articulates the key concept of the 'stakeholder' and places the narrative in the context of business theory and practice.

Kaplan, R.S. and Norton, D.P. (1996) *The Balanced Scorecard: Translating Strategy into Action*. Boston, MA: Harvard Business Review Press.

The original seminal work by the architects of the Balanced Scorecard, Kaplan and Norton provide a valuable and detailed insight into how managers can use the scorecard approach to fulfil the mission, aims and objectives of organisations by improving performance measurement systems. The book explains how the Balanced Scorecard can deliver a robust learning system for better understanding the effectiveness of a company's strategy.

Wasieleski, D.M. (2020) *Management and the Sustainability Paradox: Reconnecting the Human Chain*. Abingdon: Routledge.

The author's principal argument is about how humanity became disconnected from its ecological environment throughout evolutionary history. The narrative follows a series of discussions around the premise that people have competing innate and natural drivers that are inextricably linked to survival. Survival involves propagating the species and overcoming adversaries. This book takes a managerial perspective when analysing decisions that reflect the paradox of survival (short term) against that of sustainability values (long term).

3

STRATEGIC THINKING AND GLOBAL SUSTAINABILITY MANAGEMENT

INTRODUCTION

Strategy is a plan that supports the achievement of particular stated aims, typically over a long period of time. Many different definitions of strategy have been proposed because it is a term used in many different contexts, most commonly in business but also in the military and sport, among others. A strategy requires undertaking a series of actions to achieve stated aims. Strategic management is the use of resources required to make this happen and also involves determining the vision and mission of the organisation, setting aims and objectives; choosing the means and actions required for achieving those aims and objectives; and ensuring that the performance of the organisation is of a standard to achieve the stated aims and objectives over a set time period. Strategy can be viewed as a process involving a deliberate set of actions that are prescribed, planned and monitored. However, often strategy takes on a more emergent trajectory whereby a set of actions follows a pattern of behaviour that is consistent but without any pre-determined route to achieving stated aims (Lynch, 2018). Effective strategic management relies on feedback, knowledge, learning and analysis, which combine to contribute to the experience that managers require to make well-informed long-term decisions.

This chapter begins with a treatment of the strategy content, process and context by discussing these elements as part of a deliberate design that supports the achievement of sustainability strategic goals. The strategy process discussion focuses on the formulation, implementation and evaluation of strategy. A sustainability strategy framework is used to offer explanations and insights into the development of this process. The work goes on to highlight sustainability strategy analysis and choice, and the application of a sustainability value chain. The discussion around implementation of sustainability strategy focuses on the role of organisational structure and governance before going on to evaluate design thinking as part of the process driving strategy in this context. Key issues of organisational learning and organisational culture feature as important elements of the implementation process. The chapter is completed by a discussion of the evaluation aspect of sustainability strategy using selected tools and techniques for measuring and analysing performance.

> **Definition: Strategy** is the stated long-term aims and objectives of an organisation and the plan of action to achieve them.

STRATEGY CONTENT, PROCESS AND CONTEXT

In the context of this current discussion, strategy content refers to the added value that frameworks contribute to sustainability. It can be viewed as the discipline that underpins the requirement to satisfy business needs based on content creation. Managers involved in creating sustainability strategy content need to identify the business interests that will be met through the planning, creation and distribution of content. Here, it is necessary that the creators understand the business case for designing the content and the audience it is aimed at. The strategy process sets out the way in which the strategy of the framework, approach or project in question is formulated and designed to achieve stated content and purpose (Baumgartner and Korhonen, 2010). As part of the process, it is important to include stakeholders in the creation of sustainability strategy content. Engagement with stakeholders can help inform key areas of interest such as how the content should be used, what type of content is required, and how it should be organised. De Wit (2014) notes that the circumstances under which strategy content and process are determined reveal the strategy context (both internal and external to the organisation). Sustainability strategy has a distinct context around understanding the economic, social and environmental factors that inform the development of strategic aims and the actions that support them.

Managers need to identify the strategy context by better understanding the global and local sustainability factors and their impact on the organisation. This helps focus attention on the material issues that inform effective strategic management.

Creating and implementing a sustainability strategy poses significant challenges for managers and not all succeed. In some cases sustainability content may lack depth of understanding; in others it may be a lack of a clear resource commitment to match actions with the appropriate support. In some cases, sustainability strategy may lack focus when the emphasis is on sustainability impacts and risks at the functional level of the organisation rather than at the strategic level. This can often lead to returns on sustainability actions being limited in scope and impact. If sustainability is a strategic issue within an organisation, then it needs resourcing, suitable managerial support and the type of expertise around strategic planning and development that can deliver significant or even transformational change. Sustainability strategies can fail if the process is of marginal significance or is marginalised against that of other strategic aims. Effective strategy in this context needs to reflect corporate ambition around sustainability aims.

The strategy process

The main elements of the strategy process include formulating a mission statement and overall purpose of the organisation; undertaking internal and external analysis; analysing the range of options available; choosing a strategic option and implementing measures to achieve the aims and objectives, and evaluating the performance of the chosen strategy. Thus, typically strategy involves the three stages of formulation, implementation and evaluation as illustrated in Figure 3.1. Following a clear strategy process allows managers to set a plan of action for achieving stated aims and objectives in a systematic manner. This approach helps to clarify what is viable and desirable for their organisation and focuses attention on the key areas of analysis that support the evaluation of each stage towards achieving stated aims and objectives.

FIGURE 3.1   *The strategy process*

INTRODUCTION TO GLOBAL SUSTAINABLE MANAGEMENT

To undertake the strategy process requires strategic thinking by managers. This refers to the intentional and rational thought process that focuses attention on analysis of identified key factors that influence the ability of the organisation to achieve stated long-term aims and objectives. An important characteristic of effective strategic thinking is to understand the environment in which the organisation operates and to be able to anticipate changes in that environment (Pelard, 2020). This helps managers initiate and implement actions in a pro-active rather than reactive manner to either mitigate negative impacts from change or exploit it as an opportunity. In competitive environments this type of strategic thinking helps to formulate and implement goals, plans and aims around knowledge of market and competitive forces that help companies create a competitive advantage.

In the private sector the main strategic aim is to create a competitive advantage over rival firms. Usually, the measure of competitive advantage is financial – profit, turnover, return on capital employed, market share, etc. To achieve competitive advantage companies need to discover and implement ways of competing that are unique and distinctive from those of rivals and that can be sustained over a period of time. Michael Porter (1980, 1985) introduced this concept and emphasised the need to identify the factors that give an organisation an edge over its competitors and enable it to achieve higher levels of profitability or any of the other financial measures. This type of strategy is termed competitive strategy and is concerned with the company's position relative to its competitors in the markets which it has chosen (Kay, 2001).

Typical ways in which a competitive advantage can be gained include expanding the product line, extending market reach, differentiating products and services, being the least cost producer of products or service, adding value through creativity and innovation, superior economies from marketing and promotion of products and services, delivering high quality customer service or distribution, or building in flexibility and agility into the production process. These are just some of many ways that companies seek to gain and sustain a competitive advantage. However, in the last two decades there has been a discernible shift in strategic thinking away from the narrowly defined economic returns from strategic action towards other forms of competitive advantage that include sustainability and the myriad benefits that derive from that. The effects of changing consumer preferences, increasing awareness of the strategic dimension of sustainability, the absorption and dissemination of knowledge and understanding of sustainability issues, and a broader scope of shareholder demands have all contributed to the evolution of global sustainable managers across many different industry sectors. Global sustainability managers engage in strategic thinking that supports a long-term commitment to redirecting resources to support sustainability aims that transcend the internal organisation to incorporate all stakeholders who affect or are affected by the organisation.

Baumgartner and Ebner (2010) note that sustainability strategy comprises three elements including the economic, ecological and social. The economic element involves all the activities that ensure effective business functions and continuity including key drivers of value such as innovation and collaboration.

Ecological elements refer to environmental activities that cause or prevent environmental impacts such as recycling, carbon capture or waste management. These and a raft of others provide the basis of sustainable economic growth based on exploiting environmental value. The third element of social value has both internal and external influences. Internal to the organisation is corporate governance and employee welfare. These add value by enhancing and building trust among internal stakeholders. This links into the external environment whereby the reputation of the organisation in the wider community is one way that sustainability strategy can derive value.

SUSTAINABILITY STRATEGY: FORMULATION

A sustainability strategy sets out a series of actions that are designed to achieve long-term sustainability strategic aims and objectives (Long, 2020). Consequently, the decision-making lies in the realm of those at executive level in an organisation and those directly responsible for developing and implementing the sustainability strategy. This latter group will engage with internal managers and workers, external stakeholders including suppliers, partners, consumers, citizens, pressure groups, government, support agencies and many more. Key to effective sustainability strategic thinking is understanding the diverse needs and expectations of stakeholders; knowledge of the industry in which the company operates along with related sustainability issues; deep insight into the resources and capabilities of the organisation; and an entrepreneurial mindset for assessing risks and identifying opportunities. Beyond engaging with stakeholders, global sustainability managers need to communicate the vision and mission of the organisation's commitment to sustainability actions to gain 'buy-in' from workers and other managers (Wheelen et al., 2017). They must be able to allocate resources to support the sustainability strategy and direct the transition to sustainability that extends beyond economic returns to include social and environmental value.

So much of strategic thinking is around determining what actions to implement to achieve stated aims and objectives. Often, some hard decisions regarding the sequencing of actions have to be made based on priorities that best support these. In terms of sustainability, managers have to decide what level of commitment they want to include in their overall corporate strategy. For some companies it is clear that sustainability actions fail to reach the strategic level that commands a significant reallocation of resources to attain stated aims and objectives and that form a central part of the organisation's commitment to sustainability. In others, a sustainability commitment not only involves resourcing but also targets, key performance indicators (KPIs), monitoring and evaluation as well as learning. Here, companies integrate sustainability actions and initiatives, align them to strategic aims and communicate outcomes in the form of transparent reporting. Thus, applying a set of actions that support sustainability is not enough, they have to be linked to clearly stated strategic aims and objectives. Hart and Milstein

(2003) produced an important account of how to create sustainable value in organisations that maintains a relevance in the modern era. Figure 3.2 presents a sustainability strategy framework as a basis of explaining and discussing the strategy process in this context.

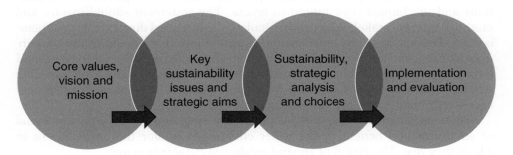

FIGURE 3.2   *Sustainability strategy framework*

Core values, vision and mission

The starting point of a sustainability strategy is to determine the core values of the organisation and the reason it exists. This may involve a single core value or a set of them. For an effective sustainability strategy, the core values should incorporate principles that underpin a commitment to sustainability whether or not it forms the central aspect of strategy or as part of a wider strategy. The commitment cannot place sustainability as a peripheral strategic issue due to the level of resource commitment it commands and the requirement for authenticity in intent. Core values govern all major strategic decisions in organisations whether they be economic, social or environment (or a combination of all three). In the context of sustainability, it is evident that more and more companies around the world are embracing the benefits associated with incorporating the actions that support it into their strategy. More than that, however, sustainability is featuring among the core values that define why these companies exist and what they aim to achieve. Large corporations such as Coca-Cola, Google and Apple have embedded sustainability principles into their core values that extend well beyond what is required by way of regulatory compliance.

This trend in defining core values around the protection of the environment has economic benefits too as it can be seen that economic performance is increasingly reliant on innovations around sustainable business practices. For example, non-renewable resources become increasingly expensive the scarcer they become making it increasingly difficult for companies to manage costs and increase efficiency. Consequently, it makes business sense to innovate around sustainable processes and practices and embedding this into the core values influences the organisational culture around sustainability practices. Core values can be developed around a wide range of themes that reflect what the company stands for. Where sustainability features as the central theme then issues of sustainable economic growth, resource efficiency, social inclusivity, equality in employment, low carbon emissions to reduce environmental impact, and zero waste policies are just some examples that may underpin the core values that permeate throughout the company.

A vision statement is a short descriptive account of an organisation's aspirations and the impact they intend to create. The statement should inspire and motivate internal stakeholders and articulate the intended direction of the organisation. The vision of the organisation is something that should attain 'buy-in' from workers and act as a unifying statement that underpins shared goals around a strategic plan. As a concise statement, the vision invariably focuses on a specific strategic aim and sets a timeframe for its achievement. It is future oriented and necessarily challenging but realistic in scale and scope.

Vision statements that feature sustainability emphasise some aspect of social or environmental benefit to the wider community and/or the environment in which they live. The vision of apparel producers Patagonia states:

> Build the best product, cause no unnecessary harm, use business to inspire and implement solutions to the environmental crisis. (Patagonia, 2021)

The vision of the company states up front that it aims to deliver the best product on the market. However, this links into their commitment to undertake business in a manner that not only does not harm but proactively seeks ways to help find solutions to the environmental crisis that many of their stakeholders perceive to be a climate emergency.

The mission statement communicates the overriding purpose of the organisation. Further to this, managers have to be able to communicate a vision of what the organisation is all about and where it wants to be in the future. The vision describes the aspirations of the organisation. The purpose, vision and mission of an organisation form the basis of determining specific objectives. By defining these, managers can clarify what the company stands for and how they can be differentiated from rivals. This clarity of purpose provides focus and direction for all involved in the activities of the organisation. Dobson et al. (2011) set out key criteria that comprise a good mission statement. These are:

- the principal business or activities of an organisation
- its key aims and objectives
- the beliefs or values of the company – defining what the organisation represents, such as the balance between profit and other values such as reputation and community involvement
- the organisation's main stakeholders.

Although mission statements are a standard item of documentation made public by companies, they have not been without criticism. Kay (2001) argues that such statements are merely part of a 'wish-driven strategy' that fails to recognise the limits to what might be possible, given finite organisational resources. This argument has some validity because there are numerous examples of firms following a strategy to achieve higher aspirations rather than what their capabilities and resources allow. In other cases, mission statements have been viewed with scepticism as being merely another public relations exercise by organisations wishing to present themselves in a positive light to internal and external stakeholders. Nevertheless, mission statements remain a staple of organisations' attempts to communicate what they stand for to stakeholders. Some general principles of effective mission statements are that they should be succinct, memorable, unique to the company, realistic and contemporary. The mission of UK consumer goods multinational company Unilever reflects these by stating 'Unilever's mission is to add vitality to life. We meet everyday needs for nutrition, hygiene and personal care with brands that help people feel good, look good and get more out of life' (Unilever, 2021).

> **Definition:** A **mission statement** is a formal summary of the aims and values of an organisation.

Sustainability has provided an opportunity for companies to spread the message of their 'green' credentials to stakeholders and has become almost a standard feature in modern times. There is much kudos attached to being perceived as sensitive to the future of the planet but there are also sound business reasons for doing so, including those of meeting stakeholder expectations and the fact that competitive advantage can be gained from pursuing sustainable business practices. However, to attain any form of credibility the statements have to be backed up by action. Also, mission statements that include sustainability as a theme require some subtle and nuanced forms of communication that build authenticity. Effective mission statements that feature sustainability have some common features including the characteristic of being easy to understand by a general audience; being succinct but specific around a key sustainability aim; being relevant to all stakeholders including the wider community; and being inclusive of economic, social and environmental commitments. Nike provide an example of a mission statement that features many of these characteristics:

> Our mission is what drives us to do everything possible to expand human potential. We do that by creating groundbreaking sport innovations, by making our products more sustainably, by building a creative and diverse global team and by making a positive impact in communities where we live and work. (Nike, 2021)

Companies like Patagonia and Nike need to craft a vision and mission statement that not only adheres to some of the effective characteristics outlined above, but also ensure that it aligns to their strategy. Where sustainability forms the central focus of that strategy then there is a need to ensure a coherent link to the identified key sustainability issues and the stated strategic aim. This forms the next phase of the sustainability strategy framework.

Key sustainability issues and strategic aims

There are a wide range of sustainability issues that companies could focus on and link to their strategy. These range from innovations for reducing carbon emissions to socially inclusive employment policies; investing in sustainability value adding activities to managing green supply chains. Sustainability aims help organisations focus attention on those areas of the business that are catalysts for growth through innovation. The development of new products or services or the creation of new business models based on sustainability issues can enhance performance by generating income from meeting social or environmental needs. Cavaleri and Shabana (2018) present a useful conceptual framework that links sustainability with strategy. There may also be reputational capital to be gained from an effective sustainability strategy by building stronger customer relationships or closer partnerships with other stakeholders. There are also a multitude of ways that a sustainability strategy can contribute to cost savings such as reduced waste, productive efficiencies, or use of more efficient energy resources. Human resources also feature in sustainability strategies by linking reputation to the attraction of new talent keen to work for organisations that have a commitment to sustainability and corporate responsibility.

There are opportunities for tackling the challenges posed by sustainability across all activities within companies; however, to align them to strategic aims requires careful consideration of how they fit within the overall aim of the organisation and the likely impact that the chosen actions will have. An important aspect to strategic management in this context is the identification and understanding of key sustainability issues that are central to driving business performance alongside meeting social and environmental aims. This is referred to as materiality and focuses the attention of managers on those issues that gain strategic priority. Materiality can inform priorities by providing the basis for determining where on the matrix each sustainability issue is positioned and the reason for that position. Formisano et al. (2018) provide a valuable insight into how the materiality matrix can be applied for prioritising sustainability strategies in a banking enterprise. Figure 3.3 uses a matrix to illustrate how priorities can be determined based on the level of impact and extent of stakeholder interest in the identified issues.

> **Definition: Materiality sustainability** is the principle of defining the social and environmental issues that matter most to an organisation and its stakeholders.

The materiality matrix is divided into four quadrants each reflecting a level of impact and interest related to the sustainability action proposed. Impact and interest relate to those of the business and stakeholders respectively. Stakeholders include shareholders, customers, suppliers, partners, regulators, employees and trade unions, among others. Thus, quadrant 1 has low impact for business and low interest to stakeholders. The sustainability actions proposed would have little effect. In quadrant 2 there is low impact on business but a high level of interest to stakeholders. Sustainability actions in this quadrant may not derive much value to the company but will meet stakeholder expectations. For example, the outcome may not improve the economic performance of the company but stakeholders may perceive value from the sustainability actions and bestow reputational capital on the company. Quadrant 3 shows high impact for the company and low interest for stakeholders. Here, it can be seen that the benefits derived from the sustainability actions benefit the company more than it does wider stakeholders. Quadrant 4 is where both high impact for the company combines with high levels of interest for stakeholders.

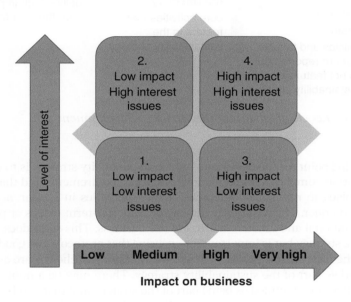

FIGURE 3.3 *Materiality matrix*

As noted in Chapter 2, much of the strategic decision-making in organisations stems from gaining a better understanding of stakeholder expectations and the relative power and influence they wield. Very often stakeholder groups have knowledge and expertise that could prove valuable to managers when deciding on what sustainability actions to prioritise. For instance, pressure groups like Greenpeace or Friends of the Earth have a vast array of different members and supporters who have developed a higher level of understanding of the impact of business activity on the environment and can often bring forward viable solutions to mitigate or remove the negative effects. It is rational for managers to seek to engage positively with such groups to improve their decision-making. Stakeholders also pose a challenge to business by exposing bad practice, exerting pressure to improve, or forcing a reassessment of priorities. Ultimately, strategic decision-makers have to prioritise certain sustainability actions over others and be prepared to argue their case to stakeholders. Although some flexibility can be built into the sustainability strategy, the core aims and objectives should be consistent throughout the timeframe identified for the achievement. Figure 3.4 outlines the three stages of sustainability strategy development that govern how managers allocate resources to support prioritised actions.

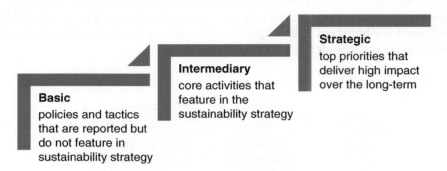

FIGURE 3.4 *Levels of sustainability strategy development*

The starting point for the development of a sustainability strategy is to ensure that the organisation complies with regulations and legal requirements and that measures are put in place to report the outcomes of their activities in a clear, accurate and transparent manner. The basic stage may involve shorter-term tactics or policies that support operational and functional areas of the business. This stage does not feature as part of the strategy but is important for ensuring that protocols and good practice is observed. The intermediary phase is where the first priority choices are assessed and implemented as part of the sustainability strategy. There may be a number of different actions that are identified as being part of the strategy and that can be considered core to the overall sustainability strategy. The third stage is where the top priorities that underpin the strategy are chosen, resourced and implemented. These will have detailed and specific targets linked to them and the outcomes will make the largest and most significant contribution to the sustainability goals of the company. It is intended that the top priorities will have the highest impact over the long-term.

Mini case 3.1: Timbeter, Estonia and Costa Rica

Tallin-based company Timbeter was founded in 2013 as a forest tech company specialising as a global industrial timber measurement, logistics and reporting platform. The company provides precise measuring and tracking of timber more efficiently and accurately. The added value of the platform is in offering the ability to track timber movements in the supply chain in real-time anywhere in the world. In a strategic partnership with the Estonian Environmental Investment Centre the company is working with the government of Costa Rica as part of that country's

INTRODUCTION TO GLOBAL SUSTAINABLE MANAGEMENT

sustainability strategy for monitoring and controlling their forestry sector. This is necessary to manage the renewable forest assets and to push back against illegal logging.

The sustainability aims of the Costa Rican government aligns to the type of solutions that Timbeter can offer and reflects the sustainability strategy developed by the company. One of the most important aspects of the Timbeter technology is the scope it provides for improving transparency in the management of forests. By applying artificial intelligence and machine-learning the company is able to monitor and control all movement of timber in any chosen forest environment. It helps to improve efficiency in forest harvesting and logistics so that the whole process is carefully controlled. This control function helps to reduce waste and cut down on pollution and carbon emissions.

The strategic fit between the development of technology at Timbeter and the aims of the Costa Rican Ministry of Environment and Energy is the basis of the synergy that drives the partnership. Costa Rica is a country that is in the vanguard of climate change and various ministries and agencies have combined forces to tackle the issue and to find solutions that help the country protect its natural assets that are so vital to the economic growth. By accessing Estonian expertise the wider strategy of supporting pioneering actions to address climate change alongside economic development is designed to manage natural resources in a sustainable manner well into the future. With deforestation now known to be a major loss for carbon capture, it has become increasingly evident that carefully managed forests are an essential for tackling the climate emergency. For Timbeter, it is yet more recognition of how their technology development can simultaneously support sustainable forests and drive company growth.

Questions and task

1. Identify the aims of the Timbeter strategic partnership with the government of Costa Rica for both parties.
2. What sustainability added value does the Timbeter forestry measurement platform deliver?
3. How does the technology developed by Timbeter help to tackle illegal logging?

Once sustainability strategic priorities have been determined there is a need to set targets and key performance indicators (KPIs) so that progress can be measured and assessed. Effective KPIs need to be accessible so that performance measurements are easily understood. They have to be relevant to managers who rely on data gained from previous measurements and be able to link them to current ones. That is, the KPIs need to be comparable to previous datasets both internally and across the industry in which the company operates. Targets link to what the company is trying to achieve from its sustainability strategy and KPIs refer to the chosen quantitative measurements that have been chosen to measure and assess the performance to achieving the set targets. Logically, there needs to be set targets linked to the identified priorities in the sustainability strategy. Figure 3.5 sets out the criteria needed for setting targets.

All strategies should take the organisation to a higher level of effectiveness and this requires decision-makers to have a vision of where they want the organisation to be positioned at some point in the future. The strategic aims and objectives have to be suitably ambitious to stretch the resources and capabilities of the organisation to effect performance improvement. In the context of sustainability, managers need to set targets around key chosen issues that significantly move the organisation beyond their existing position. For example, the strategic aim may be to reduce the carbon emissions footprint of the organisation by 50% over a five-year period. This links into the need for strategy to be impactful. The actions that support sustainability need to deliver added value and demonstrate a clear outcome based on targets or KPIs. For example, the sustainability strategy may involve all workers undertaking an accredited sustainability training programme over a four-year period. Having a qualified workforce has the potential to gain from their input into new and innovative ways to improve sustainability in their functional areas of work.

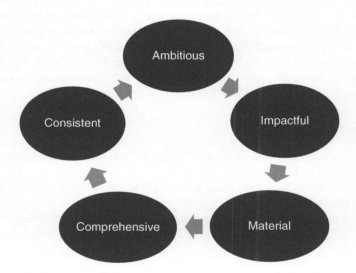

FIGURE 3.5 *Key criteria for target setting*

Finally, once sustainability strategic aims and objectives have been identified, it is essential that there is a measure of consistency around implementation so that managers and other stakeholders can determine and evaluate performance over time. Reporting on that performance in an accountable and transparent manner builds trust and helps inform future decisions.

Mini case 3.2: Backsberg Estate Wines, South Africa

One of the most proactive sectors for driving forward sustainability practices in South Africa is the wine producers of the Western Cape. Part of the success has been the close working relationships between wine producers and stakeholders across a wide range of interested and influential sectors including wildlife conservationists, water resource experts, healthcare providers, farmers and others. The strategy for developing wine as a sustainable business has also included a synergy between growers and the tourism industry, and in particular eco-tourism that combines wine tasting with tours of the South African environment.

South African wine producers have traditionally been small-scale with few opportunities for scaling the business due to restrictions on land and water uses. As part of a strategy to develop the industry, wine producers joined forces to create a national coalition between the Sustainable Wine South Africa (SWSA) and Wines of South Africa (WOSA). This has helped small vineyards to leverage advantage by tapping into the resources and knowledge of the coalition to develop a sustainable business based on wide-ranging principles including sustainable land stewardship, wildlife protection, environmental conservation and respect for farm workers. One example of a vineyard that has benefited from engaging in this coalition is the award winning Backsberg Estate.

Located on the slopes of the magnificent Simonberg Mountains, the Backsberg Estate became the country's first vineyard to be recognised as carbon neutral in 2015. Having been actively engaged in sustainability practices since 1998 the company had already built up a significant knowledge of effective means of producing world class wines in a sustainable manner. For example, the strategy involves reserving 10% of the estate for non-development and preservation status meaning that no business activity takes place on the land. The company also has a 'greening' programme to reduce carbon emissions. This followed a detailed carbon audit of all the activities of the estate to determine the magnitude of their carbon impact. The outcome proved a catalyst for a programme of tree growing as a means of carbon capture and air quality improvement that helped to improve the quality of the vines. Other carbon reducing actions included a switch to bio-mass for fuel and innovations in packaging. The strategy also featured important initiatives around social responsibility with groundbreaking initiatives such as offering housing ownership opportunities to farm workers on the estate. The Backsberg Estate has flourished as a result of their investment in sustainability practices and is often cited as an exemplar for demonstrating how a commitment to sustainability practices can derive economic, social and environmental benefits that combine to enhance global recognition and reputation.

Questions and tasks

1. What strategic advantages does the coalition of Sustainable Wine South Africa (SWSA) and Wines of South Africa (WOSA) bring to wine producers?
2. Identify three sustainable practices adopted by the Backsberg Estate.
3. Why is tree planting so important to the Backsberg Estate strategy?

SUSTAINABILITY STRATEGIC ANALYSIS AND CHOICES

The third stage of the sustainability strategy involves undertaking analysis of key issues around the strategic aims so that choices can be made regarding how to best achieve those aims. One effective tool for this process is the value chain model whereby global sustainability managers identify key linkages between primary and support activities in the organisation to add value and, ultimately, achieve stated sustainability strategic aims. The important choices to be made revolve around those combinations of linkages in the value chain that best support the sustainability strategic aims of the organisation.

Sustainability value chain

In an influential piece of work, Harvard University professor Michael Porter (1985) created the value chain model by dividing a firm into discrete activities it undertakes including designing, producing, marketing, selling and distributing its products. The value chain is applied with the purpose of diagnosing sources of competitive advantage. The value chain model is comprised of two levels of activities – primary and support activities – and when linkages are created between chosen ones then the combined effect creates added value that, if unable to be replicated by rivals, can create a competitive advantage. Although Porter designed the value chain model with a typical manufacturing company in mind, it is possible to adapt it for multiple different contexts including the sustainable value chain. In this context the value chain reveals all the sustainability activities and typically includes the:

- identification of the core sustainability activities of the organisation and their relationship with the stated strategic aims and objectives
- evaluation of the effectiveness of individual sustainability activities
- identification of key linkages between primary sustainability activities and support activities for creating added value
- identification of blockages that prevent the organisation from achieving competitive advantage based on sustainability activities.

Figure 3.6 illustrates the sustainability value chain. Primary activities include inbound logistics of sourcing, delivery and warehousing the raw materials that go into making products. In the sustainable value chain this element requires the sourcing of sustainable raw materials. For example, they may be sourced from suppliers closer to the production facilities or core markets. They may be sourced from accredited eco-friendly suppliers or from companies with a recognised high level of social responsibility.

The operations of the organisation can also derive added value in a sustainable manner. In this element the sustainability of production is the key to adding value and this can be attained through efficiency, use of renewable energy, the application of low carbon technologies, or the use of eco-friendly packaging. Following production is the distribution of products to intermediaries, retailers or wholesalers. This part of the supply chain can add value by introducing sustainability practices. Effective logistics planning can minimise the time goods spend in transit, contracts can be awarded to accredited eco-friendly distributors, and protocols can be implemented to reduce waste. The way in which products are marketed and promoted can also adhere to sustainable practices. This relates to how products are endorsed, the type of messaging that goes out to consumers regarding the purchase, use and disposal of products, the use of accreditation in advertising such as Fairtrade, or the claims made by companies regarding their green credentials. This topic is explored in more detail in Chapter 6. The final stage of the primary activities in the sustainable value chain is the service element linked to the use and re-use of products. Added value can be created in the manner in which companies demonstrate a commitment to recycling or reconstituting products after use. The effectiveness of this relies on consumers returning used products or packaging in a way that allows companies to create further value from the product thereby reducing waste, managing the effective use of resources and reducing carbon emissions.

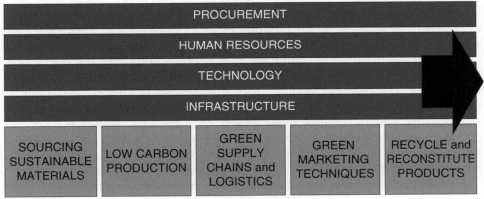

Primary sustainability activities

FIGURE 3.6   *Sustainability value chain*

Support activities in the sustainability value chain include the procurement of all materials required to run the organisation, the recruitment, training and support of human resources, technology development, and organisational infrastructure including the organisational structure, planning and quality assurance. Each should be undertaken within the sustainability ethos and should support the primary sustainability activities. For example, it will be necessary for the organisation to recruit talent based on a range of criteria such as communications, analytical and problem-solving skills but they also need to demonstrate a motivation and commitment to supporting the sustainability ethos of the organisation. Technological development must also adhere to sustainability principles and deliver green solutions to the organisational activities that improve products and service as well as operational efficiencies. Procurement must proceed based on not just 'best value' principles but also the green credentials of suppliers. The infrastructure of the organisation must be set up in a way that delivers effective process support based on low carbon and low waste principles.

By applying the sustainability value chain, managers gain a better insight into what sustainability activities the company should undertake, and how they should perform them. It also reveals information that helps managers configure sustainability activities in a way that enables added value to the products which, in turn, improves competitiveness. It is the role of strategic managers to choose the most appropriate elements of the value chain to focus resources on, build capabilities and leverage the added value into a competitive advantage.

SUSTAINABILITY STRATEGY: IMPLEMENTATION

The implementation phase is where strategy is put into action. Strategic decisions are made at the corporate level of a business but actions to implement them need to be carried out at operational level. This is why a sustainability strategy needs to permeate all levels of an organisation as its formulation and implementation affect all internal stakeholders. The success of implementation depends on the effectiveness of the lines of communication between corporate and operational level. Very often the value of the business level of management is most evident in this process. The business level of a company consists of middle managers who oversee functional areas of the business (such as finance, marketing, logistics and warehousing, human resource management, etc.) but who also act as a conduit of communications between corporate level (executive board) and operational level (shop floor level) and it is that link that bounds the sustainability strategy together. Allio (2005) provides a useful practical guide to implementing strategy.

It should be noted that not all sustainability strategies reach the implementation stage in the same form as they were originally devised. Some are abandoned completely due to rising costs, changing circumstances and environment, changes in management or a change of focus. More commonly they evolve into something different from the original plan. An 'implementation deficit' refers to the gap between intended strategy implementation and that which is actually carried out. An implementation deficit is typically caused by changes to the external environment, lack of time to fully implement sustainability strategic plans, too few resources or lack of communication. Internal political factors can also have a limiting effect on implementation and this is especially the case where strategy involves resource allocation or when financial issues are a consideration.

Sustainability strategy implementation involves the transition from strategic formulation to strategic management. Strategic management is an organisation-wide task involving both the development and implementation of strategy and brings together formulation, implementation and evaluation. Although wide-ranging and complex, it is possible to identify and discuss some key elements of implementation.

Key elements of sustainability strategy implementation

The key elements of implementation include organisational structure: organisational governance; design thinking and innovation; organisational learning; and organisational culture.

Organisational structure

Successful implementation of a sustainability strategy requires an appropriate organisational structure to determine how activities and tasks are divided, supervised and coordinated. An organisational structure acts as a controlling mechanism by formally detailing lines of authority, span of control, responsibilities and duties, the allocation of tasks and different levels of management within the organisation. Whereas large, complex and bureaucratic organisations are traditionally characterised by tall, hierarchical structures with an emphasis on rules, regulations, procedures and clearly defined levels of authority, modern organisations tend to adopt a more flexible, collaborative and changeable structure. In organisations where sustainability is either a core or integral part of strategy there needs to be a structure that supports the communication and processes aligned to sustainability actions. A typical structure is illustrated in Figure 3.7 where the sustainability strategy is developed and agreed upon at executive leadership level. This will occur after consultation with the board of directors and perhaps some managers.

Generally, executives act on behalf of shareholders. Effectively, executive managers act as agents for the shareholders and are committed to developing and implementing strategies that deliver outcomes in the best interests of the shareholders. Traditionally there has always been some distance between executive managers and shareholders as much of the relationship is built on trust. However, in the modern era, it is increasingly evident that the views of this important stakeholder group will be absorbed by executive managers as part of a due diligence procedure whereby the rationale for any long-term strategy requiring significant resourcing is explained. The emergence of social and environmental value as key competitive factors has necessarily changed the focus of attention of many shareholders leading to closer scrutiny of executive managers' strategies that traditionally emphasised economic targets and returns.

The sustainability strategy is communicated to other internal stakeholders such as middle and functional managers who then, subsequently, explain the actions that are required to support it to employees whose duties it is to carry them out. Soderstrom and Weber (2019) provide an interesting example of how organisational structure links to situational interactions in a bio-medical

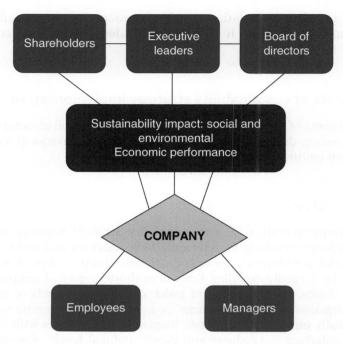

FIGURE 3.7 *Organisational structure of a sustainable company*

company seeking to become more sustainable. Importantly, the sustainability strategy should have positive impacts on social and/or environmental aspects. The economic imperative will also be recognised and the sustainability strategy will include those actions from the sustainability value chain analysis that add value, help to gain a competitive advantage and contribute to achieving long-term economic performance goals.

Organisational governance

In an era when sustainability has gained in profile it is increasingly important that organisations put in place effective governance measures to deliver the level of accountability and transparency that helps build trust with stakeholders and to offer a true reflection of their sustainability performance. Good governance requires a formal system of accountability linked to the sustainability strategy. Chapter 4 provides a detailed discussion of reporting mechanisms for organisations. Another relevant reason why good governance is essential is the information that it provides to managers regarding how effective their chosen sustainability strategy is performing. It may flag up weaknesses or areas requiring further resourcing that allows managers to make necessary adjustments. Often, companies will seek the advocacy and guidance of external experts as part of their governance process. These may include industry experts, advisory panels, consultants, accreditors, among others. At the micro-level there should also be a designated manager or point of responsibility for each identified sustainability target linked to the strategic aims.

Mini case 3.3: TATA Group, India

Founded in 1868, TATA Group is an Indian multinational conglomerate with a wide range of interests including chemicals, steel, communications, consumer goods, automotive, energy and many more. Each TATA company operates as a strategic business unit with independence in decision-making under the guidance of their own board of directors. However, as a group, the company has a distinct and integrated approach to sustainability with a policy that details how TATA companies create long-term stakeholder value by integrating economic, environmental and social considerations. The sustainability strategy has a mission to aspire for global sustainability leadership in the sectors in which it operates. This commits the companies to integrating sustainability actions into processes and activities and to ensure that sustainability principles are embedded in product stewardship throughout their life cycle. Underpinning these principles is the distinct governance structure that oversees sustainability compliance, strategy, targets and performance. The identified areas of sustainability at group level include investors and regulators, environment, community, employees, value chain partners, and customers.

Sustainability governance structure at the TATA Group consists of two tiers – the TATA Group Sustainability Council (TGSC) and the Sustainability Working Councils (SWC). The former consists of Chief Executive Officers (CEOs) of the large TATA companies and is chaired by a Group Chief Sustainability Officer. This tier provides strategic direction to the sustainability policy and sets priorities in support of achieving global sustainability leadership in each of the group industry sectors. The Sustainability Working Councils report to the TGSC and comprises Chief Sustainability Officers of the TATA Group companies. The council proposes sustainability policies, positions and targets to the TGSC to inform decision-making. It can be seen that the two tiers perform distinct but mutually reliant roles in governance. At the strategic level the TGSC defines the sustainability philosophy, advises and approves group level sustainability policies, allocates resources, controls communications on sustainability issues and related brand management, and applies networking influence to shape the regulatory framework around sustainability policy. The SWC is an important support group for the strategic decision-makers. This role involves proposing policies, identifying appropriate processes and systems for targeted sustainability interventions, advising on good practice, and engaging in group advocacy to external stakeholders.

(Continued)

The governance structure of TATA Group has been used as a template by many organisations around the world seeking to manage their sustainability strategy within principles of accountable and transparent best practice. TATA Group is one of the key influencing organisations driving forward the global sustainability agenda and the company collaborates with a wide range of other companies, non-governmental organisations (NGOs), pressure groups and government agencies to tackle the challenges of climate change and environmental protection. Some critics point to this proactive approach as the means by which the company shields itself from some of the controversial initiatives it has pursued throughout its long history. In particular, the company has been accused of land grab policies in West Bengal, Orissa and Kerala states in India, of manufacturing military transport vehicles for the repressive Burmese (Myanmar) regime and investment in environmentally damaging soda ash plants in Tanzania. The company has strongly refuted these claims and points to its robust governance structure as evidence of its commitment to sustainability.

Question and tasks

1. Outline the role of the TATA Group Sustainability Council (TGSC).
2. Explain how the Sustainability Working Councils support the TGSC.
3. What are the six identified areas of sustainability at group level that feature as part of the TATA Group governance strategy?

Design thinking and innovation

Design thinking is a method for developing innovative solutions for complex problems by purposively including the concerns, interests, and values of humans in the design process (Meinel and Leifer, 2011). It is necessarily iterative and has the aim of quickly developing and testing multiple innovative solutions that allow users to determine the optimal one for their specific purpose. The five key characteristics of design thinking are a human-centred approach; integration of experimentation artifacts; multidisciplinary team collaboration; a holistic and integrative view of problems; and a process of understanding, observing, defining, ideation, prototyping and testing as illustrated in Figure 3.8.

FIGURE 3.8 *Design thinking process*

Although presented in a linear format, the design process can link different elements separately and distinctly from other elements before the combination contributes to the whole process. For example, lessons learnt from prototyping can inform new ideation whereby further innovative ideas are generated based on the outcomes of the prototyping process. Similarly, testing informs the next iteration of prototyping. This in turn improves understanding and may redefine the problem and so on. This process supports the goal of design thinking by developing creative solutions that have a positive impact on the future. Hence, it is a strategic issue that requires the allocation of resources to effect a significant or transformational change.

Design thinking can be viewed from different perspectives including a human-centred lens that focuses on human wants and needs; a research-based perspective; broader contextual views where the problem question is expanded to a wider frame of reference; or an iterative delivery and prototyping perspective similar to the one outlined above. In the context of sustainability, the design thinking needs to focus on innovations that contribute to a future that addresses the social and environmental needs of humans (it could also be argued that this principle should extend to other species in the eco-system). The ultimate goal of the design thinking needs to generate a positive outcome in support of the identified future.

Organisational learning

Implementation of a sustainability strategy requires organisations to effectively leverage advantages from organisational learning. According to Argyris (1992), organisational learning occurs through experience, building and sharing knowledge, expertise, ideas and insights, and is closely linked to leadership, organisational structure and culture. As noted previously, organisational leaders are responsible for creating a vision for the future and that should incorporate the learning process. Senge (2006) was a pioneer of organisational learning in the early 1990s and produced a seminal work on the subject in 1990 and subsequently updated. He argues that leaders need to set the tone for developing an organisational culture around learning. The organisational culture should embrace change and seek continual sustainability improvement through the learning process. One way of influencing culture is to build an organisational structure that facilitates the key features of a learning culture. This may include work projects around small groups or teams of workers that focus on ways to build-in sustainability actions into their functional area, empowering those workers to take charge of their project and creating an integrated and free-flowing communications system that incorporates internal employees and external suppliers, partners and customers. Sustainability is an evolving process with new techniques, tools and processes constantly being developed, tested, adapted and implemented. The scope for learning is immense and the key to improvement lies in the way in which learning outcomes are fed back into the organisation to catalyse new learning and continuous improvement.

Organisational culture

Organisational culture develops from shared values and beliefs that coalesce to deliver what is understood to be the dominant culture within organisations. Values and beliefs refer to consensual, enduring and implicit assumptions held by groups within an organisation that influence behaviour and ways of doing things within the environment. These determine how people perceive and react to changes within various environments. These values and beliefs manifest themselves in many different ways but will merge around the formation of norms of behaviour and conduct. In the context of sustainability, many organisations seek to influence the formation of a dominant culture that reflects their mission and vision.

As it is not possible to replicate cultures across different organisations, each organisation has its own unique culture that sets it apart from others. The norms of behaviour inform and link into both individual and group behaviour. Various reinforcing outcomes ensure that the dominant culture is maintained. These may range from formal codes of conduct (as drawn up in some professional organisations such as solicitors and accountants) to more informal reminders of expectations regarding behaviour.

The process of forming an organisational culture that has sustainability as a central theme invariably begins with the core beliefs, values, vision and philosophy of the leaders in the organisation (Combe, 2014). They set the tone and belief system that others follow. Sometimes these dissipate over time and are replaced by new ones; other times they endure the test of time and dominate for many decades. What is clear is that they have a strong influence on the formation of culture by guiding the behaviour of managers at all levels of the organisation, informing recruitment criteria and the types of staff they employ and determining the socialisation process that matches new recruits' values and beliefs to those of the organisation. The influence of culture is of sufficient importance as to merit a more in-depth treatment and this forms the basis of the discussion in Chapter 9.

SUSTAINABILITY STRATEGY: EVALUATION

Once the performance of a sustainability strategy has been measured, the evaluation needs to address reasons for the performance outcome linked to set targets. This will reveal the relative strengths or weaknesses associated with the sustainability actions that have been implemented and help to inform future sustainability strategy. Evaluation combines both internal and external factors. Sustainability actions make use of the organisation's resources and capabilities and the returns on these need to be evaluated alongside any changes to market and competitive conditions. Thus, evaluation covers social, environmental and economic returns linked to sustainability actions including reducing product life cycles, production efficiencies, and increasing the speed of sustainability technological progress (Zotova et al., 2016).

The sustainability strategy evaluation should reveal whether or not change is necessary. If change is necessary then the evaluation should also point to the extent to which change should be implemented. Change can range from minor alterations to the business model or the way the sustainability actions affect internal functions, to radical change management or even a paradigm shift in thinking about what the business is all about. Redesigning a sustainability strategy can be perceived as risky, expensive and time-consuming since it requires the redeployment of resources and capabilities. More often than not, organisations will modify their sustainability actions. Modifications can achieve desired outcomes but with limited risk and disruption to the organisation.

Sustainability strategy evaluation should focus on the longer-term aspirations of the business. An evaluation of the sustainability strategy should determine whether or not the organisation is aligned to stated aims and will focus on where the organisation is compared to where it intends to be. The sustainability strategy evaluation should reveal:

- where the company is currently positioned
- where the organisation can be positioned given current resources and capabilities
- the benefits of adopting different levels of sustainability actions
- the sustainability position that the organisation should aspire to
- the practical steps for implementing a new sustainability strategy to achieve stated aims if the existing strategy fails to achieve expected outcomes.

The evaluation of performance of the sustainability strategy will focus on the extent to which it achieves stated long-term objectives. Sustainability objectives may include:

- targets for reducing carbon emissions to set target levels
- becoming the carbon capture technological leader in the industry sector in the next five years
- acquiring the best skills available to innovate and produce the next generation of sustainability solutions for supply chains, waste management, resource usage and production efficiency
- developing a range of new sustainable products or services
- targets for customer satisfaction linked to sustainable products to be achieved year-on-year for the next five years.

The sustainability strategy of an organisation will be built on broad-based objectives that relate to where the organisation wants to be at some point in the future. The key sustainability actions to be evaluated help managers analyse the progress the organisation has made towards achieving these long-term objectives. There are, of course, difficulties in measuring some of the key elements, such as the reputational capital associated with perceptions of the sustainable organisation, so managers need to use their experience, analytical skills and intuition in order to make value judgements about the performance of actions that support these. Nevertheless, managers need to address a number of issues relating to the evaluation of a sustainability strategy including the:

- extent to which existing sustainability strategies achieve desired outcomes
- effectiveness to which the sustainability strategies were executed
- effectiveness to which the sustainability strategies were communicated
- accuracy of the sustainability value chain analysis
- extent of managerial commitment to the chosen sustainability strategy
- depth to which alternative sustainability strategies were analysed
- extent to which the results were monitored, recorded and analysed
- level of proper diagnosis of trends and the level of consistency between strategic choices and implementation
- extent to which the sustainability strategy was properly resourced.

There are a number of useful tools and techniques for helping managers evaluate sustainability issues. Figure 3.9 highlights four of the most commonly used ones.

FIGURE 3.9   *Tools and techniques for evaluating sustainability*

A sustainability assessment is often the first opportunity that organisations get to fully understand the needs and expectations of external stakeholders such as customers, investors or supply chain partners. A sustainability assessment is designed to match the sustainability actions to the needs of stakeholders such that any gaps can be identified and managed. This can often highlight weaknesses in the current sustainability strategy or areas where greater investment or quality needs to be channelled.

Benchmarking is an important tool for determining the effectiveness of the sustainability strategy set against that of rival firms. This helps managers better understand the effects of other approaches to sustainability, identify gaps in their own strategy or consolidate strengths linked to sustainability actions.

A risk analysis is an important tool for supporting entrepreneurial decision-making based on sustainability actions. The outcomes of the analysis often improve the understanding of key economic, social and environmental factors that feature as part of the sustainability strategic aims.

Finally, an impact measurement tool helps managers understand the current environmental footprint associated with the organisation's activities. The outcomes of the impact measurements can often be the catalyst for change in organisations seeking to improve their sustainability performance.

CASE STUDY

Toyota, Japan

Founded in 1937, the Toyota Motor Corporation is a Japanese multinational automotive manufacturer. The company is the world's largest car maker employing nearly 400,000 workers on a global scale. In terms of annual revenue, the company is the tenth largest firm in the world with regular output registering around 10 million cars. Toyota is the market leader for global sales of hybrid electric and hydrogen fuel-cell cars. These represent part of a commitment by the company to invest in green technology and fits into the overall Environmental Action Plans that the company updates every five years. Key areas of investment include fuel consumption and efficiency, emissions, noise and production, usage and disposal. Results from the myriad environmental interventions have been mixed with the company being awarded 'top company' status on the Carbon Clean 200 list of the world's cleanest energy companies in 2016. However, in 2021 the company received the biggest ever fine of $180 million for violating US Environmental Protection Agency (EPA) regulations on emissions. The company

was found to have delayed required filings regarding emissions and failed to inform the EPA on recalls related to emissions defects. This has increased scrutiny of the company's environmental plans with monitoring and evaluation standards at unprecedented levels both from internal and external analysts. Key elements of the strategy and management of the company comprises a clear statement of intent regarding the fundamental approach towards the environment; environmental materiality analysis; environmental challenges to 2050; and the Toyota Environmental Action Plan to 2025. Six main challenges have been identified and these are highlighted in Figure 3.10.

The six environmental challenges feature aims that are within the management scope of the company and reach requires the deployment of sustainability actions. The emphasis is on reducing carbon emissions across all activities including production, plant operations, product life cycles, and waste and recycling. To meet these challenges requires investment in new technologies, education and knowledge sharing in the workforce, managerial commitment, resourcing, and

▶

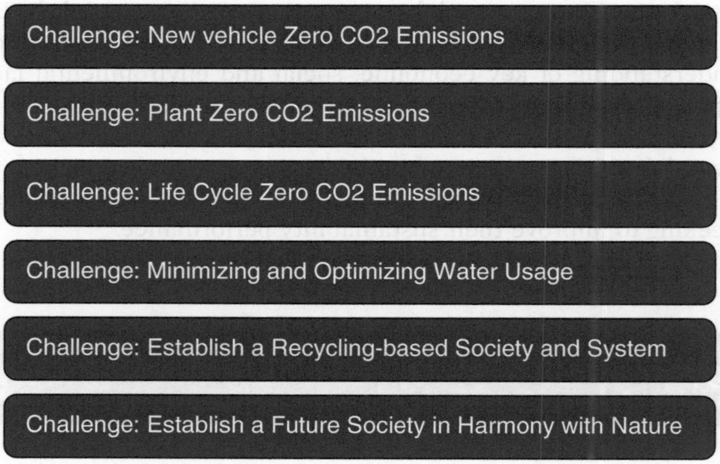

FIGURE 3.10 *Toyota's six environmental challenges*

Source: Toyota Environmental Challenge 2050 - Toyota Europe

an embedded culture around sustainability. Integrating sustainability strategy throughout the organisation is key to meeting the challenges presented and this requires high-level and coordinated management skills and attributes featuring communications, analysis, problem-solving, motivating, networking, among others. These skills and attributes combine to encourage workers to think and act in a sustainable manner in the course of their duties.

The environmental vision of Toyota is set out in their statement around the company's fundamental approach towards the environment. Here, the company commits to adopting sustainability practices for the sustainable development of society and the world. Key to this is ensuring that all workers, including those in subsidiaries, act in accordance with the company sustainability policies. The process also involves the development of an Environmental Materiality Analysis (EMA) that helps to identify risks and opportunities.

Perhaps appropriately, one of the identified risks is the imposition of fines for failing to achieve fuel efficiency regulations. The company is clearly keen to avoid repeating the financial and reputational costs of sanctions for non-compliance that it has suffered in the past. Opportunities include the growing demand for electric and fuel-efficient cars that the company has invested so heavily in. In 2020 there were 4.5 million registered electric cars in China compared to 3.2 million in Europe with both markets showing rapid growth until the Covid-19 pandemic of 2021 (www.iea.org, 2020). The EMA involves a four-step procedure starting with the identification of global environmental issues that are pertinent to the Toyota fundamental approach to the environment. The second step is the prioritisation of environmental issues based on the relevance to stakeholders and impact on the company. The third step is validating a common understanding of the environmental policy with all plants and subsidiaries that comprise the corporation on a global basis. The fourth step is to undertake a review process every five years that supports the development of the subsequent five-year action plan. The Environmental Materiality Analysis is a key outcome that helps managers formulate strategies that are designed to meet long-term aims such as the Toyota Environmental Challenge 2050.

Toyota Environmental Challenge 2050

The scale and complexity of environmental challenges facing the world in the twenty-first century are both concerning and immediate. Evidence of climate change is now a daily reality for many of the world's citizens, the loss of bio-diversity has upset the natural balance of the eco-system, and the unsustainable exploitation of resources has had economic and environmental consequences that threaten the security of societies around the world. Organisations have a role to play in addressing these issues and Toyota have been proactive in making a contribution. The Toyota Environmental Challenge 2050 was created in 2015 and is linked to the UN Sustainable Development Goals with milestones set for 2025 and 2030. The six challenges outlined in Figure 3.10 align to a series of specific actions that support the achievement of selected SDGs. For example, there is a target of a 90% reduction in carbon emissions from new vehicles by 2050 that links to SDG 7 (affordable and clean energy) and SDG 13 (climate action). These also feature in the commitment to reach net zero carbon plants by 2050 with this also supporting SDG 9 (industry, innovation and infrastructure). Perhaps the most challenging of all is the commitment to completely eliminate all carbon from the vehicle life cycle by 2050. This links to SDG 12 (responsible consumption and production).

Companies of the size, scale and scope of Toyota have a moral duty to act sustainably to help tackle climate change. Consumers and citizens are more aware of the responsibilities that corporate bodies have in this regard and this plays out in the way in which they perceive commercial organisations and their products and services. Consequently, there are sound business reasons for investing in sustainability and building strategies around it. The drive towards sustainability is characterised by innovation and creativity, improved efficiency, and better and more effective use of resources. These are key areas of competitive advantage for those firms with the vision, experience and know-how to exploit the opportunities that they present. Toyota has been at the vanguard of automotive manufacturers in striving to meet the challenges of addressing environmental issues and maintaining an economic growth ambition. The Toyota Environmental Challenge 2050 represents a commitment to making a significant contribution to protecting the eco-system which all species depend on whilst simultaneously meeting demand for vehicle transport into the future.

Questions and task

1. What three challenges set by Toyota link to reducing carbon emissions?

2. Access the Toyota Environmental Challenge 2050 and identify three actions that support identified UN Sustainable Development Goals (see https://global.toyota/en/sustainability/esg/challenge2050/).

3. What is the purpose of undertaking an Environmental Materiality Analysis?

SUMMARY

This chapter has used a typical strategy process to explain the ways in which sustainability strategies can be formulated, implemented and evaluated. The explanations of how sustainability strategies are developed have used theoretical frameworks including the value chain and the materiality matrix. Other frameworks have been used to offer insights into how targets are set and an example of an organisational structure. The discussion started with a critical evaluation of the core aims, mission and vision of organisations that are committed to sustainability strategies. This section emphasised the need to gain stakeholder 'buy-in' to the sustainability strategy aims and objectives. In particular, it was revealed just how important it is to integrate sustainability throughout the organisation.

The materiality matrix was used to explain how identifying levels of impact the sustainability strategy has and the interest among stakeholders can inform decision-making and help managers focus on appropriate levels of strategic intent and apply resources accordingly. The value chain framework was used to explain how managers can analyse sustainability actions to link with chosen support activities to combine and create added value. This process allows managers to determine the choices that support the aim of achieving competitive advantage alongside social and environmental aims. The implementation aspect of sustainability strategy featured organisational structure, governance, learning and culture. The discussion emphasised that these elements should be interrelated and implemented as a cohesive and integrated set of aims and objectives based on interconnections between them. The chapter was rounded off with the presentation of some of the most commonly used tools and techniques for evaluation of sustainability strategy.

REVIEW QUESTION AND TASKS

1. Explain the difference between operational and strategic management.
2. Give three examples of how organisations can add value by undertaking sustainability actions.
3. What is materiality and why is it important in the context of sustainability?

FURTHER READING

Rosenberg, M. (2015) *Strategy and Sustainability: A Hardnosed and Clear-Eyed Approach to Environmental Sustainability for Business*. London: Palgrave Macmillan.

The author addresses some of the tensions and challenges of bringing together the business world with that of environmental issues. The work presents some of the complexities of sustainability and links them to some of the difficult strategic choices that business managers have to make. The book contains some thought provoking examples and case studies from a number of different industry sectors.

Sroufe, R. (2018) *Integrated Management: How Sustainability Creates Value for Any Business*. Bingley: Emerald Publishing.

Using the principles of management integration across functions within organisations, the author explores ways in which individuals, organisations or even whole cities can integrate management around sustainability to improve competitiveness, efficiency and effectiveness. The book uses cases where this integration is already evident and presents examples of opportunities for enterprises to incorporate sustainability into their value propositions that include environmental, social and governance criteria.

Williams, E.F. (2018) *Green Giants: How Smart Companies Turn Sustainability into Billion-Dollar Businesses* (special edition). New York, NY: AMACOM.

The book examines nine cases that have successfully and simultaneously achieved profitability and social responsibility. Key factors driving the success are highlighted that act as useful insights and inspirations for those business managers who seek success based on sustainable strategies.

4

TRIPLE BOTTOM LINE, ACCOUNTABILITY AND TRANSPARENCY

LEARNING OUTCOMES

- Critically understand the principles of the Triple Bottom Line.
- Understand the concepts, principles and limitations of accountability and transparency.
- Comprehend the different types of support for reporting mechanisms and their limitations.
- Critically evaluate the management of accountability and transparency.

INTRODUCTION

The Triple Bottom Line (TBL) framework developed by Elkington (1994) provided the basis around which managers could think about more than economic value from their activities but also include social and environmental factors. In particular, in the modern era companies are implementing strategies in response to challenges ranging from climate change to human rights with more alacrity and intensity than witnessed previously (Esty and Bell, 2018). This chapter begins by setting out the principles of the TBL and how companies have responded to it before reviewing the progress made in light of the creator's own judgement that a review of the framework was necessary. There follows a treatment of accounting and transparency as key underpinning principles of reporting. This includes a critical analysis of social accounting as a means of incorporating social and environmental impacts into the reporting mechanism of companies. This section reveals some of the key motivations for engaging with social accounting and the limitations of the approach. The critical approach continues following the presentation of reporting mechanisms and the efforts to integrate reporting for the common good. The chapter also features the management of transparency and offers a critique of progress made in light of major developments at the policy level to address the United Nations Sustainability Development Goals (SDGs).

TRIPLE BOTTOM LINE

The Triple Bottom Line (TBL) was developed by John Elkington in 1994 and suggested a change in the way that business performance is assessed. The theory arose from the perceived limitations associated with measuring business performance by the narrowly defined profit metric only and the lack of organisational focus on sustainable results (Elkington, 1998). Elkington argued that the business organisation should work simultaneously on the three bottom line dimensions of economic, social and environmental which would ultimately allow for a more balanced and holistic approach in measuring performance.

> **Definition: Triple Bottom Line** is a framework for accounting for economic, social and environmental factors.

An adaptation of Elkington's concept is represented in Figure 4.1. This means that organisations could measure business performance on more tangible factors such as emissions or use of sustainable inputs which could be relevant to a wide range of organisations across multiple different industry sectors. However, it has been argued that this could bring organisations under the radar of scrutiny which could lead to negative outcomes on corporate reputation. An example is the scandal involving Volkswagen and their installation of 'cheat devices' inside diesel vehicles to fake emission results and therefore appear more environmentally friendly and appealing to consumers (Schiermeier, 2015).

Although this concept focuses on different measurement types for business performance, the economic dimension of the TBL concept recognises that organisations must achieve continuous profits to enable them to pursue long-term social and environmental projects. Furthermore, in terms of the social dimension, businesses need to be aware of social, as well as financial factors. According to Elkington (1998), societies differ from region to region and therefore present their own social factors that the organisation needs to adapt to in order to act sustainably and satisfy social needs. This means that in order to achieve social sustainability, organisations should be proactive in collecting data from national authorities concerning social factors such as the pollution levels in society in the area in which the business operates.

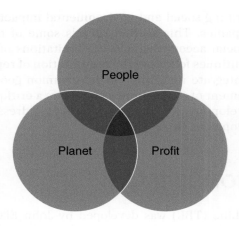

FIGURE 4.1 *Triple Bottom Line*

Source: Adapted from Elkington (1998)

The environmental dimension of the TBL considers environmental sustainability and discusses the importance of providing the same quality of life to the next generation as societies enjoy today. This aspect of the TBL concept focuses on organisations' activities in relation to environmental laws and the consumption of natural resources. The TBL concept helps to focus the minds of global sustainable managers on implementing social and environmental strategies in a sustainable manner. However, Slaper and Hall (2011) highlighted the difficulties in putting the TBL into practice. Although this theory encourages organisations to be more involved with sustainability and socially responsible practices, it has brought criticism from the fact that there is no legal requirement to operate in such a way. Difficulties in consistently and accurately measuring performance based on environmental results are also problematic. Significantly, in 2018, Elkington encouraged a re-think of the TBL concept.

Uppermost in the mind of Elkington's re-think was the purpose to which the TBL theory was being applied. In particular, he asserts that the success of the TBL cannot be determined by economic factors such as the level of profits. Whilst recognising the economic benefits of the industry that has developed around sustainability, the key performance indicators need to be measured in the wellbeing of citizens and the health of the planet. On both those criteria it is clear that all stakeholders including business managers, citizens, government and institutions have failed. According to naturalist and broadcaster Sir David Attenborough (2020) we are now at a tipping point in the Earth's history whereby the actions of mankind have placed the very existence of the planet at risk. Deforestation, species loss and polluted oceans are just some of the characteristics of the relentless drive towards industrialisation to feed an insatiable demand for goods and services. As a result, increased carbon emissions have warmed the Earth to dangerous levels and initiated weather pattern changes that result in floods, droughts and extensive fires as part of the process of climate change. If the TBL

INTRODUCTION TO GLOBAL SUSTAINABLE MANAGEMENT

was designed to help organisations shift their focus to people and planet, then it has failed in that mission.

Part of that failure is explained by the narrowly defined interpretation that many organisations adopted for understanding the TBL. In many cases, the perceived aim was to use the TBL framework as a means of measuring the economic, social and environmental performance of companies over a set period of time. Thus, most managers who incorporated TBL thinking into their performance criteria could satisfy themselves that they were indeed making a contribution to sustainability challenges. However, the intent of Elkington was to broaden this interpretation by developing the means by which organisations could track and manage economic, social and environmental value that is either added or destroyed by their actions. Platforms were created and designed to support this, such as the Global Reporting Initiative (GRI) and gave impetus to attempts to incorporate accounting, stakeholder engagement and strategy into the response by companies. For the most part, the TBL was considered a useful accounting tool for measuring economic, social and environmental factors. The data was often used as a justification for trading one element off against another.

The introduction of the TBL framework initiated a flurry of other frameworks for measuring the three key elements of economic, social and environmental factors. The most widely used are Integrated Reporting (see section below on reporting), the Social Return on Investment (SROI), Environmental, Social and Governance (ESG), and the Boston Consultancy Group's Total Societal Impact model. Other concepts have also gathered pace, such as the circular economy (first cited by Boulding in 1966) where the economic system supports the elimination of waste and the continuous use of resources, biomimicry whereby knowledge and learning are gleaned from nature as a basis for solving human challenges, and carbon productivity that provides a measure of the return on carbon employed in the production of materials. Elkington recognises the value of these developments but notes that their combined impact has not been benchmarked or evaluated in terms of real-world performance. Ultimately, the level of adoption and use by managers has not manifested itself in the form of new strategies for sustainability at a level that could be considered transformational. The emphasis on the economic performance remains the predominant one across many organisations and societies. This narrowly defined understanding of the purpose of the TBL may be a convenient boundary for companies seeking some engagement with the concept of sustainability but, in total, the efforts fall well short of systems change (a redesign of the capitalist system) that Elkington had envisioned.

ACCOUNTABILITY AND TRANSPARENCY

Since the turn of the millennium there has been a discernible growth in the number of initiatives developed around corporate accountability (Yan and Zhang, 2020). This is partly explained by the raft of irresponsible corporate actions that have undermined confidence among stakeholders. In particular, the environmental impact of energy companies exploring and exploiting carbon emitting fossil fuels has left a devasting legacy on local communities in terms of pollution and related health issues. Reckless lending by financial institutions throughout the 1990s and beyond led to the global financial crash of 2008 leaving many citizens unemployed and financially stricken. Global brands, such as Nike, GAP and Apple have been embroiled in reputational damage limitation exercises after a series of revelations about working conditions in their outsourced manufacturing plants in developing countries. Nike had to revamp their manufacturing strategy to address the issue of child labour in factories, GAP reassessed their relationships with suppliers after safety concerns in textile factories in Bangladesh, and Apple had to work on re-establishing trust after the exploitative working conditions at their supplier firm Foxconn became widely known (Pun et al., 2016). Simultaneously, efforts to make corporate business more accountable and transparent in their activities have gathered momentum.

It should be noted at the outset that corporate engagement in accountability reporting is voluntary and this cannot help but colour the efficacy of the developed initiatives. However, there are compelling reasons for participation as access to knowledge and data can better inform decision-making about how to manage sustainability strategies, build trust with consumers, suppliers and other stakeholders, act as a boost to reputational capital, and support performance enhancing actions that can lead to competitive advantage. Managers may also be motivated by the notion that in the context of the climate emergency, it is the moral and correct thing to do. Although each is a distinct motivator, they are all interconnected and should be viewed from that perspective. It has already been noted that the Triple Bottom Line framework has become more of an accounting tool rather than being a mechanism for systems change as its originator had intended. As a consequence, it can be seen that corporate social responsibility has become inextricably linked to accountability reporting for the purposes of transparency in reporting how companies address their social and environmental impacts to a wider constituency of stakeholders beyond that of shareholders.

Social accounting

Social accounting is a means by which companies can communicate their activities and impacts on social, ethical and environmental issues relevant to stakeholders alongside (or included with) financial reporting obligations. It is a means by which companies can improve accountability and transparency and is distinguished from financial accounting by the inclusion of non-financial issues, a broader range of stakeholders and the voluntary nature of it. Mook (2013) provides an effective insight into accounting for social value by focusing attention on some of the innovative ways in which accounting can lead to benefits for a wide range of stakeholders. There are a number of key principles that underpin effective social accounting that begin with clarifying the purpose and scope of the social account. To ensure effective coverage requires engagement with relevant stakeholders beyond shareholders. It is important to determine the issues to be included in the social account to derive sufficient coverage to make it meaningful.

This will invariably include economic, social, ethical and environmental factors. To maintain efficacy, the social account needs to make all efforts to measure outcomes where possible. This will ensure benchmarks are set for future performance targets and to compare with other companies. Finally, the social account needs to be transparent, verifiable and be part of an on-going accounting process within the organisation. Figure 4.2 highlights the key principles of social accounting.

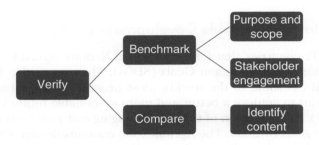

FIGURE 4.2 *Principles of social accounting*

Whilst the intension of social accounting is laudable, it has some limitations. Gray et al. (2010) explored some of the challenges and issues linked to social accounting as a practice in the mid-1990s and many of their findings remain relevant in the modern era. One of the most obvious and salient limitations is that there are no regulations obliging companies to disclose information. It is entirely within the decision-making process of managers to determine what social, ethical and environmental issues are to be included. On that level, social accounting does not guarantee transparency. There is also no mandated technique for measuring impacts or analysing performance. For example, it may be evident that a company is responsible for increasing carbon emissions through an expansion in production to meet increasing demand. The increase in carbon emissions may be measured but the full impact of the consequences for the environment and communities may remain unknown.

The qualitative nature of social accounting limits the understanding of impact as it invariably contains issues that are measurable (data on carbon emissions) and non-measurable (the effect of carbon emissions on the health of local communities). It is also relevant to note that different organisations have different aims, objectives, strategies and pressures from different stakeholders. The motivation for engaging with social accounting may vary quite markedly and will often reflect these differences. Thus, social accounting methods vary according to the needs of individual companies and that can make comparison difficult. Indeed, the methods and tools adopted by companies may evolve over time as more and more adaptations are built in to reflect the changing environment and their own changing needs. Managers always have to review the purpose and aims associated with social accounting and determine the value derived both internally and externally. Schilit and Perler (2018) provide a fascinating insight into some of the more questionable practices linked to reporting including tricks companies pull to exaggerate revenues or techniques for manipulating cash flow. Even so, there are good moral reasons why social accounting may remain a feature of company reporting of their actions and impacts. The transparency that derives from these ensures that the company can be held accountable for their actions and this level of scrutiny helps to improve performance in relation to sustainability challenges.

REPORTING MECHANISMS

United Nations Sustainable Development Goals

In 2015 all 191 countries that form the United Nations agreed to participate in the UN Sustainable Development Goals (SDGs). These comprise 17 interlinked goals that address some of the world's most pressing problems and is considered 'a blueprint to achieve a better and more sustainable future for all' (United Nations, 2017). The intention of this broad ranging and ambitious programme is to achieve the goals by 2030. The Agenda 2030 contains details of the targets set for each of the 17 goals outlined in Figure 4.3.

Indicators were established for most of the goals that measure progress towards the set targets. Monitoring and evaluating progress is an important aspect of the

FIGURE 4.3 *United Nations Sustainability Development Goals*

Source: https://www.un.org/sustainabledevelopment/. The content of this publication has not been approved by the United Nations and does not reflect the views of the United Nations or its officials or Member States.

SDGs programme as this makes data publicly available, creates accountability, transparency and trust. It is now possible for all citizens to track the progress of each country in its efforts to meet the set targets and goals.

Each of the 17 SDGs has between eight and twelve set targets and goals with each target allocated indicators to measure progress towards the goals. The targets are either based on 'outcomes' or 'means of implementation'. The indicators are reviewed and revised intermittently with a total of 36 changes being approved in 2020. The Triple Bottom Line factors feature as the basis of achieving sustainable development. The economic, sociopolitical and environmental factors have been identified as key sectors that require interdependency and multidisciplinary collaboration to meet the challenges of the SDGs. This necessarily involves multiple stakeholders including government, citizens, universities, NGOs and institutions, among others. Scheyvens et al. (2016) explain how private-sector organisations and their managers play a significant role too with global sustainable managers particularly focused on demonstrating practices that either directly or indirectly support the achievement of the SDGs.

Mini case 4.1: Siemens in Oman

Siemens is a German multinational conglomerate and is Europe's largest industrial manufacturing organisation with core interests in telecommunications, energy, healthcare and appliances, among others. The company is one of the most diverse and successful industrial organisations in the world with operating revenues close to €100 billion. The company has a long history of innovation and technical expertise that has helped gain a formidable reputation on a global scale. However, Siemens has also been embroiled in several scandals in its illustrious history including a finding in 2008 in the USA that led to the biggest ever fine for bribery placed on a corporation up to that time. Evidence from one manager pointed to a slush fund running to tens of millions of dollars for the purpose of securing deals with corrupt government officials on a global scale. Since then the company has been active in restoring its reputation and one way it pursues this aim is to engage with the UN SDGs.

One area of operations for Siemens is Oman in the Middle East where the company is proactive in not only developing business relationships but also contributing to Omani society in meaningful ways. The company has been operating in the country since 1972 and has played a key role in developing the energy infrastructure culminating in €200 million contract spanning 25 years for the supply of an integrated power and water supply system. The company is involved in the ambitious diversification plan for the country by deploying technologies that support

(Continued)

infrastructure, telecommunications and digitalisation. There is also a commitment to sustainability through environmental projects (SDG 11: Sustainable Cities and Communities and SDG 13: Climate Action). For example, Siemens provides technologies that help monitor and analyse carbon emissions and treat industrial wastewater in industrial zones. The company also develops new technologies to improve the quality of life of Omani residents (SDG 3: Good health and wellbeing and SDG 12: Responsible Consumption and Production) through healthcare, education and social interventions such as job creation and the economic security it brings.

Key to the initiatives introduced by Siemens is the *Business to Society* programme that is designed in alignment with the UN SDGs. This provides a map for a sustainability focused method that helps measure the contributions that the company makes to specific goals. The programme also aligns to the vision for the future developed by the Omani government. Many of the UN SDGs are evident in the Oman Vision 2040. Partnership is a key strategic issue in driving forward the initiatives that support the vision and Siemens is an important contributor as the country seeks to develop its people and create a knowledge-based economy built on creativity, innovation and technology.

Questions and task

1. Identify four UN SDGs that are aligned to developmental projects of Siemens in Oman.
2. How does Siemens report on its progress towards achieving their identified UN SDGs?
3. How does Siemens contribute towards achieving UN SDG 13: Climate Action?

UN Global Compact

Established in 2000, the UN Global Compact is a voluntary initiative set up to encourage chief executive officers (CEOs) and other managers to support and implement universal sustainability principles and the UN Sustainability Development Goals. Importantly, the initiative is aimed not only in raising awareness of the SDGs, but also ensuring momentum in the actions that support the achievement of the stated goals by 2030. It provides support and guidance for managers to help them implement activities and strategies that help towards the achievement of the SDGs. The initiative is designed to bolster corporate sustainability by supporting companies in linking their strategies with ten universal principles based around human rights, labour, environment and anti-corruption as well as taking actions to advance societal goals. The ten principles are listed in Table 4.1.

The UN Global Compact initiative provides a framework for helping companies engage in best practices and provides a range of support resources and networking events to better inform managers how to undertake business responsibly and to demonstrate commitments to society. In 2019 the initiative created the SDG Action Manager programme that presents opportunities for managers to learn, manage and improve their sustainability performance by accessing a range of tools for self-assessment, benchmarking and actions for improvement. The initiative allows managers to identify a starting point to better understand which SDGs matter the most based on company profiles. From this, managers can then use the range of tools and techniques to better understand the impact their company operations and supply chain has on the SDGs. By undertaking support or remedial actions, managers can track the progress in support of identified SDGs. The SDG Action Manager supports collaboration and knowledge sharing between managers to support learning and encourage a culture of collective action to tackle sustainability challenges.

TABLE 4.1   *Ten principles of the UN Global Compact*

Principle 1 Human Rights	Businesses should support and respect the protection of internationally proclaimed human rights.
Principle 2 Human Rights	Business should make sure that they are not complicit in human rights abuses.
Principle 3 Labour	Businesses should uphold the freedom of association and the effective recognition of the right to collective bargaining.
Principle 4 Labour	The elimination of all forms of forced and compulsory labour.
Principle 5 Labour	The effective abolition of child labour.
Principle 6 Labour	The elimination of discrimination in respect of employment and occupation.
Principle 7 Environment	Businesses should support a precautionary approach to environmental challenges.
Principle 8 Environment	Undertake initiatives to promote greater environmental responsibility.
Principle 9 Environment	Encourage the development and diffusion of environmentally friendly technologies.
Principle 10 Anti- corruption	Businesses should work against corruption in all its forms, including extortion and bribery.

Source: United Nations Global Compact

The SDG Action Manager initiative was hailed as a significant move to get more managers involved in supporting efforts to address the 17 SDGs. Although progress has been made within the business community, it is clear that more needs to be done with UN Global Compact Director Lise King noting that 'there is clear recognition that action is not measuring up to the size of the challenge'. This barely disguised rebuke to the business community reflects a growing consensus that businesses in general, and managers in particular, need to focus more attention on strategies that deliver positive impacts around sustainability goals. To lend emphasis to the urgency of participation, the roll out of the initiative coincided with the publication of an open letter to world leaders from 2,000 activists (including high profile campaigners Malala Yousafzai and chimpanzee expert Dr Jane Goodall) committed to monitoring and reporting on progress.

Integrated reporting

There have been significant efforts to integrate reporting mechanisms. Multiple tools are available for helping companies identify value creation opportunities and several are specifically aimed at sustainability. Integrated reporting helps to deliver a more cohesive and comprehensive array of tools for providing accurate and valuable information on a wide range of performance enhancing factors that better inform decision-making and, ultimately, benefit stakeholders. This approach developed as a consequence of a growing realisation that a large swathe of company assets are not valued in formal reporting mechanisms. Assets such as reputation, goodwill, intellectual capital and trust were not formally recognised in profit and loss accounts or other accounting records. Whilst attempts to address this gap gathered pace, a further omission became increasingly evident. That is, companies did not recognise the value of the natural environment where their premises are located, their raw materials extracted, and their transport logistics exploit. Efforts have been made to develop frameworks for integrated reporting that can be implemented effectively by managers seeking to more closely represent the range of different activities and outputs evident in their organisations. Romolini and Gori (2017) provide a useful review of integrated reporting research that helps fill the gaps in development. The integrated reporting initiatives outlined in Figure 4.4 present some of the approaches taken to address these gaps.

The International Integrated Reporting Council (IIRC)

To facilitate communications about value creation in corporate reporting, the International Integrated Reporting Council was established in 2010. As a global non-profit organisation, core thinking within the IIRC is to transform reporting from a marginal administrative task to one that features as part of mainstream activity in both the public and private sectors. This fits with the vision of creating a business environment where capital allocation and corporate behaviour support the achievement of financial stability and sustainable development. The coalition that comprises the IIRC includes companies, financial institutions, regulators, policy makers, the accounting profession, reporting developers and academics. Representatives from a range of civil society organisations are also included.

FIGURE 4.4 *Integrated reporting*

The Global Reporting Initiative (GRI)

The Global Reporting Initiative (GRI) was established to encourage responsibility and transparency of impacts of organisations by setting standards for sustainability reporting. There are a wide range of standards that can be used including those aimed at anti-corruption, health and safety, biodiversity, carbon emissions and many more. Aligned to the TBL criteria, the GRI helps managers and stakeholders to understand their impact on the economy, society and the environment by facilitating increased transparency and accountability around their sustainability practices. This is mostly achieved by providing the tools that allow companies to produce a sustainability report based on the standards. Alternatively, it is possible for companies to use selected standards to produce a report for identified users or specific purpose. For example, a company can produce a report on the carbon emissions linked to the development and market entry of a new product as a means of demonstrating their sustainability credentials to consumers. This may have economic benefits in the form of attracting environmentally aware consumers to the brand, but it also demonstrates a commitment to actions that support sustainability such as reducing waste, working with green suppliers or reducing carbon emissions.

Customer Data Platform (CDP) reports

A not-for-profit charity, the Customer Data Platform (CDP) is a global disclosure system that was created in 2000 to help the management of environmental impacts by a range of stakeholders including investors, companies, cities, states and regions. The CDP provides access to an extensive database on the actions that these various stakeholders are taking to address environmental challenges, undertake sustainability actions and reduce carbon emissions. The key aim of the organisation is to increase transparency and accountability of reporting by providing the basis for improved learning around environmental impacts and management actions that address them. The CDP has a presence in around 50 countries with companies from over 90 countries disclosing information via the platform. There are significant benefits for disclosing information for all identified stakeholders. For example, city authorities can access a centralised database of information that helps them better understand environmental impacts of their wide-ranging service provisions. It facilitates tracking and monitoring of impacts and the information feeds into better informed decision-making. The data provides benchmarking opportunities for peer performance analysis that can form the basis for remedial or new actions to meet stakeholder expectations. At the company level, the CDP provides the information that managers need to create strategies that include sustainability targets. Beyond that, reporting allows companies to demonstrate regulatory compliance (and by consequence build trust with investors and consumers), manage risk more effectively and design new and innovative solutions to support their sustainability actions. These can often combine to help create a competitive advantage too, so it is evident that engaging with the platform has the potential to deliver economic, social and environmental benefits.

Task Force on Climate-related Financial Disclosures (TFCD)

Established by the Financial Stability Board, the Task Force on Climate-related Financial Disclosures (TFCD) aims to help companies deliver accurate climate-related disclosures that promotes decision-making by investors, creditors and insurers and enable stakeholders to better understand concentrations of carbon-related assets in the financial sector. In essence, the task force aims to improve transparency in financial markets and deliver the type of information that encourages companies to include climate-related risks and opportunities into their strategies for meeting environmental challenges. The initiative is an important means by which knowledge and understanding of the financial consequences of climate-related change is enhanced across financial markets such that managers are better able to identify opportunities related to sustainability actions.

Sustainability Accounting Standards Board (SASB)

The Sustainability Accounting Standards Board (SASB) was established in 2018 as an industry-specific sustainability accounting standard covering relevant financial factors. The purpose of the standard is to support managers in their quest to identify and communicate opportunities for sustaining long-term value creation. The standards are a means of focusing attention on the key sustainability factors that are most likely to have financial impacts for a company. They provide a means of measuring, managing and reporting on value-adding sustainability factors that improve the economic performance of companies. Although the standard has economic performance as the key design aim, it can be applied in conjunction with other sustainability frameworks such as the Task Force for Climate-related Financial Disclosures and the Global Reporting Initiative.

Mini case 4.2: Etsy, USA

Etsy is an American e-commerce website specialising in handmade craft items such as home décor, bags, jewellery, clothing, furniture, toys, art and much more. The company is also known for its range of vintage items that must be at least 20 years old. The site is an online version of a craft fair whereby sellers are allocated a storefront from where they sell their wares for a fee per item. With tens of millions of items in the marketplace, the e-commerce model has proven to be highly lucrative with an average of $4 billion of merchandise sales annually.

In 2019 Etsy delivered its first integrated sustainability and financial report. The company decided that the time was right to expand the reporting data to non-financial information to align with the commitment to ecological and social impacts alongside economic ones. The integrated reporting makes progress towards stated goals more transparent and with metrics adopted from the Sustainability Accountability Standards Board (SASB) delivers consistent and comparable data that stakeholders value. The integrated report is an addition to the company's Impact Report that details a range of effects linked to company activities. The move to integrating reports can also be viewed as a strategic effort to align practice with the expectations of investors who are increasingly pressuring companies to deliver consistent and accurate reports on social and environmental factors. The Etsy strategy is a sign that the management are responsive to changes in investor requirements with a majority now factoring in social and environmental impacts to their investment portfolio decision-making. To retain the confidence of investors and other stakeholders, the company has been assured for carbon and energy reporting by auditors PwC. Data on social factors such as gender equality and diversity in the workforce are similarly externally verified.

There are also sound operational reasons for the switch to integrated reporting. Etsy has benefited from a much more streamlined and efficient reporting system when data is collected, collated, organised and reported as part of a project management process. The new approach also allows the company to deliver data and information in a format that suits the needs of stakeholders. The legal requirement to file reports for the US Securities and Exchange Commission (SEC) is met alongside

(Continued)

a deeper and more engaging understanding of the company impacts whereby background, context and analysis of stories and events that underpin their social and environmental impacts can be communicated using visuals, graphics, and other appealing design formats.

Questions and task

1. What benefits does Etsy perceive of producing an integrated sustainability and financial report?
2. Are there any external pressures that have influenced Etsy to report on social and environmental impacts of the company?
3. Access an integrated report produced by Etsy and identify four disclosures linked to social or environmental factors.

Limitations of integrated reporting

In 2020 the five reporting organisations featured here announced a collaborative approach that would coalesce around a shared vision for a comprehensive corporate reporting system. This is formally set out in a Statement of Intent (2020) facilitated by the World Economic Forum and Deloitte. The aims of the collaboration are to create greater consistency in the way that sustainability-related factors are reported, analysed and interpreted across the entire value chain of companies. This holistic approach is designed to better support managers and stakeholders in their sustainability efforts so that knowledge and learning is transformed into action. However, the initiative has not been without critics who point to a number of limitations.

The first integrated reporting framework was proposed by Eccles and Krzus (2010) and formed the basis around which the International Integrated Reporting Council (IIRC) framework was developed. Their *One Report* was distinctive in that it emphasised the use of the internet as a means of integrating reporting and analysis of financial and non-financial information that would be of interest to different stakeholders. That is certainly true, but as part of the Dumay et al. (2017) discussion on barriers to implementing integrated reporting notes, the key stakeholders who control the initiative all come from the accounting profession and a few large and powerful multinational enterprises in the form of Deloitte, KPMG, Price Waterhouse Cooper and Ernst & Young. Flower (2015) refers to 'regulatory capture' to describe the concentration of control between these private sector organisations and the industry accreditors the Association of Chartered Certified Accountants (ACCA), the Chartered Institute of Management Accountants (CIMA) and the International Federation of Accountants (IFAC). Consequently, there is a discernible focus on business performance and investor value with corporate social responsibility and sustain-ability issues being marginalised (Milne and Gray, 2013). For companies seeking to access a more comprehensive framework, the Global Reporting Initiative (GRI) or UN Global Compact remain the dominant ones. In response the IIRC opened a dialogue with stakeholders to seek ways in which this imbalance could be addressed.

Perhaps the most telling criticism of the Integrated Reporting initiative is the voluntary nature of it. The vast majority of companies do not use the Integrated Reporting framework, preferring instead to adopt ones that more closely reflect their needs. This freedom of choice risks the drift towards 'impression man-agement' where there is an effort to control the perceptions of companies (or individuals) by third parties. Melloni (2015) highlights a tendency of reporting to use data selectively and present them in a favourable light to manipulate audience perceptions of corporate achievements. Without mandatory reporting regimes, significant differences in reporting will persist leading to ambiguity, uneven dis-closure, and difficulties in making effective comparisons between companies. Also, different regulatory regimes will take different perspectives on the value of integrated reporting with some supportive of the principles, such as the European Union, and others less so. For example, the regulatory regime in the USA requires companies to report on operations, risk and financial performance, each of which features in the Integrated Reporting framework. Consequently, there is no real incentive to adopt the framework as it has little effect in changing current practice. These are just some of the arguments put forward that highlight the limitations of the IIRC framework and need to be evaluated against the guiding principle of the initiative which is to help deliver a comprehensive and holis-tic approach to reporting that improves accuracy and transparency, and offers a means by which issues of corporate social responsibility and sustainability can be properly recognised.

SOCIAL AUDITS

The development and use of social audits started in the 1950s in an effort to make companies more accountable to the societies they serve and to better represent the impact they have on communities. A key motivator for the development was the growing size and global reach of companies and, as a consequence, the level of impact (both positive and negative) they exerted on societies. Many different definitions of a social audit have subsequently emerged but the essence of it is captured by Geddes (1991) who suggests it is an attempt to embrace not only economic and monetary variables, but also social ones. As the concept devel-oped, so standards started to emerge whereby companies had to report on the likely and actual impact on the environment. This ran concurrently with the rise of ethical investment where companies were scrutinised for the impact that their use of funds had on society and the environment. Interest in corporate social responsibility intensified throughout the 1990s and extended beyond the ideal of 'doing well by doing good' to include improvements in accountability and transparency. In the UK in 2000, the Social Audit Network was established to manage a register of approved social auditors. In the EU there have been a number of initiatives put forward to encourage the use of social audits and there have been attempts to introduce similar frameworks to that set up in the UK in Asia, Canada and South Africa.

There are a number of distinct benefits that can be derived from the use and delivery of social audits for society, companies and organisations (some parts of the public sector are also active in providing social audits). First, social audits provide a focal point for bringing to the attention of managers the social and environmental impact of the activities of their organisation. The associated outcomes link to transparency of those impacts such that stakeholders can evaluate and appraise the social performance of the organisation. Accountability and transparency are key objectives of a social audit and place pressures on management to strike a balance between pursuing economic goals (such as profit) against that of social goals (such as attaining gender equality in the workplace). Thus, social audits need to be comprehensive and detailed around policy, strategy and actions that support them throughout all activities in the organisation. Social audits also improve organisational governance and give a voice to those who may be marginalised from the decision-making process but who are affected by those decisions. Low-paid workers or those on zero hours contracts should feature as negative impacts in a social audit. This may influence management to make the necessary adjustments to redress these types of imbalances. Here, it is evident that a social audit has the potential to improve decision-making and ensure that management is better informed of where inequalities and negative social impacts are evident. This helps to improve the efficiency of the organisation and, ultimately, the reputation and goodwill of stakeholders.

Although the advantages of providing social audits is well known, they are by no means prolific across the public and private sector. There may be unease among management regarding the level of scrutiny that they come under as a result of publishing a social audit; managers may perceive the transparency as a risk that jeopardises efforts to achieve a competitive advantage. This has led to doubts regarding the efficacy with which social audits can be used as a means of driving sustainable change. Although social audits have the potential for helping companies map supply chains, encourage a zero-tolerance policy on child labour and deliver health and educational benefits, there is widespread abuse of the auditing process, malpractice on recording work and pay, and the prevalence of unregistered workers on premises. The extent to which forced labour, harsh treatment, unsafe working conditions and low pay prevails in many countries around the globe is still largely unreported. Furthermore, many companies view social audits as a cost that has to be passed on to the consumer. The social audit industry is now worth over $100 million per annum making it a lucrative service but one that can be viewed as adding to costs as much as value.

SOCIAL ENTERPRISES

There has been a considerable increase in the growth of social enterprises since the millennium with many focusing on social and environmental needs. A social enterprise is a trading business that sells goods and/or services but where the primary aim is to achieve social and/or environmental benefits. They differ from charities due to their financial independence in income-generating activities based on applying their business model. Social enterprises are geared to make profit like any other commercial business; however, any profit derived is reinvested in the social enterprise. In contrast, charities rely on donations from citizens and/or organisations who support their cause. There are many different types of social enterprises, including credit unions, cooperatives and community-owned enterprises, among others. Each has the aim of delivering social returns for their investments. Very often the success of a social enterprise is determined by their ability to demonstrate a social value linked to their activities and there are a number of advantages of doing so. First, it gives the social enterprise a better understanding of the measurable results linked to their activities. Often this is linked to the application for funding from various public and private sector bodies who need to see measures of social value to justify support. In effect, measuring social value helps to build a stronger case to stakeholders for support and to demonstrate that the organisation is achieving its mission. The second key advantage is that measuring social value increases awareness of which social intervention programmes deliver the best returns. This informs decision-making regarding what areas of intervention deliver best social value and helps distribute resources to those areas of social need that deliver best returns. However, this has proved a controversial aspect of social enterprise development as there are some social needs that do not deliver high levels of social value but are, nevertheless, needed to improve the lives of citizens.

Some challenges need to be addressed when undertaking measurement of social value. The idea behind social enterprises is to deliver social value by doing 'good'. However, defining what 'good' is can be fraught with difficulty as it is an overarching term that can be ambiguous or even broad ranging. Relating 'good' to financial values is challenging and open to interpretation. Also, identifying the cause and effect of doing 'good' is also problematic. The sheer diversity and overlapping nature of social enterprise domains makes this particular ecosystem complex and difficult to measure and assess. Nevertheless, there has been a significant amount of effort put in by academics and practitioners to create measurement tools that are effective in deriving social value. Perhaps the most widely used method of measuring social value is that of the Social Return on Investment (SROI) model that uses data to measure social impact and to help decision-makers better understand the outcomes of social innovations. The SROI model can be used for evaluative purposes, where previous initiatives are measured, and the forecasting purpose where estimates of social value are measured dependent on attained outcomes (SROI Network, 2013). Nichols et al. (2009) highlight six stages which are involved in conducting an SROI analysis as set out in Figure 4.5.

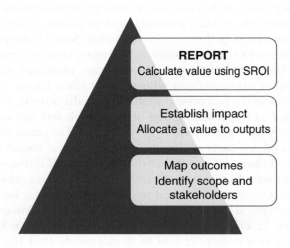

REPORT
Calculate value using SROI

Establish impact
Allocate a value to outputs

Map outcomes
Identify scope and stakeholders

FIGURE 4.5 *Stages in conducting an SROI*

Source: Adapted from Nichols et al. (2009)

1. Establishing scope and identifying key stakeholders.
2. Mapping outcomes.
3. Evidencing outcomes and giving them a value.
4. Establishing impact.
5. Calculating the SROI.
6. Reporting.

The longevity and widespread use of the SROI model is testimony to its simplicity and ease of use. However, there are limitations associated with it, most notably the lack of a benchmark for comparative purposes and the lack of a standard for measurement. This has led to inconsistencies in outcomes that have hampered rather than improved understanding and knowledge of the social impact of social enterprises. Nevertheless, the prevalence of this form of business set up to address social and environmental needs points to a wider confidence in communities of their added value.

Mini case 4.3: Sistema Cymru (Codi'r To), Wales

Sistema Cymru is a community regeneration project located in Wales and aimed at improving the education and wellbeing of children. The project is based on the founding principles of the world renowned El Sistema project established in Venezuela in the 1970s that used music as a means of transforming the lives of disadvantaged young people. The format of El Sistema has been rolled out in communities around the world with the key driving force being the power of music to instil values of discipline, responsibility and creativity that combine to enhance social cohesion and personal development. The project gives children access to musical instruments and allows them to play as part of a music group. The original El Sistema formed an orchestra of young people, whereas the Sistema Cymru includes a wide range of formats including a samba band, brass band, and music and movement sessions. In one example in Gwynedd, professional musicians delivered classes to nearly 300 pupils in two schools. With almost 30% of children in Wales living in poverty and community service provision being subject to budget cuts, the project aimed to lessen the impact of economic and social decline by bridging the gap between poverty and educational attainment. Music can help children develop confidence, concentration, listening skills, communications and social skills and there are also benefits for physical and mental health from being motivated, engaged and stimulated. The project also improved social cohesion by bringing together families for a shared experience of supporting the children as they transitioned towards active participation in music perhaps for the first time in their lives.

Assessing the effectiveness of the project was important as a means of demonstrating the social value that it created. For this, a Social Return on Investment (SROI) analysis was undertaken to reflect the economic, social and environmental impact that the initiative generated. The dimensions considered included inputs (time and contribution), mechanisms (social interaction, shared experiences and creativity) and outcomes (joy and sense of belonging). Positive or negative change was recorded for a range of stakeholders including pupils, family members, the wider school community, the wider local community and the organisers of the project. The SROI was compiled using quantitative and qualitative data gained from a series of methods including questionnaires, interviews and focus groups. By measuring the total value of impacts created (and discounting the values estimated to last longer than one year), the total and net present value of the project was calculated as a ratio. The final SROI revealed that for every pound spent on the project the social value was £6.69 (Winrow and Edwards, 2018). Interestingly, the greatest

(Continued)

social value per stakeholder group revealed that families were the greatest recipients at 51% of total social value compared to 48% for pupils. It is important to report on the extent of social value created as it validates the investment and enhances prospects for future funding. In the final analysis, it is evident that participating in playing music as part of a group or orchestra can be used as a means of creating positive social value in communities.

Questions

1. How does a social enterprise differ from a private sector commercial company?
2. What types of social value does Sistema Cymru deliver?
3. What are the advantages of using a Social Return on Investment model?

MANAGEMENT OF ACCOUNTABILITY AND TRANSPARENCY

From the previous discussion, it is clear that concepts of accountability and transparency are inextricably linked and have a mutual dependency. They are also the means by which stakeholders can access information about companies that otherwise would be beyond their reach. This enables them to voice opinions, initiate change by influencing decision-making, and hold organisations to account for their actions. In the context of sustainability this has become ever increasingly important as the immediacy of climate change challenges requires greater awareness of the impacts that organisations have on the wider society and environment. To meet the challenge of the need for greater accountability and transparency it is necessary for managers to explicitly state their company's level of engagement with these concepts and, in particular, to follow through by demonstrably delivering on those disclosures that support sustainability commitments.

Effective management of accountability and transparency relies on trust forming relationships between companies and stakeholders and can be enhanced by delivering robust reports that are clear, accurate and accessible to consumers, suppliers, regulators and a host of other interested stakeholders. Companies also benefit from increased accountability and transparency by better understanding the impacts that their activities have on society and the environment and using the information to improve management decision-making and strategic development. The development of frameworks (such as the ones featured in this chapter) are useful in supporting managers' efforts to improve accountability and transparency of reporting and are built around some guiding principles as outlined in Figure 4.6.

FIGURE 4.6 *Principles of accountability and transparency of reporting*

There are a number of key attributes that underpin the effective management of accountability and transparency. In an age when there is an abundance of information, it is necessary to ensure that material used for disclosure purposes is relevant and capable of making a difference to the decisions made by users of the information. This necessitates filtering information to meet the needs of the company and its stakeholders. Ultimately, it is a judgement of managers to determine what information to disclose and in what format and quantity. There is always a risk that 'filtering' information is perceived as controlling what is revealed but managers need to balance the need for accountability and transparency against the practicalities of managing large amounts of information.

To enhance confidence in what is disclosed it is necessary to ensure authenticity and accuracy of the information provided. Material errors in the information reported undermines trust and hinders effective decision-making. Linked to this is the principle that information must be understandable and free of jargon or ambiguous phraseology. This helps to underpin confidence that the information provided is unbiased and a true reflection of the activities and outputs of the company. Here, it is necessary to secure the reliability of preparing the information processes and internal controls that ensures that the thresholds of quality of information is met. There is also a need to ensure that the information is capable of being compared and, therefore, the reporting should consistently follow the same or similar format year-on-year. Finally, within the proviso of managing large swathes of information, managers are expected to disclose all material information in a comprehensive manner that demonstrates a commitment to accountability and transparency standards.

CASE STUDY

Huawei, China

The Chinese company Huawei was founded in 1987 and provides information and communications technologies (ICT), infrastructure and smart devices to consumers and industry on a global scale. The company has made a significant contribution to digital connectivity around the world with operations in 170 countries using a workforce of almost 200,000 people. Although Huawei is a privately owned company, there has always been close governmental interest in its affairs owing to the important strategic significance of its operations and reach. In some instances, the sensitivity of its operations has led to tensions with third-party governments such as the USA where the company has been banned from participating in the development of 5G broadband infrastructure for security reasons. The UK government similarly reduced its reliance on Huawei for 5G rollout.

Huawei have ambitious targets to 2025 around key sustainability strategies that include digital inclusion; security and trustworthiness; environmental protection; and healthy and harmonious eco-systems. Taking environmental protection as a key sustainability factor, the company has identified risks and opportunities linked to efforts to address the challenge in a manner that reduces carbon outputs whilst maintaining high levels of service quality. For example, a new and innovative means of reducing energy consumption and minimising the associated negative impacts have been developed such as carbon capture technologies that reduce emission but maintain network performance. Huawei is also diligent in monitoring the green credentials of their suppliers. Non-compliance with agreed standards on sustainability (such as packaging, carbon emissions, energy usage, waste, etc.) may negatively impact the reputation of Huawei. To circumvent this the company contributes to standard setting to ensure that suppliers align their processes and activities to levels that support a range of sustainability criteria including carbon emission limits.

To help deliver on aims linked to these strategies, the company established a sustainability management system that meets international standards (ISO 26000 and SA 8000) and provides the basis for meeting accountability and transparency standards by published policies, processes and baseline targets. Huawei have invested in planning, implementing, monitoring and improving their sustainability actions. Leadership involves overseeing the sustainability strategies and principles that underpin the policies, rules and standards set for each action. The organisational structure supports a tiered sustainability management authorisation process as a means of ensuring accountability. Importantly, it is expected that the leadership at Huawei set the tone for others to follow across all their sustainability efforts. This requires effective communication, a passion for innovation, a belief in the drive for sustainability and a strategic and entrepreneurial mindset to advance the vision of the company as one of the world's leading digital network and telecommunications organisations. The planning aspect is designed to assess risk and opportunities linked to sustainability planning and actions. Process operations ensure that sustainability is built into the whole value chain of the organisation. Crucially, the performance appraisal monitors customer satisfaction, engages in measuring, analysing and evaluating progress towards the set strategic targets and undertakes sustainability reviews.

It is important that the company is able to identify and assess the maturity of their sustainability actions over time in terms of providing effective solutions and contributions to strategic aims. This is the relationship between understanding the requirements and the level of satisfaction evident in the business environment, and among stakeholders and customers. To enable this, a sustainability maturity assessment is carried out annually to check progress and identify areas where improvements are required. This informs decision-making and ensures a level of quality that forms the basis of creating brand loyalty and, ultimately, better performance. Thus, the quality of service, combined with a demonstrable commitment to sustainability actions combine to present consumers with an organisation that accounts for economic as well as social and environmental factors.

Openness and transparency

Managers at Huawei are acutely aware of the sensitivity that some of their operations around technology-based infrastructure development has on some governments who fear compromising communications security.

Suspicions are raised when the relationship between the company and the Chinese government is scrutinised. Both parties claim the company is entirely independent of central government interference. Consequently, there have been concerted efforts on behalf of Huawei management to improve accountability and transparency as a means of allaying such fears. For example, the company cites recognition of privacy protection laws such as the GDPR in the EU as evidence of compliance. There have also been white papers published by the company relating to policies on privacy and security related to technology developments such as artificial intelligence (AI). Nevertheless, some high-profile cases have undermined these efforts, such as the charges brought against the company in the USA in 2018 for the alleged theft of trade secrets linked to a cell phone testing robot developed by T-Mobile (Whalen, 2020). In the UK suspicions of cyberattacks by the Chinese State using Huawei technology were a feature of an Intelligence and Security Committee report as far back as 2013 (HMSO, 2013).

Despite these concerns, the management at Huawei are increasing efforts to provide evidence to support claims of actions that address security concerns as well as social and environmental impacts. These are viewed as important ways in which the company can build trust and retain the confidence of investors. The sustainability reports compiled by the company are independently verified and comply with Global Reporting Initiative (GRI) standards. The company points to a number of awards for sustainable impacts such as the 2019 Best Practice award given by the Global Compact Network China for recognition of

▶

progress towards UN SDGs in environmental protection and climate action. All 17 of the UN SDGs feature as part of the Huawei strategy for delivering ICT solutions that support socioeconomic development, environmental protection, and the wellbeing of humanity. For example, the company has worked in partnership with US-based non-profit organisation Rainforest Connection (RFCx) to create acoustic monitoring systems that help tackle illegal deforestation. This contribution to slowing the loss of biodiversity and carbon-capturing forests plays a vital role in tackling climate change. The technology picks up the sound of logging and traces the location. If the location is not part of licensed logging activity the forest rangers are alerted to intervene.

Technology to support environmental protection is just one of numerous interventions that Huawei are part of around the world. Others include waste sorting standards on smart phones, technologies that detect eyesight impairment in children, and safer 5G-enabled mining operations using remote digital trucks. These are just a few examples of the vast array of technology-enabled solutions that Huawei have developed and deployed on a global basis to enable sustainability actions, improve the quality of life and address the challenge of climate change. These types of innovations are driving the company forward in its quest to meet its sustainability goals by 2025. However, few of these interventions make headlines in the global media dominated by private sector companies in Western democracies. The tensions that have occasionally surfaced between the West and China is one reason why Huawei's achievements have been largely underplayed. Huawei management point to the verification of the company's sustainability reports by a recognised independent source as one means of securing redress to this perceived imbalance.

Questions and task

1. Identify one of the UN SDGs and explain what actions Huawei undertakes to address the challenge.

2. By what means does Huawei try to demonstrate accountability and transparency?

3. Why do some Western governments (such as the USA and UK) mistrust Huawei?

SUMMARY

This chapter started with a reflection on the Triple Bottom Line framework devised by Elkington (1998) and offered an explanation as to how it can be used and the purposes of its application. The discussion then featured an update on the relevance of the framework recommended by the author himself and the consequent clarifications of its purpose. It was found that the original purpose was to act as a catalyst for change to the capitalist system but that, in reality, it was being applied as an accounting tool. The chapter then turned attention to issues of accountability and transparency and the reporting regimens evident in supporting these concepts. There was an insight into the value and limitations of social accounting and social audits. The development of reporting mechanisms linked to the UN Sustainable Development Goals (UN SDGs) and the UN Global Compact were discussed alongside a critical evaluation of the moves and motives to introduce integrated reporting. Reporting on the impacts of social enterprises was also included to offer a useful overview of how reporting in different organisational settings plays out. The chapter closed with discussion around the effectiveness of the management of accountability and transparency.

REVIEW QUESTIONS AND TASKS

1. Is the Triple Bottom Line relevant to a modern understanding of sustainability?
2. What are accountability and transparency?
3. Outline three main challenges associated with the effectiveness of social accounting.
4. Account for the trend towards integrated reporting.

FURTHER READING

Idowu, S.O., Schmidpeter, R. and Zu, L. (2019) *The Future of the UN Sustainable Development Goals: Business Perspectives for Global Development in 2030*. New York, NY: Springer.

This book uses case studies and critical reviews to examine business perspectives around all 17 UN Sustainable Development Goals. The authors predict developments to 2030 by using a range of evidence-based data on how companies have adopted the goals across Europe, Africa and Asia. The main theme of the book is the link between monetary value and investment for sustainable development.

Lehman, G. (2021) *Accountability, Philosophy and the Natural Environment*. Abingdon: Routledge.

The author uses an interdisciplinary and philosophical approach to examine how accountability can contribute solutions to some of the world's most pressing environmental and political problems. By focusing on perspectives of authenticity and expressivism, the book delivers a radical new way of thinking about our understanding of being in the world. The discussion provides a starting point for exploring ways in which individuals and communities should address the political challenges of dealing with accountability and ecological crises.

Villiers, C. (2019) *Sustainability Accounting and Integrated Reporting (Finance, Governance and Sustainability)*. Abingdon: Routledge.

An important work featuring a theoretical and practical treatment of sustainability accounting and integrated reporting from perspectives of voluntary external disclosure, stakeholder engagement, organisational focus and assurance. The book articulates the value of these concepts and provides useful insights about organisations that engage with sustainability accounting and integrated reporting for the benefit of both the business and wider society.

5

SUSTAINABILITY SKILLS AND COMPETENCES

LEARNING OUTCOMES

- Gain an understanding of the types of skills and competences linked to sustainability actions in organisations.
- Critically evaluate attempts to integrate sustainability into business education.
- Critically assess the role of government in supporting access to sustainability skills and competences training.
- Determine the role of the corporate sector in supporting sustainability skills and competences.
- Understand the role of support bodies and accreditors in developing sustainability skills and competences.

INTRODUCTION

Sustainability skills and competences are wide ranging, potentially complex and apply to all workers, practitioners and professionals within business organisations. It is important that global sustainable managers understand that the knowledge, skills and competences that support sustainability actions must permeate throughout their entire organisation. That means effective communication of the sustainability strategy is a prerequisite for addressing sustainability challenges in any business setting. Beyond that, there is a requirement to deliver the training and knowledge that help to develop skills and competences that support sustainability performance both at the individual and organisational level.

This chapter begins with an overview of the relevant skills and competences linked to sustainability practices and processes. The role of education in the development of key skills and competences is discussed with examples, such as the United Nations Principles for Responsible Management Education (PRME), used to lend context to selected interventions to boost knowledge and understanding around sustainability education. The chapter then focuses on the input and support mechanisms from government and the corporate sector for the development of skills and competences for sustainability practices. The chapter further elaborates the role of these institutions and the business community by drawing together some of the key collaborations between education, government and corporate bodies to support sustainability skills and competences. The discussion concludes with an overview of the role of support bodies and accreditors in enhancing the professionalism surrounding support for sustainability skills and competences.

SKILLS AND COMPETENCES

Research by Bhutto and Auranzeb (2016) points to the 'green' training of employees as having a significant effect on company performance. Thus, managers need to consider how, what and where that development will play out. In the first instance, it is useful to determine what level of skills and competence exists within the organisation. These may vary widely but tend to follow a trajectory between basic through to expert and strategic as outlined in Figure 5.1.

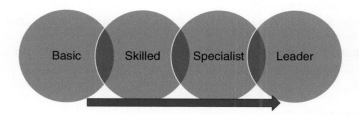

FIGURE 5.1 *Sustainability skills and competence levels*

The basic level of understanding of sustainability will not be sufficient to add value to the organisation in ways that support the sustainability strategy. Training will be required to develop workers, practitioners or managers to achieve a level where they can apply skills and knowledge in a meaningful way.

The skills may be technical, knowledge-based, experiential or a wide range of other learning development formats. They may vary according to the types of skills and competences required by the organisation to meet their sustainability strategic aims. Over time, when training is combined with experience, workers, practitioners or managers may become specialist in delivering value-added sustainability returns to the organisation in specialist areas of the business. This may include a wide range of activities including managing green supply chains, waste management, responsible marketing, carbon reducing production techniques, and so on. These may include those involved in functional roles that support core business processes within the organisation. Here, the key to improving sustainability performance depends on the effectiveness with which workers, practitioners and managers at the functional level understand how their role links to sustainability outcomes. Accessing skills and competences to enable this is a necessary part of this process. Ultimately, as sustainability actions become embedded in the organisational culture, effective leadership will deliver transformational types of value that support the achievement of the organisational sustainability strategy. There is a wide range of skills and competences linked to sustainability actions. Some are regulated and require accreditation to demonstrate minimum standards, some are optional in terms of acquiring qualification and others need only low-level training or knowledge acquisition. Table 5.1 lists some examples.

As a minimum it would be expected that workers, practitioners and managers have a basic understanding of sustainability issues pertaining to their organisation and perhaps within the industry in which they operate. Here, it is necessary to ensure that staff have a basic level of comprehension around environmental issues linked to their organisation's activities and that they are familiar with the protocols and regulations that underpin the implementation of sustainability actions. This basic level of compliance is a mandatory element of the organisation's overall sustainability strategy as negligence at this level may lead to environmental and reputational damage. Staff should also be encouraged to better understand sustainability issues and 'buy into' the ethos of sustainability that managers embed into the organisational culture. This can be achieved by access to training, experiential learning, work-based learning and the influence of mentors or change agents (Armstrong and Sadler-Smith, 2008). Staff at this level receive instruction and are expected to undertake basic compliance actions. Of course, not all companies will have in-house expertise to deliver training to staff and will, therefore, rely on consultants, external trainers or work in partnership with NGOs, accreditors or other companies.

Staff who can be considered practitioners around sustainability issues take on more responsibility and ensure that compliance is observed. This often involves managers at functional levels within organisations and their remit extends to incorporating sustainability monitoring, evaluation or actions into their sphere of influence. As practitioners they may be motivated to gain accreditation or qualifications that enhance their knowledge of sustainability in the context of their functional

TABLE 5.1 *Sustainability skills and competences*

Non-regulated	Optional	Regulated	Strategic
BASIC	**SKILLED**	**SPECIALIST**	**LEADER**
Environmental awareness	Sustainable business practices	Environmental Management Systems auditor	Sustainability innovation
Sustainability practices awareness	Waste best practices	Energy resource manager	Change process leadership
Understanding of and compliance with sustainability protocols	Accessing sustainability training and knowledge sharing	Sustainable procurement	Long-term sustainability targets
Attending sustainability learning workshops	Carbon monitoring, evaluation and reporting	Environmental legislation	Embed sustainability in organisational culture
	Recycling practices	Community engagement	Assess sustainability risk and opportunities
	Reconstituting products	Waste management	Integrate skills and specialist knowledge
		Water resource management	Influence industry change
		Business resilience	Integrate value chain activities for sustainability
		Sustainability Impact Assessment	Achieve sustainability targets

area. Examples include overseeing sustainability practices, waste management, recycling protocols or organising training and knowledge sharing programmes. They may also be involved in the process of monitoring and reporting on trends in carbon emissions linked to their functional area to facilitate decision-making at managerial level. Rajput and Pachauri (2018) discuss the perception of employee sustainability roles and initiatives as important drivers of organisational culture.

Specialist practitioners operate at the next level whereby sustainability management defines the roles. It would be expected that practitioners at this level have had formal training or have acquired accredited qualifications. This typically includes Environmental Management Systems and auditing, specialist roles around energy usage, waste management, water resource management, procurement, and so on. Understanding and acting upon legislative measures may also feature at this level and is a vital element of the compliance process. For example, managers have to ensure that there is compliance with international standards such as ISO 14001 that uses an Environmental Management System (EMS) for environmental performance. Research by Darnall and Kim (2012) and research reviews by Tourais and Videira (2016) into why, how and what organisations achieve by implementing EMS both link its use to effective sustainability and eco-management performance. Managers and practitioners at this level will also be actively involved in community engagement activities where information on the sustainability plans, strategies and performance can be disseminated to stakeholders. They will also gain feedback from stakeholders what to include in future plans for sustainability actions. This may be linked to the compilation of a Sustainability Impact Assessment where the effect of the organisation's activities on the environment and communities is recorded and presented. This is a specialist task requiring a high level of understanding and knowledge around measurements of impact and the analysis of data and information.

Specialists are also involved in the innovation process since they are best positioned to understand how new ideas can enhance sustainability performance in their functional area. This may include new and better ways of packaging, production, design, distribution, marketing and sales. They may also consider better ways of informing consumers on sustainable actions linked to their product use such as recycling, disposal or reducing waste. Specialists may also generate new ways of adapting products or reconstituting them after use. Whatever the area of intervention, this level delivers the added value that makes a significant contribution to the achievement of the sustainability strategic aims of organisations.

Leadership in sustainability can incorporate those with specialist skills too. However, much of the leadership around sustainability actions are played out at the strategic level. This may not necessarily involve technical expertise but rather the ability to drive forward the change necessary to achieve sustainability strategic aims. The type of leadership referred to in this context links to leadership, analytical skills, decision-making, influencing and communicating ideas and goals. Necessarily, this type of expertise requires inter-personal skills, a deep understanding of where the organisation needs to be positioned in terms of sustainability goals sometime into the future, and a clear strategy of how to achieve those goals. Leadership expertise in this context will involve a superior understanding of how innovation can be the catalyst for change, how collaborative networks across supply chains can add value to sustainability goals, or how a systems thinking approach (an integrated and holistic view of the component parts of a system) can help deal with complex issues. Metcalf and Benn (2013) provide a compelling account of just how complex sustainable organisations can be and how they require extraordinary forms of leadership. This form of leadership is also expressed in the entrepreneurial mindset whereby an understanding of risk and opportunities that sustainability challenges present can deliver improved economic performance for the organisation whilst addressing environmental and social needs.

Perhaps one of the biggest challenges facing managers with this type of expertise is to embed the values and beliefs around sustainability into the organisational culture (Polman and Bhattacharya, 2016). Leaders need followers to validate their position and much of this will depend on how well they communicate the vision, mission, ideas and concepts around sustainability to key stakeholders both inside and external to the organisation. The deployment of these types of leadership skills and competences will prove pivotal to the extent to which strategic aims are achieved. Ultimately, the success of any sustainability strategy will rely on how coherent and collaborative the combined and interrelated actions are across the entirety of the organisation. The issue of leadership is of such importance to the process of change required to drive forward sustainability actions that a more in-depth treatment of it comprises Chapter 10. For this current chapter, the focus is on the triple helix of education, government and business contributions to developing sustainability skills and competences. The role of accreditors and support bodies are also included to reflect the valuable contributions made from those sources.

EDUCATION

The educational sector plays an important role in supporting the skills and competences that the next generation of practitioners and managers will need to address the challenges of sustainability as a means of reducing carbon emissions and averting a climate catastrophe. Sustainability is a feature of curricula across schools, higher educational institutions and universities around the globe. It features as part of the learning process in many different contexts including business, engineering, healthcare, fashion, construction, transport, and many more. The modes of learning have also developed significantly and now include formal lectures, e-learning, the virtual classroom, distance learning, work-based learning and applied learning, among others. There are a number of important support bodies that have been created to improve understanding and knowledge of sustainability and responsible management across the globe. Many emanate from educational institutions such as business schools in universities or educational support organisations. One of the most high-profile initiatives has been the Principles for Responsible Management Education (PRME) created by the United Nations.

Principles for Responsible Management Education (PRME)

Developed in 2007, Principles for Responsible Management Education (PRME) is a United Nations Global Compact-backed initiative to promote and inspire responsible management education and research in academic institutions around the globe. As PRME signatories, universities have to declare their willingness to progress the implementation of key principles as outlined in Figure 5.2. The purpose of PRME is to equip the next generation of leaders and managers with the skills and competences to deliver change based on the UN Sustainable Development Goals (SDGs) for a better future. The initiative is designed to raise the profile of sustainability across educational institutions around the globe. There are over 800 signatories to the initiative, which now forms the largest of all relationships between the UN and the management-related educational sector. The PRME vision is to 'create a global movement and drive thought leadership on responsible management education' (www.unprme.org).

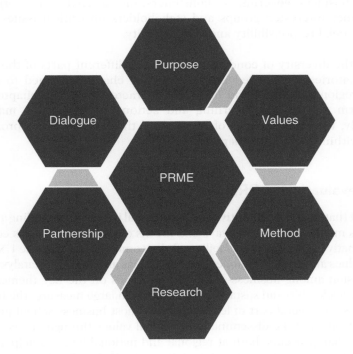

FIGURE 5.2 *Principles of PRME*

Source: www.unprme.org/what-we-do

Purpose: to develop the capabilities of students to be future generators of sustainable value for business and society at large and to work for an inclusive and sustainable global economy.

Values: to incorporate into our academic activities and curricula the values of global social responsibility as portrayed in international initiatives such as the United Nations Global Compact.

Method: to create educational frameworks, materials, processes and environments that enable effective learning experiences for responsible leadership.

Research: to engage in conceptual and empirical research that advances our understanding about the role, dynamics and impact of corporations in the creation of sustainable social, environmental and economic value.

Partnership: to interact with managers of business corporations to extend our knowledge of their challenges in meeting social and environmental responsibilities and to explore jointly effective approaches to meeting these challenges.

Dialogue: to facilitate and support dialogue and debate among educators, students, business, government, consumers, media, civil society organisations and other interested groups and stakeholders on critical issues related to global social responsibility and sustainability.

To reflect the diversity of conditions that affect different parts of the world, the PRME signatories are divided into 14 regional chapters aligned to geography, national, regional, cultural and linguistic characteristics. The chapters provide the platform for dialogue, learning and action on responsible management. Importantly, the six principles of PRME (and the UN SDGs) are promoted and actioned within each of the chapters.

Critical evaluation of PRME

It is evident that the PRME initiative has had a global impact by providing a framework that unifies membership in the ways and means of changing business education in a transformative manner. It has facilitated the communication of the UN SDGs and the core values and goals that underpin them. It has also been the catalyst for debate and discussion among business-school professionals on the key themes of ethics, responsible leadership and sustainability. Indeed, in large measure, the topic of sustainability is an integral part of learning across most business school programmes. PRME has facilitated the dissemination of global values through an ever-increasing network of change agents, both at regional and national level, to help advance the role of social responsibility and sustainability in business education environments.

There has been significant progress among signatories in embedding the principles into teaching and research and, although the extent of this varies between different institutions, the initiative continues to evolve. Hamid and Johner (2010) suggest that a minimum number of principles should be established to ensure acceptable levels of progress. They also point to a lack of comparison between institutions as a weakness of the existing format. Alcaraz et al. (2011) take a critical view of PRME and conclude that membership comes with certain ideological, integration and implementation tensions. For example, signatories are expected to align their strategies to a paradigm shift based on a rethinking of the relationship between business and society. Consequently, the previously held pre-eminence of profitability, shareholder value and growth has been replaced by issues of sustainability and social responsibility. Porter and Kramer (2006) put forward arguments on how these issues cannot only co-exist, but thrive in a mutually advantageous manner.

Louw (2015) questioned the notion that PRME initiated paradigm change in business schools and claimed that, in fact, there had been little real scrutiny of the initiative. A key argument presented was that business school signatories to PRME are servants to the corporate sector. Forray et al. (2015) present a different view by highlighting the rigour to which PRME membership is assessed and point to some institutions being de-listed as evidence of the standards required for inclusion. Debate around the efficacy of the PRME initiative continues apace with some arguing that it has failed to produce business leaders with the capacity to deliver on the challenges of sustainability (Crawford-Lee and Wall, 2018). This assertion follows that of Wall (2017) who believes that business education programmes produce graduates more interested in profit than people or planet. Miller and Xu (2016) produced empirical evidence to suggest that MBA students from a sample typically exhibited more self-serving graduates compared to other programmes.

Despite some well-formed criticisms of PRME, some of which have been presented here, it is clear that the champions of the initiative have set an evolutionary tone to its implementation with adaptations and improvements being sought constantly. The initiative calls on expertise from multiple different disciplines on a global basis to effect the paradigm change around social responsibility, ethics and sustainability. The initiative has invigorated campus teaching through transformations in the business education curriculum, reconfiguring learning methodologies for deeper thinking of key issues by students, and supporting effective and practical research. Much of the success of PRME depends on faculty actively engaging with the principles in meaningful ways that reframe the way in which business education is taught. The challenge is to inform, educate and facilitate faculty for engaging with PRME so that the associated values can be transferred to students as next generation business leaders.

Mini case 5.1: Intentional Sustainable Communities

Carla Nogueira (University of Algarve, Portugal) and Hugo Pinto (University of Coimbra, Portugal)

Intentional Sustainable Communities (ISCs) are self-organised groups that are agents of change contributing to the transition to a more sustainable environmental, social and economic paradigm. There has been a significant rise in the number of ISCs around the world in recent decades as more and more people seek a more sustainable lifestyle. ISCs are characterised by their focus on sustainable lifestyles based on principles and concerns consistent with the ecological movement. The pioneers

(Continued)

of this movement began to experiment with new ways of living in the community and reflecting diverse areas of life including consumption, production, organisation and governance (Bang, 2005). According to the Global Ecovillage Network (GEN), these intentional communities are consciously designed through participatory processes, with local ownership, for the regeneration of social and natural environments. They are based on three main dimensions of sustainability – environmental, social and economic – integrated into a holistic perspective (Bang, 2005). Although there is a great diversity within the family of ISCs, it is also possible to identify some common pillars: the community impulse, the citizen initiative of resistance and action, the sharing of values, research and training. As they assume an experimental and laboratory character, these communities tend to combine forms of governance, production and technology in a creative way.

There is consensus that ISCs should be based on founding principles including the social or political dimension (since people must feel simultaneously supported and responsible for the group), building a sense of belonging through the ability to be part of the decision-making process in a transparent way; the ecological or environmental dimension through the interconnection between the individual, group and land that satisfies needs within respect for the cycles of nature; the cultural or spiritual dimension through the promotion of activities that enhance the artistic and creative spirit; and the economic dimension, based on the principles of redistribution of resources within a solidarity economy framework.

These communities have contributed to developing experiences at a societal level to build management skills and competencies that contribute and adapt to contemporary contexts of sustainability. ISCs have developed practices that directly align with the United Nations Sustainable Development Goals (SDGs), particularly in the social dimension (Barani et al., 2018). More precisely, all ISCs offer education in areas related to sustainability (SDG4), gender equality (women occupy at least 40% of decision-making roles in 90% of cases) (SDG5), 80% have established conflict resolution procedures and 100% provide training in the decision-making processes (SDG16 on responsible institutions, peace and justice). The governance dimension, decision-making process, management and the resolution of conflicts are structural features for these communities' development and success. Many of them use alternative formal governance methods. Others prefer informal methods that are better suited to their characteristics. In all cases, the ISCs thrive under the premise that these organisations, and/or communities, have collective intelligence and are capable of self-organisation.

Question and tasks

1. What are the characteristics of an Intentional Sustainable Community?
2. Identify three UN SDGs that an Intentional Sustainable Community supports.
3. Identify an example of an Intentional Sustainable Community and explain the guiding principles and ethos of the community.

GOVERNMENT SUPPORT

As many economies around the world transition towards a more sustainable future, the role of government has become increasingly important in supporting skills and competence development in the workforce and management. Governments pass legislation (such as carbon emission regulations) to underpin the development of sustainability as part of wider economic growth strategies. Alongside this, governments around the world have been proactive in designing policies to support the transition towards what has been termed a 'green economy'. In the UK, the low carbon and renewable energy economy employed almost a quarter of a million people in 2018 with a total investment of £8.1 billion, a 48% rise since 2015. Energy, manufacturing and construction accounted for over 80% of the turnover in the sector. In Australia, a country with a relatively high carbon emission output per capita, the government has been proactive in setting out plans for the transition to a net zero carbon target by 2050 in alignment with the Paris Agreement. Research from the University of Melbourne in 2019 points to a $549 billion saving for the Australian economy by transitioning to a clean economy with all the social and environmental benefits that would also accrue (Kompas et al., 2019). In the US, research by the World Resources Institute showed that clean energy investment in the US reached a record high of $78 billion in 2019, a 20% increase from the previous year (Jaeger and Saha, 2020). Similar trends are evident in other parts of the world too as increasing numbers of governments turn their attention to climate change policies. Part of these policy trends has been governmental support for developing the skills and competences that help implement sustainability actions and drive the transition towards a net zero carbon economy by 2050.

Government support for sustainability skills and competence development

Governments have authority and a wide range of policy tools to support the development of sustainability skills and competences. These need to be used collectively and in an integrated manner to deliver a coherent strategy that supports skills and competences in all settings including the workplace, higher education, training facilities or online. Figure 5.3 presents a framework for government support for sustainability skills and competences development. Effective support requires government leadership to drive forward the goals and aims linked to identified needs. This means establishing a coherent and coordinated government effort that spans multiple departments including those overseeing industry, environment, education, technology, communities and others.

Some organisations, such as the Greener Jobs Alliance in the UK, have called for the establishment of a specific post dedicated to coordinating efforts for the transition to a low carbon economy. For example, the UK government has separate ministerial posts covering environment and climate change and each have separate remits and aims, even though stakeholder interests may overlap. Similarly, there are separate posts covering education and communities and local government. There are sound reasons for having these posts separated due to the size and complexity of the remit covered in each. However, sustainability issues are relevant to all and, therefore, to meet the challenges of climate change there is a strong argument for effective coordination between departments if a coherent skills and competences strategy is to be realised.

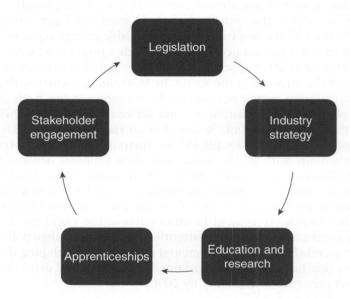

FIGURE 5.3 *Government support for sustainability skills and competence development*

Governments apply policy tools and legislative power to address the pressing need to identify and fill gaps, and enhance sustainability skills and competences. Legislation may be necessary to drive forward strategies where voluntary initiatives fail to deliver. Pressure to meet net zero carbon levels by 2050 has increased the pressure on governments to deliver on the skills needed to achieve this and it may require increasingly robust legislative measures to enforce compliance across all public bodies and industry sectors. However, this form of enforcement sometimes proves unpalatable for some decision-makers who favour a more collaborative approach based on an effective industrial strategy designed to form the catalyst for delivering the skills and competences required to meet aims and objectives. Industrial strategies need to have skills training at the core of implementation so that the benefits help drive future economic growth around sustainability actions. This links to funded apprenticeship schemes, education and research where sustainability features wholly, or in part, to the learning process. Combined with the formal qualifications for industry professionals and practitioners delivered

INTRODUCTION TO GLOBAL SUSTAINABLE MANAGEMENT

by accredited bodies, governments have policy opportunities for supporting the generations of skilled and knowledgeable managers and workforce that are so vital to shaping the way industry tackles the challenges of sustainability into the future. Here, the relationship with stakeholders forms another important aspect of government intervention by creating the mechanisms for working with local communities on identifying opportunities for accessing skills and competence-based employment, training and education.

Mini case 5.2: Greener Jobs Alliance, UK

Established in the UK in 2012, the Greener Jobs Alliance (GJA) is a partnership organisation comprising local authorities, trade unions, training providers, employers, housing associations and campaign groups with the aim of promoting skills training and job creation to meet the needs of the industries as they transition to a net zero carbon economy. Having been initially funded by Battersea and Wandsworth Trades Union Congress, the organisation has become an important contributor to the local and national effort to develop the workforce skills and competences required to deliver on carbon reduction targets to 2050. This necessarily involves liaising and working with partners in policy and investment decision-making and with multiple stakeholder groups including local and national governments.

The Greener Jobs Alliance also works closely with colleges and universities to advise on how curricula can be developed to reflect the need for skills and competences across different sectors of industry. The organisation also delivers a range of training modules themselves in topics such as climate change awareness and air quality. Other important partnerships include the Institute of Public Policy Research (IPPR), the Trades Union Congress (TUC) and the environmental campaign groups Friends of the Earth and Greenpeace. The partnership with the TUC has been aimed at developing 'green apprenticeship partnerships' for low carbon skills in construction, waste management and horticulture, among others.

The organisation is a key contributor to debates on all aspects of skills development policies linked to a low carbon economy. In particular, there has been scrutiny and critique of the UK government's 'Green industrial revolution' strategy launched in 2021. The Greener Jobs Alliance has been vocal in pushing for a clear link between the strategy and the follow-up actions that create green jobs. For example, in 2020 the organisation responded to the consultation on green jobs set up by the UK Parliament Environmental Audit Committee (UK Parliament, 2020) by highlighting the lack of clarity in official forecasts of green job creation. The debate has highlighted the gulf in political thinking between the UK government under the premiership of Boris Johnson and the perspective of the Greener Jobs Alliance with

(Continued)

the former viewing the private sector as the main drivers of the 'green revolution' whereas the latter believe that only greater public sector ownership can deliver the scale of change needed to meet net zero carbon targets by 2050.

Questions and task

1. What are the main aims of the Greener Jobs Alliance?
2. Identify four partner organisations of the Greener Jobs Alliance and outline how they combine to help job creation in the low carbon economy.
3. What training courses do the Greener Jobs Alliance deliver?

Skills for a sustainable economy

As noted, governments play a key role in driving change through introducing policies that support skills and competences as part of wider economic and industrial strategies. Central to many government policies is the identification of the types of skills needed to build sustainable economic growth. Although the specifics of what skills are deemed necessary vary between different countries, it is possible to determine some common themes that feature in decision-making at governmental level around identified skills and competences. These themes are highlighted in Figure 5.4.

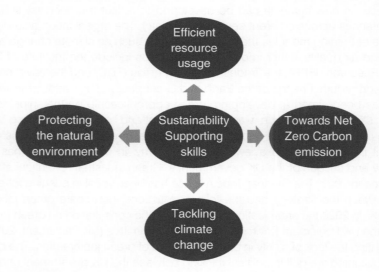

FIGURE 5.4 *Skills for a sustainable economy*

The Earth has finite resources and it is clear that human consumption of those resources has extended far beyond the planet's capability to replenish them.

This trend has been especially marked since the 1950s with an exponential rise in consumption and carbon emission output leading to dangerous increases in global warming. Perhaps the most immediate area of need for skills development is in supporting new and innovative ways to be more efficient in resource usage. At industry level the government has scope for addressing this pressing need by introducing regulations that limit carbon emissions by companies. Other regulatory measures can ensure minimum standards of compliance are observed in numerous other sustainability actions such as water resource efficiencies, health and safety, pollution limits and so on.

Alongside regulation as a policy tool for more efficient resource usage is the development of skills and competences that support new and innovative ways of managing resources and consumption. Resource-efficient business requires the specialised knowledge and skills that transform ideas and concepts into actions that deliver benefits to the environment through lower carbon outputs linked to resources and consumption. Examples include the development of new technologies that capture carbon, support lean manufacturing of products, support project management based on sustainable practices, and waste-reducing processes that lower the overall consumption of resources. The skills and competences around better use of resources can also extend to professional services such as finance and accounting whereby environmental and social factors are included in the audits and reports.

Governments around the world have agreed to sign up to the ambitious target of net zero carbon emissions by 2050. To achieve this requires the deployment of skills around sustainability actions that delivers innovative solutions to the myriad challenges facing global managers and practitioners. Skills and competence development needs scientists and engineers to design and implement technological solutions for everything from carbon capture to renewable energy, from green supply chains to waste management systems. The investment in training is geared towards creating and sharing knowledge that gives impetus to delivering better and more effective sustainable solutions across all industry sectors. Skills and competences need to be most fully deployed in the development of new technologies, products and processes specifically designed to reduce carbon emissions.

The overarching objective behind the investment in skills and competences is to tackle climate change. There is already an increasing level of skills evident in the way in which climate change is monitored and evaluated and the knowledge gained helps managers and policy makers make better informed decisions on a global basis. However, understanding such a complex system requires a long-term approach and one that involves multiple collaborations around the world. The management of these interactions and collaborations continues apace with many influential organisations such as the United Nations leading the way in terms of coordinating efforts and channelling resources to areas that deliver best returns in terms of knowledge and expertise. A wide range of other skills and competences make valuable contributions too, such as risk management, impact assessment, investment planning, environmental management, and designing. These skills support the efforts linked to creating new products or processes that drive sustainability actions, many of which support environmental protection. Managing natural resources involves a wide range of skills both in situ (forestry and land use) and support services (consultants, lawyers, accountants, design services, ecologists, water management engineers and many more). Government plays a crucial role in policy making, industry support and coordination of resources to help deliver the skills and competences needed for the transition to a net zero carbon economy.

CORPORATE SUPPORT

Corporations provide the platform for developing the skills and competences required to address sustainability challenges. Many business leaders around the globe have been proactively seeking ways in which their organisation can contribute to this. In many ways, it can be seen that businesses are at the cutting edge of managing economic wealth creation within the parameters of environmental and social protection. There are opportunities for corporate bodies to engage with sustainability actions as many of the skills and competences can lead to the development of new products and services, cost reduction technologies, less resource-intensive manufacturing techniques and so on. Competitive advantage may be determined by the effectiveness with which workers and practitioners can contribute to these developments. Global sustainable managers need to access new skills and training too. Many of the processes described above rely on a range of key management skills and competences such as strategic thinking, systems thinking, a global entrepreneurial mindset, critical thinking, networking and collaboration, and, most crucially, an understanding and commitment to embedding the sustainability ethos throughout the organisation they lead. In many industry sectors these management skills and competences deliver economic, social and environmental benefits.

Corporate bodies also need to offer opportunities for the workforce and practitioners to gain new skills and competences around sustainability actions. Many of the innovative solutions to sustainability challenges stem from specialists across different functions both internal and external to the organisation. At the basic level, all workers need a basic understanding of how sustainability development adds value to the organisation and how they can contribute to it. At the strategic level corporate bodies need to be proactive in investing in the sustainability capability of the workforce to enable sustainability development through innovation. First, though, companies need to determine the context within which skills and competences training is developed. The training needs to be designed around key activities and processes that form the core aims and objectives of the business. It is important that targets linked to these remain achievable and uninterrupted while skills and competences training takes place. In many instances, sustainability skills and competence development takes place 'in-house' to minimise the disruption during the training phase.

It is also important that businesses demonstrate the value they place in education by making skills and competence development a strategic priority as they transition to a net zero carbon trading environment. This means better understanding of what skills and competences are needed to drive the transition by implementing human resource policies that support sustainability actions. The Aldersgate Group are a multi-stakeholder alliance that supports a competitive and environmentally sustainable economy in the UK. A report published by the group in 2020 called for urgent action to plug the gap in skills that undermines the growth of a low carbon supply chain across the UK economy (Aldersgate Group, 2020). Corporate bodies can channel resources to fill skills gaps especially in those areas that drive change such as engineering and technical skills, cognitive adaptability skills that support innovation, and problem-solving skills that help tackle the challenge of delivering low carbon products and services whilst maintaining competitiveness. The sustainable value framework in Figure 5.5 illustrates the process that corporate bodies need to follow to address the skills and competences challenge as part of the transition to a net zero carbon economy.

In some countries, such as the UK, there may be an imbalance between current skills and those needed to attain future low carbon targets. The first stage in the process of identifying the skills that will be needed is to determine the current position. This can be assessed in the context of the projections made on a range of economic, social and environmental criteria that influence the anticipated skills requirements for the future. The insights offered by these assessments provide the basis for a sustainability value framework that identifies opportunities for businesses to create value based on the alignment to anticipated skills. Schaltegger et al. (2016) note that this process helps to create business models that present a sustainable value proposition to customers and stakeholders that captures economic value whilst maintaining or regenerating natural assets.

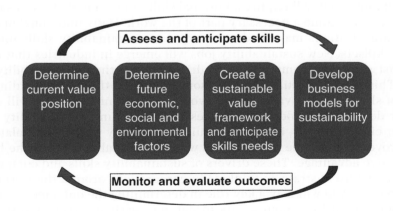

FIGURE 5.5 *Sustainability value framework*

One of the biggest challenges facing corporate bodies is to anticipate what skills and competences will be required in future. Much will depend on how accurate managers can identify the types of jobs needed in different parts of the economy while they transition to a net zero carbon future. Figure 5.6 outlines the four key drivers of sustainability skills and competences.

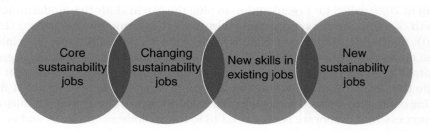

FIGURE 5.6 *Drivers of sustainability skills and competences*

A great many jobs already have a sustainability aspect to them and require some specialised skills and competences in engineering, design, waste management, environmental management, and so on. It is likely that many existing sustainability jobs will evolve to become changing sustainability jobs or even new sustainability jobs. As the challenges and opportunities increase so the demand for new skills and competences will evolve too; many will replace existing ones or be adapted to add value to a maturing sector of industry based on sustainability actions. For example, the installation of low carbon boilers will require new skills by heating engineers. New skills in existing jobs are similar but refer to areas where there is not a specific sustainability focus. These are jobs that will require additional skills and competences as sustainability actions become a necessary part of the work. Many functional managers within organisations may need to incorporate sustainability skills into their overall skillsets. New sustainability jobs will emerge in industries that require specialist skills and competences to drive forward their sustainability strategies. This driver of skills requires some strategic thinking regarding what types of skills will add value in the evolving environment. Much will depend on how demand for goods and services evolves around sustainability issues. In other circumstances, it may be required to comply with new regulations or to improve performance in industries where sustainability forms the basis of competitive advantage. These drivers of sustainability skills and competences will be a feature of strategic thinking in corporations around the world in the years to come and will play a key role in determining the outcome of the challenges presented by commitments to net zero carbon targets across a wide range of industries.

INTRODUCTION TO GLOBAL SUSTAINABLE MANAGEMENT

Mini case 5.3: KPMG in India

KPMG is an Anglo-Dutch professional services multinational company with headquarters in the Netherlands. One of the 'big four' accounting firms alongside Deloitte, PwC and Ernst & Young, the company has offices in 147 countries and employs over 200,000 people. The main service provision is financial accounting and audits, tax and management consultancy and key to the organisation's success is the quality of staff it recruits in all of its specialist areas of business. Much of the quality is derived from bespoke in-house training programmes which cover a wide range of technical, business and strategic skills. To meet client expectations, the company has partnered with the non-profit organisation Global Reporting Initiative (GRI) to access a specific programme on sustainability to help staff gain the necessary knowledge and expertise around sustainability reporting. The programme has been rolled out in offices in India under Climate Change and Sustainability Services leading to the award of the Global Reporting Initiative (GRI) certificate. It is primarily aimed at staff with responsibilities in the development or assessment of sustainability reports and may include managers in finance, communications, information technology, human resources, legal, marketing and operations, among others. There are six key learning and skills development parts to the course including:

- An introduction to sustainability reporting and GRI
- Planning the GRI sustainability reporting process
- Initiating and conducting dialogue with stakeholders
- Focusing efforts towards the key aspects of the report
- Building the report
- Checking progress and communications

The training programme is a response to the skills required to meet the challenges of ensuring long-term stakeholder value around sustainability issues. KPMG look to next-generation managers and consultants to better understand and manage risk, and identify opportunities brought about by economic, social and environmental change. Indian companies are increasingly including corporate responsibility and sustainability into their strategies and many rely on skilled and knowledgeable KPMG staff to help them navigate an appropriate route to integration. These core skills can be deployed effectively in the process of ensuring that client businesses that build sustainability into their operations and establish goals and measures of sustainability performance are capable of reporting outcomes in a manner that complies with recognised accountability and transparency standards.

(Continued)

COLLABORATIONS: EDUCATION, GOVERNMENT AND BUSINESS

Each of the organisational settings covered in this chapter make valuable contributions to skills and competences development for sustainability across the globe. Each has a distinctive role to play and level of knowledge and expertise that can support the myriad ways in which skills and competences can be improved. There is also value to be gained from these sectors collaborating to achieve common goals. For example, universities and colleges need to work closely with business to better understand what forms of learning support their sustainability development needs. In particular, educational programmes need to be designed to fit with career pathways and, therefore, require the input from business on course design, methods of teaching and a range of experiential learning opportunities. Government also needs to have an input by introducing educational policies around skills and competences for sustainability development and economic strategies for growth.

Collaboration is also necessary for creating the next generation of business leaders. Here, companies can collaborate with the educational sector to embed responsible leadership into established programmes such as the Master of Business Administration (MBA) or executive programmes. They can also encourage workers to participate in educational programmes by giving access to work-based learning opportunities that directly link the learning to ways in which sustainability development can support the company's aims and objectives. Importantly, all sectors can benefit from the shared learning from teaching and research around sustainability development. Thus, educators, business managers and government decision-makers can all gain from knowledge sharing linked to business practice, research outputs and policy evaluations. A common sense of purpose encourages companies to share knowledge of the insights gained from sustainability development initiatives and innovations.

SUPPORT BODIES AND ACCREDITORS

Support bodies

Support bodies such as non-governmental organisations (NGOs), associations, community groups and campaign groups play important roles in the development of sustainability and environmental causes. Some may partner with public- and private-sector organisations, or social enterprises to further their specific area of interest. Figure 5.7 highlights different types of support bodies. There are many thousands of small-scale support bodies that proliferate around the world and each makes a contribution to social and environmental causes with sustainability at the heart of many of their activities. However, NGOs provide some of the most influential and effective support bodies such as CERES, an organisation that promotes sustainability business practices; the World Resources Institute which works with world leaders to action solutions linked to climate change, energy usage and food waste; and the Carbon Trust that works with companies to help the transition to a low-carbon economy.

NGOs are often well placed to engage with communities, business and civil society to address challenges to sustainability caused by a wide range of factors including over-consumption, resource extraction, deforestation, industrialised fishing, pollution and waste, population growth and the effects all of these have on climate change. NGOs can help by using their influence, knowledge and expertise to undertake research that supports better decision-making and resource allocation, building institutional capacity and engaging with communities to educate on how to live more sustainable lives. There is a growing awareness of environmental issues across many societies and this has led to an increasing demand for acquiring the skills and knowledge required to manage sustainability actions that protect communities and the planet. NGOs can play an important support role in leading and promoting initiatives and opportunities for accessing skills and knowledge.

FIGURE 5.7 *Types of sustainability support bodies*

The many thousands of support bodies that have been created in recent decades have reflected the growing awareness and concern over social and environmental factors that has led to a climate emergency. The role of support bodies will become increasingly important in the future as the transition towards a net zero carbon target gathers pace. These support bodies are broad-ranging in their areas of interest but each makes a valuable contribution to sustainability efforts. Some support bodies are well funded and can rely on institutional support such as business associations and government agencies. These support bodies are well placed to generate information and disseminate to relevant stakeholders. Some support specific functions and specialist areas of business such as accountancy, engineering, design and conservation. Others rely on donations to support their preferred causes, such as pressure groups and community groups. Nevertheless, they play an important role in furthering understanding of environmental and sustainability causes or issues around these that impact on local communities. Not-for-profit organisations and research organisations can harness the skills, knowledge and expertise of a wide range of supporters and employees to deliver the insights and new understanding of environmental and sustainability issues. This helps inform decision-makers and other important stakeholders including business managers. Table 5.2 lists some examples of support bodies around the world.

Accreditors

Accreditation is the process of evaluation and approval for organisations involved in sustainability practices including services. The purpose is to ensure minimum levels of quality are observed by practitioners and managers and is usually managed by a non-governmental agency comprising trained external peers with expertise to enable a thorough evaluation of standards of practice at both individual and organisational level. Although accreditation is often voluntary, the reputation and standing of an organisation may be affected if their operations and professional practices have not been certified by accreditors as being in compliance with set standards. Stakeholders including customers, suppliers, partners and industry support agencies may check organisation's accreditation status before engaging in business.

Accreditation services have grown in number and reach in tandem with the exponential rise in sustainability practices in the last two decades. The management of accreditation quality and effectiveness has been the source of interest to managers, practitioners, governments and other stakeholders as the drive for quality in sustainability practices has become a strategic issue in many settings. A key driver is the increasing attention paid to identifying the factors that most commonly derive from quality management in sustainability practices. This is one reason why accreditation has gained in importance as it is often viewed as crucial leverage for sustainability management performance linked to the development of strategies and the use of management tools that enable organisations to meet stakeholder expectations whilst simultaneously remaining competitive. There are many accrediting bodies linked to sustainability and responsible management around the globe and each delivers a service linked to standards relevant to their own environment and country characteristics. One such example in the UK is the Institute of Environmental Management and Assessment (IEMA).

TABLE 5.2 *Sustainability support bodies*

Organisation	Country	Support type
Accounting for Sustainability	UK	Practical guide and tools for embedding sustainability into reporting and decision-making.
Business in the Community	UK	Development of frameworks for responsible business.
Capitals Coalition	UK	Supports ways to ensure value created from nature, society and people informs public and private sector decision-making.
Carbon Trust	UK	Supports businesses and the public sector in reducing carbon emissions using carbon technologies.
CERES	USA	Coalition of investors, environmentalists and social advocacy groups working with companies on sustainability.
International Society of Sustainability Professionals	USA	Works towards empowering professionals to advance sustainability in organisations and communities.
Sustainable America	USA	Non-profit organisation working towards making the fuel and food systems more efficient through public education.
American Sustainable Business Council	USA	Business organisation supporting public policy interests of responsible companies.
Chinese National Platform for Voluntary Sustainability Standards	China	Platform to improve public awareness of voluntary sustainability standards.
Clean Ocean Foundation	Australia	Environmental organisation committed to stopping all forms of ocean pollution.
Canadian Business for Social Responsibility	Canada	Aims to help Canadian business and government build a sustainable future.

Institute of Environmental Management and Assessment (IEMA)

With around 15,000 members, the Institute of Environmental Management and Assessment is the largest professional body supporting environmental practitioners in the UK. IEMA was established to lead change in global sustainability standards and supporting professionals in delivering sustainable solutions in business practice. The organisation provides resources, tools and techniques, and knowledge alongside formal qualifications to meet the needs of members. These are often requirements for compliance with sustainability regulations, but they also provide the basis around which practitioners can gain a better understanding of how to address skills gaps, drive innovation, and shape career pathways to incorporate sustainability as a core knowledge-based asset. Membership also encourages new ways of thinking about sustainability and its impact on cutting carbon emissions and reducing the negative impacts of climate change. Knowledge sharing is also an integral part of the global network created by IEMA with transferable skills and knowledge being a feature of the global connections of mobile resources that drive change. The organisation also provides recognition for meeting standards and acquiring a level of skill, knowledge and competence that is so important to managing business in a sustainable and responsible manner. Skills development is one of many support activities delivered by IEMA. Figure 5.8 outlines the three key areas of skills development training provided by the organisation.

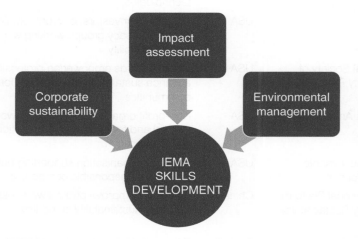

FIGURE 5.8   *Skills development training by IEMA*

Source: www.iema.net/skills/training

Impact assessment (IA) is designed to ensure that social and environmental factors are included in any impact assessment alongside economic values. The skills development helps in the identification of relevant social and environmental factors that support effective policies, plans, design and consenting processes that ensure the social value for communities and the economic value to investors is met without harming the natural environment. Environmental management helps organisations deliver goods and services in a sustainable manner by focusing on design, packaging, manufacturing, distribution, recycling, readaptation, waste and disposal, and other carbon-reducing activities. Corporate sustainability focuses on developing skills that help managers identify critical economic, social and environmental risks and opportunities that typically impact on organisations and their stakeholders. The emphasis is on strategic thinking around innovative solutions to sustainability challenges.

CASE STUDY

Glasgow Caledonian University, Scotland

Glasgow Polytechnic was awarded university status in 1993 and became Glasgow Caledonian University with a mission to deliver good quality undergraduate and postgraduate courses. The university has always had close links to the community and this has been a major part of the vision of the organisation and how it communicates its core values. The mission of the university states that 'Glasgow Caledonian University (GCU) is the University for the Common Good. Our mission is to make a positive difference to the communities we serve and this is at the heart of all we do, especially in our social innovation teaching and research'. The university has made a transformative change to the way it achieves its aims by developing and implementing Common Good principles. Common Good principles help staff when they develop courses for teaching or do research. It also helps them to make contact with the wider community in Scotland and abroad. These help the university to differentiate from other universities and attract more fee-paying students at postgraduate level who are attracted to a university with a good social mission. Thus, it is evident that the mission not only sets out the core values of the university but also helps the process of growing the number of students as an important source of income for the university. This means that the Common Good principles act as an economic driver as well as a means of building reputational capital as an institution that embeds social value into its wide-ranging activities. The main goals linked to the Common Good principles are high-quality teaching; research

that has Common Good values; activities that enhance the reputation of the university; and an increase in student recruitment at postgraduate level.

As part of the Common Good ethos, the university has been proactive in embedding social responsibility, ethics and sustainability into teaching and research as part of a commitment to develop future business leaders with skills, knowledge and mindset that support these values. The university is a signatory to the United Nations Principles for Responsible Management Education (PRME) and demonstrates a willingness to progress the principles by developing teaching and learning programmes that are informed by the values of PRME, many of which align closely to the principles of the Common Good. The commitment also extends to research outputs where issues of social justice, gender equality, climate justice, responsible leadership, and many others are key features of the research strategy. Dr Alec Wersun is the GSBS Lead for the Common Good and recipient of the inaugural UN Pioneer Award at the Global Forum in New York in 2017 for 'leadership and commitment' to PRME. Dr Wersun sums up the GCU contribution by stating that:

> The potential of higher education institutions to make significant contributions to this UN agenda is widely acknowledged, be that through research, community engagement and education, to produce the responsible citizens and leaders of tomorrow. GCU is playing a leading role in this area and is committed to delivering economic

▶

and social benefits at home and across the world. It is important that higher education institutions, business and civil society come together to discuss matters of wider public concern and GCU is delighted to create a space where these important conversations can take place.

There are also opportunities for students to extend their experience of sustainability actions by participating in many of the initiatives developed with partner institutions. For example, students are encouraged to tackle some of the world's most pressing challenges through a leadership programme backed by the Clinton Foundation. GCU is part of the Clinton Global Initiative University Network, set up by former US President Bill Clinton, to help young people turn their ideas of how to make the world a better place into practical action. Participating GCU students receive support to develop projects to reduce consumer waste, tackle poverty in the developing world, and promote sustainable food production. The students, who will join scholars from institutions including Cornell University, the University of California, Berkeley, and the University of Chicago, will have access to a wide range of networking, mentoring and funding opportunities throughout their year of study.

As part of GCU, the Glasgow School for Business and Society (GSBS) is a member of Business in the Community (BITC), a Prince of Wales charity that promotes responsible business. The school aims to contribute through:

- developing a new generation of business and community leaders capable of managing the complex economic, social and environmental challenges faced by business and society in the twenty-first century
- leading relevant research and sharing findings with policy makers, business leaders and community leaders
- increasing engagement of staff and students with the wider community.

Membership of BITC is an important means of reinforcing connections in international networks that are committed to building a sustainable future for people and the planet. BTIC members come from both public and private sectors and commit to transforming communities by tackling key social and environmental issues where organisations can make a real difference. The expertise, resources and capacity of BITC and its members helps GSBS to become recognised as a socially responsible school that serves both business and society.

In research, the UN Sustainable Development Goals (SDGs) inform the ethos around the research strategy which addresses three major societal challenges of inclusive societies, healthy lives and sustainable environments. To support these developing areas of expertise, GCU management created thematic inter-disciplinary research centres that are underpinned by research groups using an inter-sectoral approach to addressing societal challenges locally and internationally. As the output and recognition from the groups has developed, the reputation of the university as being a centre of excellence in business, social and environmental research has gained traction. In the Times Higher Education Global Impact rankings for 2020, GCU was placed 43rd in the world out of 766 universities and 8th in the UK (THE World University Rankings, 2020).

Alongside GSBS, two other schools that comprise the university are similarly involved in taking forward the Common Good ethos and aligning teaching and research to the principles of the SDGs. For example, the School for Computing, Engineering and Built Environment is actively engaged in addressing sustainable environments through the Built Environment Asset Management research centre which tackles climate change issues affecting man-made structures. The centre for Climate Justice addresses climate inequality and promotes a transformative approach to tackling the root cause of climate change. The School of Health and Life Sciences hosts the Research Centre for Health (ReaCH) and draws on expertise from other schools and the Yunus centre for Social Business and Health.

The vision of GCU to be recognised as a world leading university for social innovation by 2030 forms the basis of the Strategy 2030. The commitment to SDGs provides the guiding framework for the delivery of the strategic aims. The examples highlighted above give an indication of the direction of travel and some of the achievements that have already been recognised. The Common Good ethos is one that is supported, recognised and embedded within teaching, research and management at the university and sets guiding principles that make Glasgow Caledonian University a distinct and socially valuable educational asset.

Questions

1. What is the Common Good mission of Glasgow Caledonian University?

2. What three major societal challenges feature in the GCU research strategy?

3. What are the benefits for students of GCU membership of the Clinton Global Initiative University Network?

SUMMARY

This chapter set out the context around which skills and competences development play a crucial role in meeting the challenges of sustainability as economies transition to net zero carbon targets agreed as part of the Paris Agreement. The discussion started with actions that support different levels of sustainability skills and competences from basic to skilled, specialist and then strategic leadership. The discussion revealed the important role that practitioners and managers play in supporting skills development and creating the added value that the deployment of skills and competences delivers in the context of sustainability strategies.

The chapter then focused on the triple helix of education, government and business by critically evaluating the attempts of each to contribute to the transition to a net zero carbon economy by 2050. In education, the focus was on the impact of the Principles of Responsible Management Education initiative as a means of supporting educational institutions to deliver transformation change in the paradigm of business education that places social and environmental issues alongside that of the economic imperative driving business. The chapter also outlined the role that government plays in supporting business to engage with sustainability actions and with education in designing curricula for sustainability skills development. The third element of the triple helix is business itself. Here, the chapter focused attention on the application of a sustainability value framework to determine how corporate bodies can identify and anticipate skills requirement and then monitor and evaluate their impact. Key drivers of sustainability skills development were also highlighted to provide some clarity on the evolving sustainability skills needs across industry. Discussion followed on how these three areas of support can collaborate to achieve the range of goals and targets linked to the development of sustainability skills and competences. The chapter was completed by a treatment of the role of support bodies and accreditors in the process of delivering the skills and competences required by future generations of practitioners and managers.

REVIEW QUESTION AND TASKS

1. Identify the three components of the triple helix of support for sustainability skills and competences.
2. Using the basic, skilled, specialist, and leading levels of sustainability skills and competences, provide details of a specific role for each level.
3. Why is accreditation important for sustainability skills and competences development?

FURTHER READING

Principles of Responsible Management Education (2012) *Inspirational Guide for the Implementation of PRME: Placing Sustainability at the Heart of Management Education* (The Principles for Responsible Management Education Series). Abingdon: Routledge.

This book highlights the process of continuous improvement in the design and implementation of responsible management educational institutions in order to develop the next generation of business leaders capable of meeting the challenges of twenty-first century business.

Rimanoczy, I. (2020) *The Sustainability Mindset: A Guide to Developing a Mindset for a Better World*. Abingdon: Routledge.

This book is a useful contribution to understanding how the challenges of sustainability intersect with the discipline or professions that are chosen. It focuses attention on the range of cognitive skills that support the development of a sustainability mindset including beliefs, values, assumptions and mental processes.

Stibbe, A. (2009) *The Handbook of Sustainability Literacy: Skills for a Changing World*. Totnes: Green Books.

Although over a decade old, this book provides the reader with a valuable insight into the many skills, attributes and values that support understanding of sustainability issues including those that drive ingenuity, creativity and new ways of thinking in changing environments.

INTRODUCTION TO GLOBAL SUSTAINABLE MANAGEMENT

6

SUSTAINABILITY MARKETING

LEARNING OUTCOMES

- Understand the five key principles of sustainable marketing.
- Understand the key drivers for sustainability marketing.
- Critically assess the integration of traditional and sustainability marketing.
- Evaluate strategies for green marketing.
- Comprehend the design of a green marketing plan and marketing mix.

INTRODUCTION

Sustainability marketing refers to a specifically designed form of marketing that links products and services to positive social and environmental impacts. The aim of sustainability marketing is to enhance the quality of life through the promotion of products and services that do no harm to the environment. Belz and Peattie (2012) view the concept of sustainable marketing as being one that an organisation is compelled to meet to fulfil the needs of present consumers without compromising the ability of future generations to fulfil their own needs. There is an appetite among consumers to orientate their buying behaviour towards products and services that are eco-friendly and the marketing and promotion of these plays a role in that process. Organisations are similarly motivated to seek positive social and environmental impacts and the marketing strategies they adopt reflect this. There is a symbiosis in the relationship between consumers and producers to seek ways in which these positive effects can happen. Consumers demand that promotion of products and services reflects their expectations and organisations implement marketing and promotional campaigns that not only meet those expectations but also help encourage more consumers to engage with the concept.

Some of these issues reflect the growing importance of sustainable marketing in the consciousness of producers and consumers. It is in the interests of both these stakeholders to be transparent and more aware of the source of materials used for products and services, the manner in which they are acquired and the associated impact on the environment and humans. These have combined to ensure that brand loyalty is firmly entwined with efforts of organisations to demonstrate sustainability practices and the marketing communications around the promotion and use of products and services (Schultz and Block, 2015). Consequently, these principles of sustainability necessarily extend beyond producers to incorporate all organisations along the supply chain. They also feature beyond the commercial sphere to include the provision of public services.

> **Definition: Sustainability marketing** is the promotion of environmental and socially responsible products and services, practices and brand values.

This chapter focuses attention on the development and implementation of sustainability marketing in organisations. The discussion starts by outlining the five key principles that underpin sustainable marketing before going on to discuss the key drivers of sustainability marketing. The chapter then presents a theoretical framework for critically evaluating some of the criteria that support organisations' integration of traditional and sustainable marketing. This includes a discussion of consumer behaviour and sustainability including consumer values, emotions, and new forms of buying behaviour including ethical consumerism. The chapter then focuses attention on the formation of green marketing strategies that support organisations' efforts to build relationships with consumers based on the concept of sustainability before concluding with a treatment of how sustainability can be incorporated into the formation of a green marketing plan and marketing mix.

FIVE PRINCIPLES OF SUSTAINABILITY MARKETING

Organisations need to become proactive in creating initiatives to support sustainability and the marketing function has an important role to play in that. When organisations demonstrate a commitment that is followed up with practical action and value-adding new ideas and innovations, technologies and designs, then consumers are more likely to engage positively with the concept of sustainability and adapt their preferences accordingly. That relationship between producer and consumers is a strategic issue as it needs to be nurtured carefully over time through the reallocation of resources. Thus, the performance of the organisation is partly determined by the effectiveness with which it applies the sustainable marketing strategy based around five key principles as outlined in Figure 6.1.

FIGURE 6.1 *Five principles of sustainability marketing*

Consumer-oriented marketing determines that marketing activity should be informed by, and aligned to, the perspective of the consumer. This is the basis around which effective relationships can be built. Consumer dairy brand Müller devised a consumer-centric organisation based on four pillars of sustainability. These include responsible sourcing, reducing environmental impact, developing staff on sustainability practices, and inspiring healthier lifestyles. Each has a role to play in the marketing strategy of the business and relies on a superior understanding of how consumers perceive each of these key pillars. Consumer-value marketing refers to the extent to which the organisation allocates resources to support value-adding activities for consumers. Much depends on how consumers perceive value and is often determined by functional, monetary, psychological or social factors. Sustainability and ecological factors add another dimension to perceived value and are an increasingly important aspect of consumer buying behaviour. White et al. (2019) provide a useful literature review of research carried out in this field of study.

In some instances, consumers will perceive value from one factor or a mix of them and effective marketing strategies identify what these are and communicate the product value to them. For example, Hilton hotels and resorts use marketing strategies to communicate the core values of service and quality to customers, but they also use sustainability marketing to emphasise the company's commitment to sustainability practices with the aims of cutting their environmental impact in half by 2030. This aligns to perceptions of social and environmental value that their marketing research confirms their customers' favour. Innovative marketing determines that the organisation must be engaged in the process of continuous improvement and innovation. This invariably links to customer-value marketing as the added value is what drives brand loyalty and the acquisition of new customers. Apple has built a reputation around innovation to the point where the next phase of technological development for their range of devices is eagerly awaited by many consumers. Organisations that embed sustainability innovation into their marketing could similarly engender enthusiasm and brand loyalty from consumers. For example, ice cream manufacturer Ben & Jerry's has an established reputation for using the brand to champion a range of social and environmental issues and now consumers look out for what cause comes next. The company's 'Love Our World' campaign used advertising to raise climate change awareness by using the imagery of a melting ice cream to reinforce the message.

The sense of mission marketing centres the core aim and objectives of the organisation around social values rather than the more narrowly defined product values. This lends a greater prominence to the quest for positive social impacts as a consequence of the activities of the organisation. Cosmetics brand Lush has proactively sought to use its marketing strategy to champion the cause of many different campaigns including the Global Climate strike of 2020 when all their shops were closed for a day. The brand is now synonymous with campaigning in support of a wide range of social and environmental issues. This links to societal marketing whereby the combined interests of the consumer, the organisation and the wider community drive the marketing strategy. Soft drinks giant Coca-Cola now features sustainability across many of their advertising campaigns to inform their consumers of their efforts to address some of the climate change emergency issues. For example, the company has invested in new technologies that allow for up to 25% of their soda bottles to be manufactured using recycled marine plastic. This strikes a resonance with many consumers as awareness of marine pollution becomes more globally recognised. For some, however, the size, scale and economic power of large corporations such as Coca-Cola, means they should be doing more across all their manufacturing and supply chain activities to support sustainability practices and contribute to achieving net zero carbon in advance of the 2050 target date set by signatory countries to the Paris Agreement. Societal marketing also extends to the way an organisation upholds core values of equality, diversity, fairness, and other key attributes that reflect the expectations of stakeholders. Many organisations embed images or content into their marketing, advertising and promotional efforts to reflect their proactive approach to meeting those ideals and shaping the dominant organisational culture around them. This builds trust, empathy and loyalty among customers and ensures that the structure of the workforce reflects the society they represent.

Mini case 6.1: Qantas, Australia

Qantas is the national airline carrier for Australia and has a workforce comprising over 90 different nationalities and 55 different languages. Managing diversity is a key component of the organisation's wider sustainability strategy and features as part of the personalised marketing effort across multiple different media including social media, television, apps, web and inflight wifi. The consistent emotional marketing is based on ideas of 'home' and 'belonging'. These concepts feature as part of the human resource strategy where developing an inclusive and integrated workforce is key. The 'Feels like Home' brand campaign ran between 2014 and 2018 and included real customers and employees in the adverts that emphasised the emotional connection Australians have to their homeland. Apart from creating a harmonious workplace and reflecting the values of their core customers, the organisation also believes that this approach has the potential to deliver economic and competitive advantages as a consequence of attracting the best quality recruits to deliver added value services to their global consumer base. The organisation has called on creative talent to produce compelling imagery that reflects a globally engaged, modern airline.

The strategy also extends to the management of the recruitment process at Qantas and reflects high standards of equality and diversity informed by strict adherence to Equal Employment Opportunity and anti-discrimination guidelines. Employee candidates are supported by guidance on the process which is provided in a number of different languages. Hiring on merit is the key theme throughout the selection process and is closely monitored to ensure that decisions are based on that criterion. The company is proactive in implementing tailored programmes to support equality and diversity such as gender balance where the organisation has initiated the Nancy Bird Walton (renowned Australian aviator) initiative that aims to recruit 38% women in senior management roles and 40% female cadet pilots by 2028. The initiative also introduces work/life balance solutions by introducing flexible working arrangements and the establishment of childcare centres. These initiatives are all designed to encourage a wide range of people from different backgrounds to make the company an 'employer of choice'. They help to build loyalty and facilitate the integration of a diverse workforce that is the basis of a strong social dimension to their sustainability strategy of which marketing plays a key role.

Questions and task

1. What emotional responses was the 'Feels like Home' advertising campaign of Qantas designed to tap into?
2. How does the Qantas human resources strategy fit with their sustainability marketing strategy?
3. Research and highlight the current gender balance of employees at Qantas.

Consumer behaviour and sustainability

There has been an evident shift in consumer behaviour in the last two decades driven by technology and the increased awareness of the importance of sustainability in lifestyles. Where some consumers remain stubbornly aloof from the concept of sustainability for reasons mostly to do with apathy or lack of understanding, the majority have transitioned to varying degrees to the changes required to install sustainability choices into buying habits. Technology in the form of mobile devices, social media, apps, and a plethora of other platforms and software provides opportunities for consumers to shop anytime, anywhere. This has transformed the marketing of products and services to accommodate different types of consumer preferences including shopping that is planned, impulse-driven, on-site, online, and so on. The sustainability issue has also played a role in designing marketing strategies that align to consumer behaviours, attitudes and values. Research by Haller et al. (2020) for IBM notes that as the issue of sustainability matures in the minds of consumers, almost 60% are willing to change their shopping habits to reduce environmental impact with over 70% of those committed to sustainability being willing to pay a premium of 35% for brands that are sustainable and environmentally friendly.

There are four main consumer segments that characterise modern shoppers which comprise consumers that are value driven, purpose driven, brand driven, and product driven. Each has a signature behavioural characteristic linked to their inclination to switch shopping habits to reduce their environmental impact. This is illustrated in Figure 6.2.

The value driven consumer segment seeks good value and convenience over other attributes and are most likely to base their purchasing choices on price and functionality of products. This segment is the least likely (and, therefore hardest to reach for producers of sustainable products) to switch buying habits to reduce negative environmental impacts.

Purpose driven consumers are more conscious of how products and services support their lifestyle and their core values. This consumer segment are more sensitive to environmental impacts and exhibit high levels of willingness to switch their buying habits towards those products and services that have eco-friendly characteristics. They are also most likely to be proactively involved in sustainability practices such as waste management and recycling than any of the other segments. For producers of sustainable products and services this segment is the easiest to reach and to communicate the sustainability value linked to their offerings.

Brand driven consumers represent a group where the added value of the brand is the most important driver. If this added value aligns to sustainability characteristics then that will govern their choices. However, a wide array of other factors influence their purchasing including the design, quality, status, lifestyle, aspiration and other physical, functional and emotional appeals. The key to reaching this consumer segment is to effectively communicate the added value linked to the sustainability characteristics of the brand. With relatively high levels of disposable income, this segment is highly prized but requires a more intense relationship and nurturing to build brand loyalty.

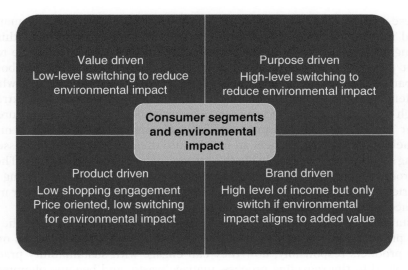

FIGURE 6.2   *Environmental impacts and key consumer segments*

Product driven consumers are the least likely to switch buying habits for environmental impact as the key motivator is price and functionality of products. This segment has a low engagement with shopping and relatively low incomes with their purchase choices most likely governed by basic needs. This consumer segment is difficult to reach for sellers of products with sustainability characteristics as they will be unwilling to pay a premium price for eco-friendly products.

DRIVERS OF SUSTAINABILITY MARKETING

There are significant business opportunities to be gained from effective sustainability marketing. Organisations that meet the requirements of consumers' expectations and values linked to sustainability can accrue wide ranging competitive benefits ranging from increased market share to improved reputation. The market based on social and environmental impacts of products and services has grown significantly over the past two decades and has allowed organisations to better understand the needs and values of consumers based on these characteristics. Consumers are exhibiting an increased interest in what products are made of, where the materials are sourced, and the carbon footprint and social cost associated with their production. Also, there has been an increasing use of public policies and regulatory interventions to encourage sustainability practices and this has added further impetus to the trend of delivering eco-friendly products and services. This acts as an important driver of sustainability marketing for organisations as they seek to maintain control of their sustainability strategy and avoid governmental or quasi-governmental interventions.

These factors have had the effect of concentrating the minds of managers around new and innovative ways their organisations can compete within this evolving eco-system, and sustainability marketing has a significant role to play in that process. This has necessarily involved participation and collaboration with partners along the supply chain to create an integrated strategy whereby eco-friendly credentials can be demonstrated and communicated from extraction through to customer sales and the recycling process. Clothing manufacturer and retailer Timberland has been proactive in developing their sustainability marketing reach by offering consumers an insight into their supply chain processes and inviting scrutiny of their supply chain partners' eco-friendly credentials. They are also product focused with much of their advertising and promotion being based on stories that engage viewers and inform on the efforts made to test their materials to accepted environmental standards.

Sustainability marketing has a role beyond simply communicating the value of the product – it is used to educate, inform and persuade consumers on how to use products responsibly, how they can engage with sustainability practices, get involved in the recycling process, manage waste, and become champions of sustainability themselves. For example, Swedish furniture designers and retailers IKEA have a mission to educate consumers such that sustainability becomes a natural and intuitive part of their living environment and everyday lives. This ethos plays a key role in the marketing strategy of the company with advertising that informs and explains how consumers can create a sustainable home using their products. Many consumers are seeking ways in which they can live healthier lives and contribute to tackling climate change. Marketing is a powerful communications tool for disseminating important ways in which consumers can more fully engage with the concept through the purchase of eco-friendly products and services. Here, there is a win–win scenario playing out as organisations initiate sales through powerful and effective sustainability marketing techniques that create value for consumers whilst simultaneously encouraging fuller participation in sustainability practices.

Another driver of sustainability marketing is the potential it has for building trust, reputation and confidence among consumers. Organisations across many different sectors, such as mining, oil, fashion, transport, fishing and others, have struggled to create a positive corporate image in the minds of consumers partly due to the nature of their business but also the emphasis on economic growth and performance ahead of any other criteria of success. For example, the link between the fashion industry and sustainability may be perceived as an oxymoron such is the reputation the industry has for negative social and environmental impacts. However, many fashion houses are now promoting their 'green' credentials via powerful marketing techniques to reposition their brands in the minds of sustainable oriented consumers. Fashion designer Stella McCartney initiated a 2020 campaign that highlighted the brand's most sustainable collection to date by communicating the value of plants as innovative materials.

Industries that were once unsustainable now have an opportunity to realign their practices and purpose to fit more closely with the values that consumers express, and sustainability marketing is potentially an effective platform that can help organisations communicate how their actions support the ideals and values expressed by consumers and other stakeholders. As a consequence of unprecedented levels of scrutiny by individuals and pressure groups who monitor the sustainability actions across a wide range of industry sectors, organisations are increasingly embracing sustainability practices and are proactive in disseminating information on their practices to a wide audience. These pressures have been evident for over a decade and have contributed to the growth in sustainability marketing as organisations rethink and reinvent their marketing strategies to meet consumers' expectations on social and environmental impacts (Kotler, 2011; Lim, 2016).

Mini case 6.2: Sustainable tourism in the Maldives

The Republic of Maldives is an archipelago of 1200 small islands in the Indian Ocean south-west of Sri Lanka. The main source of income is tourism with people from all over the world seeking to experience the white sandy beaches and crystal-clear warm waters that the coral islands have to offer. Luxury tourist brands such as Kuoni and Carrier have specialised in tailor-made holidays for many decades and have used compelling emotional marketing techniques to attract customers seeking an exotic and memorable tourism experience. However, the tourism industry in the Maldives has been presented with some modern challenges that has initiated a change of direction in how they market their offerings. The global Covid pandemic has caused safety fears that the industry has to address and the growing awareness and vulnerability of the islands to the effects of climate change has similarly informed new ways of communicating the value of the destination to customers.

The evolving tourism marketing strategy is managed by the Maldives Marketing & PR Corporation with two identified priorities of safety and sustainability being key features. The Covid pandemic has created huge uncertainty in the minds of travellers in general and governments have been grappling with advice and policy guidance on a raft of destinations including the Maldives. This has informed the marketing strategy with the use of social media (including 'The Sun Will Shine Again' campaign on Facebook) and film to communicate empathy and reassurance that the country has taken all steps possible to protect the safety of visitors including adherence to guidelines that meet World Health Organisation standards. There has also been a concerted effort to explain efforts to meet expectations on environmental impacts, something that consumers are increasingly sensitive to especially given the pristine nature of the location. The development of mass tourism has created challenges including the increasing hotel construction, exponential rises in aviation traffic, waste management problems, erosion of coastal zones, and the marine polluting effects of tourism activities (Waseema, 2017). The marketing strategy includes recognition of the increased interest in eco-tourism and many of the brochures and online offerings feature content that explains how sustainability

(Continued)

practices have been managed including supporting marine health, maintaining the tree line between accommodation and the beach, practical waste management guidance, and the designation of protected areas. Individual resorts also contribute their own eco-friendly measures to support sustainability. The marketing function is one tool of many that the authorities in the Maldives use to manage the growth of tourism whilst maintaining a commitment to sustainability practices that contribute to tackling climate change.

Questions and task

1. Identify three sustainability challenges facing the tourism industry in the Maldives.
2. What techniques have been used to communicate the environmental protection and safety aspects of the country's tourism marketing strategy?
3. What are the biggest threats to sustainable tourism in the Maldives?

INTEGRATING TRADITIONAL AND SUSTAINABILITY MARKETING

The marketing function within organisations has traditionally been perceived as a range of communications tools and techniques to influence the perception of value in the minds of consumers. This form of 'indoctrination' brought success for many and proved an effective means of contributing to the competitiveness of organisations. However, the relationship between producer and consumer evolved over time and this demanded more subtle and nuanced approaches to communicating brand values. In the modern era, partly due to the influence of social media, organisations have had to adapt their marketing strategies to new media channels, changing expectations and, fundamentally, a more collaborative relationship with consumers. Part of this process has been the integration of traditional marketing tools and techniques with those that more closely fit with consumer expectations, sustainability being one pertinent example. Belz and Peattie (2010) devised a marketing framework that integrated traditional forms with sustainability marketing as illustrated in Figure 6.3.

The framework starts with modern marketing techniques including market research, identifying customer needs, and then building relationships to create a brand loyalty. This approach to modern marketing is a holistic one that is designed to create connections between brands and customers using a blended strategy, communications technology, and analysis of market data.

A sustainability marketing strategy takes these concepts and tools to lend a sustainability focus to the approach. These may include ethical practices, eco-friendly initiatives or innovations that support sustainability. These can then be used as a basis for relationship building with consumers who exhibit preferences

FIGURE 6.3 *From modern to sustainable marketing*

Source: Adapted from Belz and Peattie (2010)

for products and services with these attributes. This gives rise to the sustainability marketing framework presented in Figure 6.4.

The sustainability framework is built on an integrated system that forms the dynamic between environmental and social factors (either narrowly or broadly defined in scope) and the focus of marketing based on relationships or commercial transactions. Taking the process of modern marketing and transitioning to sustainable marketing as the central pillars of the marketing strategy (as illustrated by the arrows in Figure 6.4), it can be seen that a range of different options present themselves depending on what the marketing aims and objectives of the organisation are. If it is a series of goals linked to sustainability then the marketing efforts should all migrate in that direction whereby the emphasis is on the broad environment incorporating the market (economic), society (social) and planet (environmental). The move to sustainability marketing relies on the generation of new ideas and innovations that support the approach. According to Belz and Peattie (2010) this transition requires some re-thinking by managers along the lines of treating socioecological problems as a starting point, taking a holistic view of consumer behaviour, reconfiguring the marketing mix (this is discussed later in this chapter), and understanding and utilising the transformational potential of marketing activities and relationships.

It is important to remember that the commercial aspect of marketing cannot be ignored as consumers continue to demand a range of added value from the transactions in which the marketing function plays a role. Issues of quality, price, value, functionality and service remain prominent features of consumer buying behaviour. Although it may be deemed laudable to pursue a sustainability marketing approach, it has to be within the constraints of economic viability for organisations otherwise they risk losing focus on the purpose of their enterprise, which in the commercial sphere is to make profits and effect growth. Managers need to understand and act upon information around the costs and benefits of pursuing a sustainability marketing strategy and what returns (economic, reputation, social, environmental) will accrue from their efforts. Organisations need to ensure that the message they convey is accurate, realistic and capable of being demonstrated. For example, fast food retailers McDonald's used their switch to paper straws as

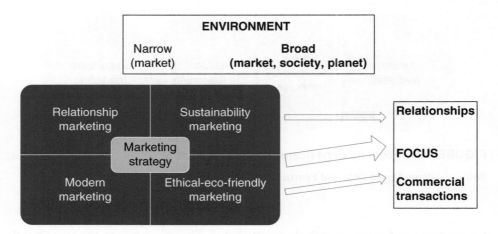

FIGURE 6.4 *Framework for sustainability marketing*

Source: Adapted from Belz and Peattie (2010)

part of an advertising campaign designed to communicate their 'green' credentials to customers only to discover that their plastic straws were capable of being recycled whereas the paper version was not. The risk of 'greenwashing' (conveying a false impression of the environmental soundness of a product) may, ultimately, harm a brand if these criteria are not carefully considered.

GREEN MARKETING STRATEGIES

There is pressure on organisations to deliver green marketing strategies that meet eco-friendly conscious consumers' expectations and to communicate the sustainability credentials of their brands. Care needs to be exercised to avoid over-claiming on the eco-friendly characteristics or functionality of products and services that are branded as being 'green'. This so-called 'greenwashing' can have negative effects on the authenticity of the brand and the resulting damage to reputation can permeate throughout the whole organisation and take some time, effort and money to re-establish. Green marketing strategies can help to spread the message about the innovative 'green' features of products and services, position the brand in the market where positive social and environmental impacts are valued by consumers, and help to demonstrate their eco-friendly authenticity as a means of building consumer relationships, trust and brand loyalty. There are many different ways in which a green marketing strategy can be devised depending on what customer segment is to be targeted, what the wider strategic marketing aims are, and what resources and capabilities the organisation has in delivering eco-friendly products and services. Figure 6.5 highlights a combination of five possible areas that can form the basis of a green marketing strategy.

FIGURE 6.5 *Green marketing strategy*

Green design refers to those aspects of the design process that deliberately add sustainability features or functionality to a product with the aim of making them as eco-friendly as possible. The construction industry is innovative in the ways in which modern houses incorporate a range of sustainability features such as insulation, recycling facilities, renewable energy sources such as solar panels, low waste, and low carbon materials. The green marketing strategies of house builders in the UK such as Bellway, Taylor Wimpey and Barratt Developments all feature these innovations as selling points to customers and provide the basis for demonstrating their commitment to a wide range of pertinent sustainability issues including renewable energy, low carbon footprint, protecting bio-diversity, managing waste, and recycling materials. Effective green design can form the basis of a compelling green marketing strategy as it not only emphasises the positive environmental and social impacts but also allows organisations to showcase the results of the innovation and creativity they have invested in to deliver sustainable products and services attractive designs and high quality functionality. These attributes are evident in the green marketing of a huge array of consumer products and services across multiple different industry sectors.

The product attributes highlighted above can be used to position the brand in the market. Green positioning is the process of building brand associations linked to communicating the social or environmentally friendly attributes of products or services. Functional and emotional associations are two types of green positioning linked to brand perceptions by consumers. Functional positioning as part of a green marketing strategy relies on informing consumers of the practical or functional attributes of the product that will meet or exceed their expectations. The car manufacturing industry uses a functional type of green marketing to explain to customers the engineering innovations that support low emissions and increased efficiency. For example, Toyota ran an effective advertising campaign with the slogan 'more green for less green' that drew consumers' attention to the range of eco-friendly innovations for the-gas electric hybrid *Prius* model. The slogan was designed to emphasise the functionality of the product, its green credentials, and the competitive pricing strategy (hence the larger letter on the end part of the slogan).

Emotional attributes are another type of positioning in green marketing strategies and offer marketeers a wide range of opportunities due to the complexity of the human mind and how it responds to certain stimuli. It could be argued that all advertising, promotion and marketing efforts are designed to spark an emotional response from the viewer. However, some are specifically designed to trigger specific types of responses based on the communication whether it be words, imagery, sounds, colours, shapes, or a combination of these forms. Tapping into this rich seam of potential presents some challenges for marketeers due to the sheer number and complexity of human emotions. Sustainable behaviours can decrease negative emotions or increase positive ones (Sun and Trudel, 2017). Some figure prominently and consistently across both traditional and sustainability marketing such as feelings of assertiveness, belonging and status, among others. In some instances, consumers have feelings of guilt associated with their lifestyle that can manifest in pro-environmental buying behaviour (Rees et al., 2014). Marketing brands with a strong sustainability characteristic has the potential for both function responses (consumer preference is governed by the practical effectiveness of the product) and emotional responses (consumer preferences are governed by the emotional trigger the product elicits). There is some debate among academics as to whether there is a trade-off between these two associations or if they can work in tandem (Matthes et al., 2014; Jang et al., 2021). Both have potential for tapping into what consumers desire or need, but the emotional element has broad potential for engaging consumers in sustainability as the subject matter exhibits a range of value-laden attributes including being topical, credible, impactful, moral and other emotive characteristics that resonate to different degrees across different customer segments.

Much of the success of sustainability marketing using emotional triggers depends on identifying what emotion to target and then designing a communication that taps into that emotion in a way that embeds itself into the sub-conscious mind of the target audience. The topic of sustainability can link to a wide range of emotional connections such as social awareness, healthy lives, morality, spirituality, economic welfare, healthy physical environment, fairness, equity, and so on. Koenig-Lewis et al. (2014) identified a range of emotions that link to friendly environments such as moral emotions and emotional affinity with nature or even the fear of ecological endangerment. Dekker (2018) also provides some valuable insights into emotional marketing that can be aligned to a sustainability marketing strategy. Figure 6.6 illustrates the key components of an emotional sustainability marketing strategy.

FIGURE 6.6 *Emotional sustainability marketing strategy*

Source: Adapted from Dekker (2018)

Market research

The first and most important step in the process of implementing a sustainability marketing strategy based on emotions is to undertake effective research to identify and understand the target audience. As noted previously, customers are driven by a range of different drivers including value, product, brand and purpose. Each of these can have an emotional association that could be tapped into by marketeers. However, it is necessary to gain an understanding of the characteristics of each segment linked to these driver groups as they will react differently to emotional stimuli. For example, customers with a close engagement with brand will be affected by imagery that communicates aspiration, whereas those driven by product functionality will be more likely to respond positively to demonstrations of how products can be used to achieve a specified outcome. Market research into how sustainability resonates with these different groups helps to design the appropriate message.

Use of colour

For sustainability marketing the colour green is by far and away the most commonly used in advertising, promotional material and marketing efforts. Brands that have a strong environmental message or sustainability function invariably use the colour green to emphasise these values. It is a colour that has strong associations with sustainability and ecological artefacts and is used extensively across many different products and services. For example, the detergent brand Tide uses a green plant on the innovative plant-based product branded Purclean. Other colours have similar effects, such as different shades of blue when associating the brand with water. This can be images of oceans, waterfalls, rivers and so on. The brand Jaws (Just Add Water), a glass cleaning product, uses a deep blue colour to symbolise the water element and also its reusable qualities. Psychologists have undertaken effective research around responses to different colours. For example, light shades of green are relaxing and harmonious and are prevalent in hospitals and other caring settings, yellow is warm and red evokes strong emotions such as passion, anger, or excitement. Black links to power, allegiance and formality such as evident in police uniforms. Whatever message marketeers wish to communicate around sustainability, the choice and use of colours plays an important role.

Storytelling

Stories are relatable and feature heavily in the marketing of sustainable products, especially around issues that engage the interest of consumers, spark a passion or elicit empathy. Issues of climate change, animal welfare, the destruction of habitats or the devastation wreaked by human actions on the planet are commonly referred to as part of a storytelling approach to connecting with audiences. Positive stories are also effective and can feature heroic efforts by mankind to tackle the climate emergency or protect the rainforests or oceans. Marketeers can use storylines to explain what the organisation does to meet expectations of stakeholders and can have an educational aspect to the dialogue. Consumer goods producers Unilever commissioned a film called 'Farewell to the Forest' to illustrate the company's commitment to tackling deforestation. The poignancy of the storyline was designed to elicit both empathy and support from audiences. Social impacts also feature in this strategy whereby organisations communicate their commitment to equality, diversity, equal pay or other workers' rights. The effectiveness of the storytelling strategy is determined by the extent to which it creates an emotional connection between the brand and the consumer and this is often achieved by focusing the narrative on shared values and beliefs.

Create a community

Sustainability has huge potential for galvanising people into action as a group, whether it be community activities to support the protection of local environments, lobbying organisations to meet their expectations or canvassing for greater decision-making power to address issues of local concern, the power of the group is tangible and real. Marketeers can harness that power by using emotional marketing to help create a movement or campaign group in communities based around brands.

This can trigger emotions linked to community spirit, esprit de corps (team spirit), acceptance and belonging, and the feel-good factor of doing something valuable for the community. Brand loyalty may be a by-product of this that is worth pursuing by organisations. The global coffee chain Starbucks initiated a community around their brand entitled 'My Starbucks Idea' whereby consumers can offer up suggestions for the company to follow through on. This has included a significant number of innovations to improve the sustainability of the company's products as well as the on-going relationship building with coffee growers around their portfolio of partner farmers. Over 300 innovation suggestions have been followed up by the company and has facilitated idea sharing and knowledge exchange on sustainability issues between the hundreds of thousands of members that comprise the community.

Inspire

Marketeers have opportunities to inspire consumers to become engaged in sustainability as it taps into feelings of being proactive around a good cause, feelings of hope and joy, or of being part of something bigger than ordinary everyday events. Sustainability practices can be linked to aspirations of creating healthier lifestyles, protecting and safeguarding the planet for future generations. The ideal of leaving a positive legacy for grandchildren and great grandchildren acts as a powerful human emotion about family, continuity and the need to protect. Emotional marketing campaigns are deliberately designed to tap into those powerful and instinctive emotions of consumers. National Geographic has created opportunities for readers to become an active supporter of their campaign to tackle climate change and to address a raft of social issues that many of their customers feel passionate about. This taps into some of the emotions already highlighted above but can also include the kudos and self-satisfaction of partnering with a global brand with a reputation for highlighting and supporting good environmental and social causes.

Mini case 6.3: IKEA, Sweden

Headquartered in Malmö, Sweden, IKEA is an iconic brand of designers and manufacturers of self-assembly furniture. Through market research the company has identified their core market as the 20–30 age group, professional, urban and supportive of sustainable lifestyles. Consequently, the marketing strategy is reflective of this demographic adopting communications channels that help support the image of being young, energetic, and cool. IKEA have become adept at using advertising and promotion of their products based on emotive colour schemes, functional but stylish design, and innovative layouts. The youthful market segment is an important one for IKEA and has formed the basis of distinct promotional campaigns designed to positively project the role of their products in the lifestyle, attitudes and beliefs of

(Continued)

young people. Issues of sustainability, climate change, healthy lifestyles and social justice all feature in the mindsets of the target audience. This has led IKEA to be proactive in harnessing the potential of social media to communicate their brand values, many of which reflect these lifestyle characteristics. For example, social networking is a phenomenon that has global reach, most evidently in the under 30 age group – the so-called Generation Y age group who grew up in the digital age.

IKEA uses a number of social media sites such as Twitter and YouTube for posting information about their products and what values they can bring to consumers. Social media is a channel that is capable of generating initial interest easily and then snowballing to gain many thousands of viewers very quickly. The viral effect of the medium supports some innovative and enticing marketing techniques. By using social media to tap into their existing knowledge of their target demographic, IKEA have been able to better understand their needs and adapt their products and marketing accordingly. For example, young buyers are interested in eco-friendly products, where they are sourced, the carbon footprint, waste, energy and water usage in their production. The company subsequently launched a line of products labelled 'more sustainable' with energy efficient appliances and water management products being two of the most prominent innovations to demonstrate their eco-friendly credentials. The sustainability marketing included staff and customers with demonstrations at festivals, living experiments, and workforce education programmes. Social media is also used to inform customers of the wide range of sustainability practices they adopt such as the use of balers to compress packing materials to make recycling easier and more efficient. The success of the IKEA sustainability marketing strategy is based on some simple but effective rules for using social media and traditional marketing techniques. First, it is ubiquitous across multiple platforms and there are innovative means of communicating core values, product attributes and lifestyle choices via stories, anecdotes, photos, case studies, customer reviews and so on. These are effective means of supporting the brand identity and gaining the attention of eco-friendly customers.

Questions and task

1. Identify the key factors that have led to the success of the IKEA sustainability marketing strategy.
2. What does 'going viral' mean in the context of online marketing?
3. What are the key characteristics of Generation Y consumers?

GREEN MARKETING PLAN AND GREEN MARKETING MIX

The marketing plan of an organisation stems from the vision and mission and aims to bring together strategic goals and marketing objectives. A green marketing plan incorporates those elements of social and environmental factors that resonate with consumers and help to communicate the sustainability features or functions of products and/or services. An effective green marketing plan requires market-eers to identify the marketing mix that simultaneously meets economic objectives (usually profitability targets) and social and environmental impacts linked to sustainability. Figure 6.7 illustrates a typical green marketing plan.

FIGURE 6.7 *Green marketing plan*

Organisational sustainability goals should be in line with the overall long-term vision and strategic plan. The sustainability strategy should clearly set out the aims linked to identified positive social and environmental impacts the organisation seeks to achieve. The green marketing objectives form part of this and should contain specific actions and targets linked to stated objectives. For example, it may state that a recycling capability built into an existing product achieves a 5% increase in market share within an identified target audience. Sustainability strategies refer to how the green marketing strategies are to be achieved. For example, a sustainability strategy may include actions that support recycling and the reduction of the organisation's carbon footprint. The green marketing mix adds details to what exactly those actions comprise and how they align to the green marketing objectives. The target market is the one that the organisation has decided to compete in and is determined by analysing the product/service life cycle from development, introduction, growth, maturity or decline. Sustainability presents many opportunities for extending the life cycle of a product or service by building in new and innovative features or solutions that elongate its lifespan at the mature level. Continuous improvements or innovations maintain the level of brand loyalty that organisations can use to remain competitive. This element of the green marketing plan requires organisations to identify the specific target audience and understand their needs and wants closely based on their engagement with the 'green' concept and the value they place on it.

The success of a green marketing plan depends on the effectiveness of the chosen green marketing strategies. Here, it is essential that a close understanding of the values and beliefs of consumers is well understood. The analysis of the green marketing mix forms the basis of the research that goes into developing this understanding and will include various indicators of consumer needs including product or service quality, functionality, convenience, pricing, packaging and other sustainability features and characteristics. A key determinant of success is the ability of the organisation to build relationships with consumers, to engage them in the process of developing sustainable solutions and to transform their thoughts and feelings into added value sustainable products and services. In order for this to be effective, the organisation needs to instil their own sustainability values and beliefs to partner organisations along the supply chain. If a supplier pays scant regard to sustainability practices then this negative environmental impact will inevitably compromise marketing efforts that demonstrate how the organisation embraces the concept.

Marketeers implement their chosen marketing strategy once the target audience has been identified using the marketing mix. McCarthy (1960) first devised the four Ps marketing mix comprising product, price, place and promotion. The framework can be adapted for the context of sustainability to create the green marketing mix as illustrated in Figure 6.8. It is the hallmark of an effective green marketing mix that each element demonstrably supports the principles of sustainability and this requires openness, transparency, honesty and credibility throughout the process. In return, consumers recognise the value of these efforts and this helps to create strong brands that improve competitiveness. Thus, an effective green marketing mix contributes to the social, environmental and economic elements of the Triple Bottom Line.

> **Definition: Green marketing mix** is an environmentally friendly reconceptualisation of the product, price, place and promotion framework for marketing.

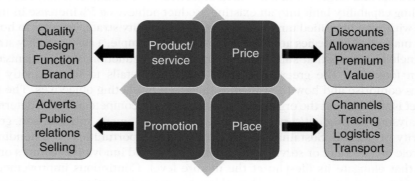

FIGURE 6.8 *Green marketing mix*

Source: Adapted from McCarthy (1960)

Product

Organisations need to offer benefits to customers or a solution to a particular need. There has been a distinct shift towards the solutions aspect and less emphasis on product in the last two decades as the demand for services has increased. Tukker (2004) also noted the trend towards product/service systems as a way of developing sustainable consumer markets. There are a wide range of opportunities for organisations to introduce innovation to support this (LED light bulbs, electric vehicles, goods manufactured using natural products, etc.). The product element should also include how materials are sourced, the type of component parts or ingredients, and how the product is manufactured including issues of energy use, waste and recycling. Even luxury brands can access the benefits of green marketing of products. High-end Italian fashion house Gucci has transformed its carrier bags and labelling in a way that retains the aesthetic but incorporates environmentally friendly materials such as recycled rubber, water-based adhesives, and dyed paper packaging procured from FSC-certified forests. Plastics, polyesters and other man-made materials have been discarded in favour of natural sources. Furthermore, customers only receive 100% recyclable gift boxes on request.

Price

The price of a product or service has to be set in line with the consumers' perception of what value it has. Consumers will value different products and services in different ways and exhibit different levels of tolerance or advantage associated with changes in price (this is referred to as elasticity of demand in economics). In classical economics, the price is determined by the intersection of supply and demand and all of these factors are influenced by characteristics such as quality, functionality, brand, utility (satisfaction), experience, emotional value and so on. The sustainability factor is another important element in this process and is often viewed as a limiting factor in gaining mass market appeal due to the additional costs incurred in the sourcing, manufacture and distribution that is usually passed on to the consumer in the form of higher prices. For example, products that exhibit the Fairtrade logo are usually more highly priced than mainstream rivals that do not support this initiative. Fairtrade is a market intervention that allows growers of crops in less developed countries to achieve a premium above the market price they could charge. Essentially, consumers of Fairtrade products pay the premium as a means of supporting subsistence farmers as a positive social impact. In manufacturing, those organisations that use renewable energy may have had to invest heavily in new technologies that support sustainable buildings or machinery and this cost may ultimately have to be absorbed by consumers in the form of higher prices. Consequently, a 'green' pricing gap emerges as there is an additional expense associated with sustainable products and services as compared to traditional and non-sustainable products.

It could be argued that this imposed additionality to price discriminates against low-income groups who cannot afford to pay the premium linked to sustainable products and services. Even for those groups who can afford sustainable products and services, there is a buying decision to be made based on assessments of what value they derive from them. It may be that the emotional value of contributing to tackling climate change or other sustainability-related issues is sufficient to persuade consumers to pay the premium price, or there may be other factors at play such as added value from the design, functionality, packaging or longevity of the sustainable product. An alternative is to find ways for sustainable products and services to be closer in price to their non-sustainable counterparts, or to gain benefits from marketing that result in higher perceived value by consumers. The beauty industry has been particularly effective in marketing the transition to sustainability such as in the widespread adoption of natural and organic materials for a range of products such as shampoos and body lotions. Companies such as Avalon and Waleda have used powerful environmental imagery and compelling storylines around sustainability to communicate the added value of their range of organic beauty products and this is reflected in the price of those products compared to ones produced in traditional and non-sustainable forms.

Place

In the marketing mix, place refers to where the product can be bought and includes the method of distribution to the point of sale, whether physical or virtual. For retailers with a physical shop there are a wide range of sustainability opportunities to explore such as energy efficient buildings using renewables, low-carbon work practices, recycling facilities, low waste, zero use of plastic bags and green marketing approaches including support for encouraging sustainable consumption among their customers. The ethos of purchasing local produce is another means of demonstrating how sustainability in distribution can permeate throughout the place of purchase. Technology is also making an impact in the way that consumers shop with online shopping becoming more social, accessible and instantaneous. As e-commerce becomes the dominant means of transacting, organisations are creating new and innovative ways of attracting consumers based on these key demands. For example, easyJet have enabled Instagram users to book holidays simply by clicking on a photograph they have seen. This innovation allows consumers to add products and services to a virtual shopping cart anytime and in any place and will become the norm across multiple sectors of commerce. It also presents the opportunity to build in important educating messages regarding different aspects of sustainability that consumers can engage with. Relating this to the easyJet example, it can be linked to information on ethical tourism and the sustainability practices that tourists can observe and practice.

Consumers are also concerned about the source of the goods they buy. Traceability has become an important factor in providing the transparency consumers seek regarding the ethical practices of suppliers, the sustainability across the supply chain and the environmental impact linked to their purchases. Here, blockchain technology can be used as part of the green marketing approach to offer consumers access to detailed information on the source of products using QR codes. French supermarket giant Carrefour has adopted this technology to support their commitment to full transparency on all their sourced products to offer consumers insight into a range of issues of concern including food safety, nutrition, animal welfare and workers' rights.

Promotion

The promotion element of the marketing mix is the communications techniques and tactics that organisations use as a means of marketing and promoting their products. These support the value of the brand and there are numerous ways in which sustainability can be incorporated into the promotion communications around positive social and environmental impacts. For example, Planet Organic is an eco-friendly retailer of organic household products and foodstuffs that support their brands of domestic cleaning products, such as Ecover, by communicating the environmentally friendly characteristics. These include the plant-based materials for packaging, no plastics, no phosphate ingredients, and how to use, refill or dispose of the product. Typical tools and media channels for applying the principles of effective promotion of products include advertising, digital marketing, social media marketing, personal selling, and consumer and trade promotion. Even organisations that operate in industries with a poor record and reputation for doing harm to the planet (oil, gas, fashion, chemicals, logging, etc.) can use these tools and media to rebrand and reposition the product in the minds of consumers. The oil company BP has struggled to meet stakeholder expectations on environmental issues as a result of their oil exploration and extraction activities including the Deepwater Horizon environmental disaster in the Gulf of Mexico. In an attempt to address the negative perceptions of the brand the company invested in sustainability planning and supported it with a change to the branding including that of the company logo which now features a flower in the green and yellow company colours. It was also followed up with an intense public relations campaign designed to inform, influence and persuade consumers that the company were proactive in minimising negative environmental impacts. BP and the industry in which it competes has a considerable challenge ahead if they seek to change negative public perceptions of their activities in an age when fossil fuels are in the process of being replaced by renewable energy.

Social media is a medium that has become increasingly important to organisations seeking to target particular audiences, particularly the so-called millennials (usually referring to those born between 1980 and 1996) or Generation Z (born between 1997 and 2015). The young people born within those timeframes have either been schooled in the age of the internet or lived their whole lives in the digital world. Social media platforms and applications such as Facebook, Instagram, WhatsApp, Twitter, and others, are the main source of information for these generations and they have become adept at navigating different online sites for what they need. This provides an ideal platform for organisations seeking to promote their products and the messages they seek to communicate to their audience regarding the product and the social and environmental issues that are important to supporting the brand. Mobile marketing is also a key part of promoting products and services as this type of device has become a ubiquitous lifestyle accessory and the main source of information on products and services for billions of consumers on a global scale.

Nike, USA

An important challenge facing organisations in the modern era is to maintain competitiveness through delivering quality products and services whilst demonstrating a commitment to sustainability. In some instances this marriage is difficult to achieve and maintain. Some industries struggle to transition to sustainability due to the nature of their operations. The Canada oil sands excavation industry in Alberta is one of the most polluting forms of energy extraction in the world leaving environmental scarring of the landscape and health risks to local communities. Companies engaged in the industry often resort to employing public relations consultants and sympathetic politicians to greenwash their negative environmental impacts. Other industries are more proactive in seeking ways to incorporate sustainability into their operations and products. Domestic detergent producers have traditionally relied on the use of chemicals as key ingredients but have now explored ways of including eco-friendly materials in their products and packaging. In other settings, organisations view sustainability as a compelling business opportunity and build it into their strategy for gaining a competitive advantage. Opportunities for creating a closer bond with the values of consumers provides good reason for engaging with sustainability and this has led to new and innovative ways in which they produce, package and recycle products. One such organisation is the US sportwear manufacturer Nike. The company has been active in rethinking their marketing strategy based on innovative new green designs for selected parts of their product portfolio.

Green design is an integral part of the circular economy and Nike have invested people and processes that help rethink their creativity in ways that support the protection of the environment and deliver high-quality, well designed and durable products. The key to driving the green design strategy is to reimagine the culture around its development by not seeking perfection but rather reimagining the process in radical ways that include experimentation, learning from mistakes and finding solutions. Designers at Nike have a broad scope for exploring creative solutions but there are also some built-in guidelines and parameters that maintain a discipline that protects the brand. One of the key principles that guide designers' thinking is that of circularity. Solutions to design challenges need to consider the materials used, how they are manufactured, used by consumers and then returned by way of recycling. Thus, one of the key challenges is to find solutions that deliver compelling design, durability and longevity of use at least waste and maximum efficiency. Some solutions include using leather scraps, linen sock liners, redesigning patterns for maximum efficiency, reinforced seams using natural materials for strength, and using recycled polyester. Materials account for around 70% of the carbon footprint of Nike so much thought and effort has gone into finding solutions that help the organisation achieve its target of net zero carbon and zero waste by 2050. Many of the design solutions are small scale individually but combine to deliver a sustainable process and end product. The iconic Air brand of trainer is one of the bestselling products in the Nike portfolio but it is also one of the most sustainably produced too with many innovations around design, materials and processes being rolled out to support the marketing development of the brand. There is also a close working relationship with an array of independent factories and material suppliers around the world to ensure adherence to the principles of sustainability including more energy efficient production methods, sourcing renewable energy, decreasing packaging, reducing shipping emissions and implementing recycling processes.

Building in sustainability to the design function at Nike has entailed influencing and shaping an organisational culture that supports it. The mindset of designers has to be governed by principles of circularity and this presents the challenge. Designers not only have to be creative but also be motivated by challenge, to thrive in a problem-solving environment, to view their domain as one that taps into their competitive spirit. In many ways the design team exhibits many of the attributes and characteristics of the sportsmen and women they design the products for. Preparation, discipline, practice, dedication, skill, and the will to win are all key features of the design team. Teamwork is another key asset that plays a role with knowledge sharing, collaboration and coordination underpinning the dominant working culture. This culture allows for new ideas and innovations to be presented, experimented upon and reworked. The ethos is one of progress rather than seeking perfection. This in itself is a radical departure from traditional thinking whereby seeking perfection was the mantra often cited in mission statements of organisations.

The green design of Nike products presents opportunities for marketeers to use as part of their advertising and promotional campaigns. The means by which the range of trainers and other sportwear products are made provides a compelling story and is something that strikes a resonance with their core target audience of young people under 30 years of age. This demographic exhibits a close affinity with sustainability and takes an interest in the actions of an organisation that demonstrably supports the protection of the planet. Nike has a positive story to tell and uses this to create an emotional connection with their consumers in ways that speak of a dual commitment to the shared core values around sustainability. The recycling capability of their products has also been used to enhance the emotional connection to the products. Each recycled sports shoe or piece of apparel has been on a journey and has had a life somewhere out in the community. This provides the basis of a story that can be used to illustrate the link between the product and the ordinary lives of citizens as they go about their daily business in many different ways. For marketing purposes these stories are a valuable means of communicating the value of the brand and the commitment to sustainability in ways that are authentic and true.

For Nike, sustainability has been a valuable pathway to re-establishing a positive reputation after a number of high-profile cases of unethical practices linked to workers' rights in overseas subsidiaries and factories, the use of toxins in

▶

materials, child labour, negative environmental impacts on wildlife habitats, and even gender discrimination against female athletes (the company had to implement a maternity policy for all their sponsored female athletes). The organisation has found some redemption through their award-winning sustainability practices that has had the effect of building trust and brand loyalty of consumers around the world.

Questions and task

1. How does green design support the marketing of Nike brands?
2. Research and comment on the current carbon footprint of Nike.
3. What attributes do Nike designers exhibit in tackling the challenge of incorporating sustainability into their design solutions?

SUMMARY

This chapter has focused attention on some of the most important aspects of developing and implementing sustainability marketing practices. The discussion provided a background to the concept of sustainability marketing by setting out five key principles that support its application. Key drivers of consumer value around sustainability were discussed and it was revealed that purpose-driven consumers are the most likely to switch to sustainable products that reflect their own core beliefs and values. The chapter also provided insights into the key drivers that encourage organisations to transition to sustainability marketing including issues of trust, reputation, changes in consumer attitudes, supply chain partnerships and the increased competitiveness it can deliver. This was followed by the presentation of a theoretical framework for creating an integrated system that forms the dynamic between environmental and social factors and the focus of marketing based on relationships or commercial transactions. From a normative perspective it was explained how organisations should align their marketing towards sustainability goals. There then followed a discussion around green marketing strategies and the issues of functional and emotional means of attracting consumers. The chapter concluded by adapting the traditional marketing mix to feature the incorporation of 'green' associations and used examples to illustrate the distinct character of the green marketing mix.

REVIEW QUESTIONS AND TASK

1. What are the five principles of sustainability marketing?
2. Give three examples of how companies can increase consumers' awareness of sustainability through marketing and promotion.
3. Is emotional marketing more effective than functional marketing for generating sales of products?
4. Define the green marketing mix. How is it different from the traditional marketing mix?

INTRODUCTION TO GLOBAL SUSTAINABLE MANAGEMENT

FURTHER READING

Altinbasak-Farina, I. and Burnaz, S. (2019) *Ethics, Social Responsibility and Sustainable Marketing*. Singapore: Springer.

The authors have produced a valuable work that offers a compelling treatment of societal marketing. The book focuses attention on social responsibility and corporate ethics to reflect consumer concerns around how business operates and the effect on society. The discussion also features an explanation of how companies can adopt corporate social responsibility as a means to gaining a competitive advantage.

Carvill, M. and Butler, G. (2021) *Sustainable Marketing: How to Drive Profits with Purpose*. London: Bloomsbury Publishing.

This book provides a thoughtful and comprehensive account of the key issues relevant to sustainable marketing including supply chain management, packaging, and responsible marketing. The authors provide a range of case studies that offer valuable practical insights into the practice of sustainable marketing.

Sharma, R.R., Kaur, T. and Syan, S. (2021) *Sustainability Marketing: New Directions and Practices*. Bingley: Emerald Publishing.

The book provides an effective and refreshing new insight into marketing practices that align to the increase in customers' desire for sustainable products. The authors focus attention on marketing strategies that deliver benefits from an ecological, social and economic perspective.

7

SUSTAINABLE OPERATIONS AND SUPPLY CHAIN MANAGEMENT

LEARNING OUTCOMES

- Understand the characteristics of sustainable operations and supply chain management.
- Understand the application of the life cycle sustainability assessment tool.
- Be able to understand and apply a theoretical framework for sustainable supply chain and the Triple Bottom Line.
- Critically evaluate circular supply chains and regulatory approaches to global sustainable operations and supply chains.
- Comprehend the development of green manufacturing, green technology and sustainable logistics.

INTRODUCTION

Sustainable operations and supply chains have become important strategic issues for organisations not only because of their duty to respond to the climate emergency by reducing carbon emissions but also because it has become a source of competitive advantage. This has ushered in a period of intense activity around how, where and why sustainable practices can be introduced to operations and supply chains. Necessarily operations and supply chain management involves reviewing the entire process from acquiring raw materials through to recycling to determine the environmental, social and economic impact of activities. Sustainability across the range of business activities and those of partner organisations can improve productivity, improve efficiencies and deliver added value to customers in the form of quicker fulfilment times, quality assurance and competitive pricing. Meanwhile, the associated positive environmental and social impacts help build brand loyalty and enhance the reputation of the organisation. However, managing sustainability in operations and supply chains presents some significant challenges as well as offering key benefits. Understanding these in the context of the circular economy alongside developments in green manufacturing and logistics forms the basis of the discussion in this chapter.

The chapter begins with an overview of sustainable operations and supply chains where environmental considerations feature recycling, effective waste management and efficient logistics to lower carbon emissions. The chapter continues with the presentation of a theoretical framework for sustainable supply chains and the Triple Bottom Line. This is followed by critical discussion of circular supply chains and regulatory approaches adopted to bolster sustainability. Thereafter the chapter focuses attention on the development of green manufacturing, green technology and sustainable logistics.

SUSTAINABLE OPERATIONS MANAGEMENT

Operations management refers to the administration of business practices to create a maximum level of efficiency within an organisation in the process of transforming factor inputs of capital, materials and labour into goods and services. In the commercial sector, this invariably involves balancing costs and revenue to achieve an optimal level of profit. Mainstream operational issues link to inventory management, logistics, manufacturing schedules, work-flow, quality control, materials handling and raw materials acquisition. Operations managers need to ensure maximum efficiency and the least waste associated with these activities. Slack and Brandon-Jones (2019) identifies five main performance objectives of operations management as cost, quality, speed, dependability and flexibility. Traditionally the focus has been on the cost factor as managers sought means by which operations could be streamlined and made more efficient as a route to competitive advantage. However, it became increasingly evident that this was a short-term and narrow perspective that failed to exploit the whole range of performance criteria in organisations. This ushered in a more systems-based approach that was more effective in reducing costs and waste through the adoption of concepts such as quality management, lean production and reduction in waste. These align closely to the concept of sustainability in operations and gave rise to the term 'lean and green' (Florida, 1996). The sustainability dimension extends the systems approach to incorporate the entire product life cycle as illustrated in Figure 7.1. Necessarily, the sustainability dimension required a further addition to the five performance objectives so as to include the environmental factor.

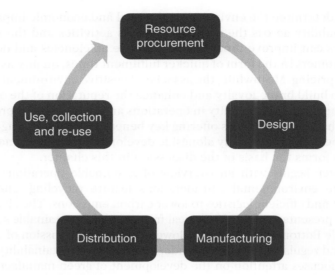

FIGURE 7.1 *Product life cycle*

Sustainability practices can feature in each of the product life cycle stages and require strategic thinking around the ways and means in which they can be integrated throughout the system. For the most part, operation managers have embraced this new way of thinking as it not only helps tackle the wider environmental challenges but it is also an effective means of gaining and sustaining a competitive advantage by introducing technologies and practices that lower costs, build brand loyalty and improve the efficiency of supply chains. These can include recycling facilities, streamlined production, greener energy use for distribution, and innovative designs for packaging that help recycling and waste reduction. Where gaps exist in adopting some of the practices that underpin this approach, regulation is sometimes imposed to ensure compliance with standards that support sustainability. This is discussed in more detail later in this chapter.

The product life cycle can be assessed by determining the impact that each stage has on the environment in terms of energy usage, carbon emissions, waste and pollution. This not only allows the measurement, assessment and analysis of such impacts, but also helps to focus attention on the means by which the impacts can be reduced to effect environmental benefits. Life cycle assessment (LCA) was devised as an environmental accounting tool with rules and regulations developed by the International Organization for Standardization (ISO). LCA comes under ISO 14040 and covers the whole of the product life cycle, sometimes referred to as 'cradle to grave'. An effective LCA identifies process steps for each stage of the product life cycle along with relevant inputs (materials and energy) and outputs (carbon emissions and pollution). The inputs and outputs are grouped into environmental impact categories which include different types of toxicity to the planet. LCAs involve four main stages of goal and scope definition, inventory analysis, impact assessment and interpretation as illustrated in Figure 7.2.

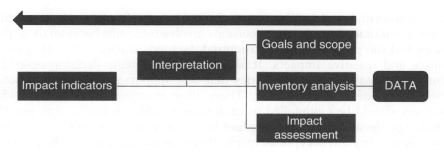

FIGURE 7.2 *Life cycle assessment stages*

Source: Adapted from Muralikrishna and Manickam (2017)

The first stage of the LCA is to determine the goals and scope of the assessment to focus attention on the main factors that contribute to environmental impacts in the process of extraction of raw materials, production, use and disposal. Managers need to determine what contributing factors to include and what they intend to achieve with the results. For example, the organisation may be rolling out a new eco-friendly product that they want to market and promote around that added value. To do so requires an understanding of how the product performs and what environmental impact it has in design, manufacturing, distribution, consumption and disposal or reuse. The LCA would provide an insight into how effective the claims of 'eco-friendly' are within the context of environmental impact. The second stage involves inventory analysis based on data (both qualitative and quantitative) of all the inputs and outputs linked to the product life cycle. Inputs include raw materials and energy, and outputs refer to emissions including air, water, carbon and soil. Data generated for the inventory analysis is used for stage three of the process, the impact assessment. Here, the inputs and outputs have been identified and measured and the data allows each to be categorised according to impact. Once this process is completed the results can be analysed and interpreted according to the objectives set for the LCA. Ultimately, this provides important knowledge around the impact indicators (carbon, pollution, waste, etc.) that help identify areas that require intervention and those that support positive outcomes.

The concept of LCA can be extended to incorporate the sustainability dimension. The Life Cycle Sustainability Assessment (LCSA) refers to the assessment of all environmental, social and economic negative impacts and benefits linked to decisions made to support sustainable products throughout the product life cycle. Kloepffer (2008) devised a model that combines an ISO compliant environmental life cycle assessment model (LCA), a life cycle costing model (LCC) and a social life cycle assessment (SLCA). Thus, LCA + LCC + SLCA= LCSA. The LCSA has been applied in many different industrial sectors including agriculture, construction, manufacturing and transportation, among others.

There are a number of advantages associated with Life Cycle Sustainability Assessments (LCSA) that managers can exploit including better understanding of the environmental, social and economic factors by organising them in a structured format. Sometimes management decisions involve trade-offs between these three factors and the presentation of structured data aids clarity of thinking around positive and negative impacts. It also supports strategic decision-making by identifying key value chain activities that best support sustainability practices or where weaknesses are evident. These allow managers to determine where resources should be channelled to exploit value-added sustainability practices or redesign those parts of the product life cycle where negative sustainability inputs persist beyond acceptable levels. By consequence, this also helps managers prioritise resources more effectively by channelling them towards sustainable technologies and products. These can have the effect of stimulating innovation, extending capabilities of workers, and supporting managers in implementing sustainability strategies.

Acquiring accurate data is a limitation associated with LCSA that managers have to contend with. Hellweg and Mila i Canals (2016) point to a high level of uncertainty in results due to the amount of measured and simulated data required to formulate the assessment as well as the simplified models used for understanding complex environmental cause and effect linkages. Tolerance of uncertainty varies between different objectives of the assessment. For example, differences in environmental assessment for product comparisons require a higher threshold of accuracy than simply identifying relatively high levels of impact across a supply chain. It is also rare that data is available across the whole supply chain of companies. Estimates are used for practical purposes, but this again only delivers an approximation. Consequently, LCSA does not deliver a single and accurate outcome but can offer insights that improve understanding of environmental impacts across different dimensions so that problems can be identified and solutions explored.

SUSTAINABLE SUPPLY CHAIN MANAGEMENT

Supply chain management is another important element to this process. This refers to the management of inventory along the supply chain. Supply chain managers need to ensure the seamless and efficient flow of materials from acquisition of raw materials to the distribution of the end-product. To coordinate all the processes along the supply chain requires knowledge, understanding and control of the logistics of this flow of materials. By streamlining activities, maximising efficiency and lowering costs, it is possible for companies to gain a competitive advantage from superior supply chain management, especially if it is combined with high-quality products, quick delivery times and excellent customer service. Traditionally, operations and supply chain management were primarily concerned with maximising efficiency and reducing costs. This meant looking for ways to improve the productive process and logistics and gave rise to a number of innovative approaches for achieving this including lean production (reducing waste whilst maintaining quality), just-in-time inventory (materials delivered just before they are required) and Six Sigma (management techniques for improving business processes that reduce the probability of error) among others.

In the modern era, the issue of sustainability has formed a further dimension to operations and supply chain management. Sustainable operations management (SOM) takes the traditional processes outlined above and connects them to environmental and sustainable development. That is, operations management needs to secure development that meets the needs of the present without compromising the ability of future generations to meet their own needs. Thus, modern operations management extends to include the economic, people and planet paradigm. Thomsen (2013) cites the World Commission on Environment and Development (WCED) definition of SOM as 'the set of skills that allow a company to structure and manage its business processes in order to obtain competitive returns on its capital assets without sacrificing the needs of stakeholders and with regard for the impact of its operations on people and environment'. The related process of supply chain management (SCM) has similarly been transformed along sustainability lines. This requires managers to integrate the environmental and economic practices into the supply chain including product design, acquisition of raw materials, manufacturing, packaging and distribution. Seuring and Muller (2008) provide a compelling definition of sustainable supply chain management by emphasising the management of material, information and capital flows as well as cooperation among companies along the supply chain while taking goals from all three dimensions of sustainable development. The goals referred to are, of course, economic, social and environmental. Pagell and Wu (2009) set a threshold of a sustainable supply chain as being one that, at worst, does no net harm to natural or social systems whilst still producing a profit.

Mini case 7.1: NHS Scotland

Angela Sutherland and Dr Niladri Palit (Glasgow Caledonian University)

The global market for medical and surgical instruments is flourishing in parallel with advances in medicine, increased lifestyle diseases (such as heart disease and diabetes) and the growth in the elderly population with 16% of the global population predicted to be aged 65 years and over by 2050 (Grand Review Research, 2021). The National Health Service (NHS), the largest procurer of medical and surgical instruments across the UK, has come under scrutiny for adopting a piecemeal approach to procuring medical equipment through a mix of local, regional and national distributors (Coyle, 2018). Distributors purchase from global suppliers who then purchase from manufacturers, some of whom are renowned for unacceptable work practices (BMA, 2020; IBIS, 2021). An estimated two-thirds of surgical

(Continued)

instruments are produced in Pakistan where labour rights' violations and occupational health risks have been recorded (Bhutta, 2017). Musculoskeletal injuries, exposure to toxic chemicals and metal dust, deafening noise-levels, and chronic diseases are among the hazards reported (Trueba, 2020). Working conditions have improved over the last decade, however, challenges remain (BMA, 2020).

The Covid-19 pandemic reduced surgical instrument sales, negatively affecting workers' incomes across supply chains as hospitals cancelled elective surgeries to prioritise the pandemic (First Research, 2021). However, NHS demand for gloves and masks rose substantially with most outsourced to factories in Malaysia and Thailand where similar working conditions exist (Trueba, 2020). Emerging from lockdown, the NHS now faces a huge backlog in surgical procedures requiring increased supplies of both gloves and surgical instruments, with demand for the latter predicted to grow at a compound annual rate of 9.8% and worth a global market value of £17.41 billion by 2028 (Grand View Research, 2021). Pakistani manufacturers argue that purchasers demand high quality but do not consider the full economic and social costs involved whereby improving the health of some comes at the cost to health to others (Trueba, 2020).

Through its recent Procurement Strategy 2020–2025, NHS National Services Scotland established a 'Sustainable Procurement Duty' to reduce health inequality and environmental harm, evidence of fair work practices within and across its supply chain and commitment to eradicating modern slavery (NHS, 2020). To achieve these goals, a range of resources are provided including prioritisation tools, sustainability tests incorporating whole-life costing, life cycle impact mapping, staff training and a Centre of Excellence, which should collectively work towards achieving effective sustainable practice across NHS Scotland's supply chain in future.

Questions and task

1. Give three examples of risks associated with procuring medical supplies from developing countries for NHS Scotland.
2. What has NHS Scotland done to address environmental harm in its procurement process?
3. Why does NHS Scotland not procure all its medical supplies from UK-based manufacturers?

Sustainable supply chain

A sustainable supply chain involves numerous business organisations specialising in different parts of the chain. These typically involve suppliers of raw materials, distributors, storage and warehousing, wholesalers, retailers and customers. Each stage adds costs and value to the process with the aim being to gain a surplus of value to drive performance. Although there are some significant challenges in terms of costs, adapting to a sustainability culture and adopting and introducing new technologies, among others, each activity along the supply chain contributes to the effective delivery of products and services and each has potential for introducing sustainability practices (Abbasi and Nilson, 2012). Figure 7.3 illustrates the sustainable supply chain.

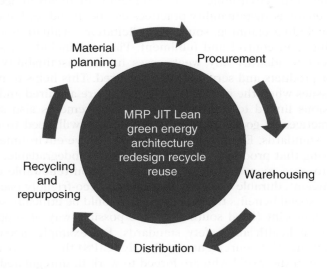

FIGURE 7.3 *Sustainable supply chain*

Material planning can be viewed as a scientific approach to determining the requirements of raw materials, components and any other items that are required for production purposes. Usually these include factors such as price, business cycles, government policy, access to funding or any other issue that impacts the acquisition of materials. Modern businesses use Materials Requirement Planning (MRP) software to plan and control the movement of materials to maximise efficiency in the production process, manage costs and control inventory. Relevant issues linked to material planning include plant capacity utilisation, inventory levels, lead times, rejection rates, and seasonality or other predictable changes in demand. One of the main advantages of MRP is the scope it provides for transitioning to a low carbon and environmental process by applying forecasts of requirements and, thereby, reduce waste. Overestimating production needs has traditionally been a source of waste that can be drastically reduced using MRP as part of a sustainable supply chain. Examples of how this can be put into action include migrating and integrating all information and data (purchase orders, packaging, invoices, reports, distribution, etc.) to the MRP system and becoming a paperless organisation, reducing energy usage and reducing carbon emissions by accurately forecasting demand so that the correct quantities of products are transported to the correct destination more efficiently. Also, being able to monitor the quality and flow of products more closely means that returns are minimised and carbon emissions reduced.

Sustainable procurement refers to that part of the supply chain where organisations acquire products, services, works and utilities (gas, water, electricity, etc.) they need in a way that achieves value for money on a whole life basis in terms of generating benefits to the organisation, society and the economy without doing harm to the environment. Procurement is in an advantageous position in the supply chain as sustainability practices can be introduced at each stage of the process including planning, sourcing, solicitation, evaluation and contracting, monitoring, and control and fulfilment. Planning includes a sustainability risk assessment to identify any weaknesses in the sustainability compliance thresholds for products and services to be acquired. This helps to pre-empt any compliance issues when the products and services are acquired and reduces the carbon emissions linked to returns. Defining requirements also supports sustainability practices as goods and services procured will need to comply with sustainability standards. Examples that support positive environmental impacts include ensuring that products are 'fit-for-purpose', biodegradable, designed for disassembly to ease recycling, contain minimum non-renewable components, are energy efficient, durable and have minimal and eco-friendly packaging.

For positive social benefits the procurement should be ethically sourced, have a low carbon footprint (local sourcing is one possible way of supporting this), and comply with health and safety standards. For example, according to the Chartered Institute of Procurement and Supply (CIPS) there are over 40 million enslaved people in the world who are forced to work in unregulated sectors that generate around $150 billion of illegal revenue per annum. Legitimate industries and organisations need to address this by closely scrutinising the credentials of their suppliers. As part of the solicitation process suppliers should be required to demonstrate sustainability credentials and compliance with set standards. The extent to which suppliers adhere to these standards and expectations should be revealed in a robust monitoring and evaluation process. There is some way to go before consumers can be satisfied that the highest standards are being met by companies they routinely buy from. The non-profit supply chain monitoring group KnowtheChain (2020) researched some of the world's best-known brands according to criteria linked to the use of forced labour and gave each a score out of 100. The average score was 37 with some well-known brands scoring relatively well such as Primark (75) and H&M (65). Both companies have received criticism in the past regarding the outsourcing of manufacturing to less developed countries with poor human rights records such as Myanmar and Cambodia. Other companies' performance was woefully inadequate with Prada scoring 5 and Hermes 17. Clearly, the procurement element of the supply chain is an area in need of significant improvement in its performance around social impacts.

Sustainable distribution involves the redesign of the process of bringing the products to consumers. Typically, this refers to storage arrangements, order processing, packaging and modes of transportation that combine to deliver products from suppliers to buyers (most likely to be wholesalers or retailers) with a minimum possible environmental and social impact. The redesign may focus on some or all of the activities along this part of the supply chain and may include continuous improvement through green technologies for eco-efficient transport and

INTRODUCTION TO GLOBAL SUSTAINABLE MANAGEMENT

energy, reduced waste in packaging, and just-in-time inventory management. For example, energy demands for warehousing and storage units is traditionally high and continuous around the clock. Sustainability can be enhanced by installing solar panels on the facility or by optimising the warehouse architecture to exploit natural light. Finally, it is useful to consider customer service in this process as there are positive environmental impacts to be gained from educating consumers on how to use and dispose of the product in eco-friendly ways and setting up processes for recycling and repurposing of products. Customer service has to incorporate sustainability practices whilst not compromising satisfaction for delivery times. This is necessary to fit with the Triple Bottom Line principle of integrating social, environmental and economic factors.

Mini case 7.2: Deutsche Post DHL, Germany

In March 2021 German distribution company Deutsche Post DHL announced an ambitious accelerated roadmap to decarbonise their operations with a €7 billion investment in climate-neutral logistics by 2030. Specifically, the focus is set for delivering alternative aviation fuels, the expansion of the company's zero-emission e-vehicle fleet, and climate neutral buildings. Technology development plays a key role in each of these aims. In aviation, DHL has invested in electrification and hydrogen technologies that simultaneously improve fuel efficiency and lower carbon emissions. In 2020 the company struck a deal with Shell for the supply of sustainable aviation fuel (SAF) for its DHL Express arm operating out of Schiphol airport in Amsterdam, a major European hub. SAF is the only viable non-fossil liquid fuel suitable for use in commercial aircraft that is capable of reducing greenhouse gases. Management at DHL views this development as an important step towards achieving decarbonisation in this part of the roadmap whilst maintaining economic growth.

Another green transport solution features the e-vehicle fleet. The company has set a target of 2030 for 60% of their vehicle fleet to be electrified and have initiated similar solutions with their subcontractors by setting standards, educating on sustainability practices and giving incentives for investment in green transport solutions. The third key area of decarbonisation is the creation of carbon neutral buildings. As a global operator, DHL has building assets in over 200 countries including warehouses, sorting centres, hubs, terminals, offices and so on. The company has committed to transitioning towards carbon neutral buildings for all new buildings by 2030. The plan also requires that half of all existing building assets use sustainable energy sources for heating by converting locally produced electricity from solar or photovoltaic fuel by the target date. Digital technology and intelligent building management systems will add further sustainability capacity by reducing energy consumption across the portfolio of building assets.

(Continued)

The entire logistics and distribution industry is facing significant challenges. The coronavirus pandemic has altered the trading landscape for all businesses and DHL have had to adapt to what is, by consensus, a new reality. Whilst many industries have experienced a downturn in demand for their products and services, distribution has become increasingly important as consumers migrate online for their purchases. This phenomenon had already made its mark prior to the pandemic but was ratcheted up throughout the period of restrictions on ordinary life. Companies such as DHL, have numerous competing demands to contend with including how to manage the transition to net zero carbon whilst continuing to experience growth and profitability. The accelerated roadmap produced by DHL reveals how investment in technology can be used to leverage competitive growth performance and sustainable supply chains into the future.

Question and tasks

1. In which part of the supply chain does DHL core business reside?
2. Give three examples of how DHL implements the accelerated roadmap to decarbonise its operations.
3. Give an example of a green transport solution implemented by DHL.

Sustainable supply chain and the Triple Bottom Line

Sustainable supply chains can be designed around social, environmental and economic factors and, therefore, align to the Triple Bottom Line framework (Carter and Rogers, 2008). This is illustrated in Figure 7.4.

FIGURE 7.4   *Framework for sustainable supply chain management*

Source: Adapted from Carter and Rogers (2008)

INTRODUCTION TO GLOBAL SUSTAINABLE MANAGEMENT

As explained in Chapter 4, there are activities that organisations can undertake that add positively to social and environmental impacts. There are also economic benefits that can derive from this link to gaining and sustaining a competitive advantage. Many of these activities can be introduced along the supply chain to form the sustainable supply chain and link to key facets of strategy, risk, transparency and culture. It should be noted that social and environmental impacts are not separated from economic ones. Indeed, as Porter and Kramer (2002) suggest, the social and environmental elements have to be considered alongside the economic imperative of the organisation of seeking a competitive advantage and securing economic aims in the form of profits and growth. In Figure 7.4 this relates to the question mark against the word 'Good' as this element is within the intersection of the social and environmental performance parts but outside that of the economic performance. It also emphasises the fact that undertaking activities that support social and/or environmental impacts comes at a cost and that this should be factored into any sustainability strategy. Thus, the intersections between the social and economic constitute a 'better' reflection of this, as does the intersection between environmental and economic. However, the optimal position for sustainability is when all three elements intersect.

The sustainability effectiveness depends on the influence of strategy, risk, transparency and culture. Sustainability has to be fully integrated into the formulated strategy and included in all practices that support implementation. Risk involves making contingencies for disruptions to business continuity that may compromise sustainability; transparency refers to how effective sustainability practices and outcomes are communicated to stakeholders, and organisational culture refers to the extent to which sustainability values and ethical practices (and ethos) are infused throughout the organisation.

CIRCULAR SUPPLY CHAIN MANAGEMENT

There are many different definitions of the circular economy. The Ellen MacArthur Foundation (2018) describes it as restorative and regenerative by design. The European Commission (2015) signals that it is where the value of products, materials and resources is maintained in the economy for as long as possible by returning them into the product cycle at the end of their use. Ekins et al. (2019) see it as an economy that has low environmental impacts and makes good use of natural resources through high resource efficiency and waste prevention. The concept of the circular economy can be viewed through a supply chain management lens. As outlined above, a traditional and linear supply chain refers to a straight pathway from acquisition of raw materials, production, packaging and distribution before consumption and disposal. This has been proven to be costly and wasteful and creates harmful effects for the environment. By contrast, a circular supply chain is where the raw materials used are recycled back into the manufacturing process. Effectively, they are repurposed so that they can be used in the production of another product.

Circular supply chains are just one area of intervention that has given rise to the wider circular economy that is designed to implement the changes necessary to reduce waste and lower harmful carbon emissions. As a contributor to this, sustainable supply chains operate on recycling principles whereby products have their constituent parts separated and the materials reused in the process of manufacturing new products. For example, a laptop computer can be dismantled to derive valuable components of metals, glass, plastic, etc. that can be used in the manufacture of another laptop or another product. Essentially, production outputs become inputs such that the sale of goods to customers is not the end point of the transaction process. Information technology can aid this process by controlling the flow of all component parts in the circular flow in real time. There is also a need for high-level collaborative relationships along the supply chain to identify recycling, repurposing and reuse opportunities. This helps in the planning and coordination of the circular flow and supports compliance with regulatory and ethical standards. The circular supply chain approach not only saves the company money in acquiring new materials for each and every product manufactured, but it is also more sustainable by lowering the need for exploiting scarce resources that cannot be replenished. The effect of this lowers carbon emissions that are contributing to global warming and climate change.

It is clear that an effective circular supply chain requires managers to rethink the whole process along the lines of resilience and no waste. This means operating an eco-system that is based on rebuilding and restoring rather than consumption and disposal. The life cycle of products should be exploited to generate future value by recycling and repurposing products. In fact, the supply chain business ethos needs to reflect the goal of raw materials being capable of endless recycling. The long-term benefits extend not only to the environmental and competitive performance of organisations but also the promotion of healthy communities and a sustainable planet.

Regulation

Now that the harmful effects of unfettered operations and supply chain practices are better understood, there have been significant moves to introduce regulatory regimes to encourage organisations to adopt sustainable solutions to operations and supply chain management. The Basel Convention on the Control of Transboundary Movements of Hazardous Wastes and their Disposal was established in 1989 in the aftermath of revelations regarding the exporting of dangerous waste materials to unregulated sites in Africa in the 1980s. Soon, it was discovered that the dumping of waste from affluent Western countries to developing countries around the world was endemic and required regulatory intervention. The Basel Convention committed signatories to be proactive in reducing hazardous waste, restrict transboundary movements of hazardous waste, and to set in place a system of regulation for the permissible transboundary movement of hazardous waste. The European Commission has also been active in setting directives linked to the management of waste across the EU.

INTRODUCTION TO GLOBAL SUSTAINABLE MANAGEMENT

The Waste Framework Directive (Commission Decision EU 2019/1004) sets out basic concepts and definitions linked to waste management including provisions to avoid harming human health, risks to water, air, soil and animal life, noise and odours, and the protection of the countryside. Figure 7.5 illustrates the EU waste management hierarchy.

FIGURE 7.5   *European Union waste management hierarchy*

Source: European Commission

The hierarchy sets out the order of preference for waste management starting with the optimal position of prevention of harm. This is followed by making provisions for reuse which include maintaining functionality, quality, safety and no harm. The next level of preference is recycling. This follows a process that allows for the safe dismantling of component parts or the safe restoration of the product without harming the environment or people. Recovery is the penultimate stage whereby disposed products are recovered before they do harm to the environment or people. The least preferable level is that of disposal. If none of the other levels are possible then safe disposal of the product must adhere to strict standards linked to landfill, incinerator sites or other disposal facilities. The Waste Framework Directive provides additional labelling, recording, monitoring and control of products from 'cradle to grave' as the product flows from production through to disposal. Some regulation is aimed at specific types of products or equipment. For example, the Waste Electrical & Electronic Equipment (WEEE) directive is designed to minimise the environmental impact of such equipment throughout the life span of the product before becoming waste. Thus, the directive sets the criteria for collection, treatment, recycling and recovery of waste electrical and electronic equipment.

Regulation can be a powerful tool to ensure that organisations within a supply chain internalise the effects of their activities (Carter and Jennings, 2011). The efficacy of regulation depends on the response of organisations and whether or not they perceive it to be an opportunity or a threat. For example, if standards of compliance are set then managers may see this as an opportunity to build brand loyalty around their reputation based on trust, accountability and transparency. Demonstrating compliance also bolsters the negotiating position that can help reduce costs and improve competitiveness. Compliance can also have shared benefits with partners along the supply chain who work collaboratively on managing sustainability practices that result in economies (increased contracts, new markets) as well as positive environmental (low carbon emissions, renewable energy use) and social impacts (gender equality, health and safety). On the other hand, if organisations view regulation as an additional cost incurred in the process of compliance then this will negatively impact on their competitiveness.

There are some barriers to regulation of the circular supply chain that need to be addressed. First, although significant progress has been made to introduce standards (such as the Basel Convention, Waste Framework Directive, or WEEE outlined above), there remain regulatory gaps that create opportunities for bad practice. Definitions of key targets are often unclear or open to different interpretations. The lag in implementation of legislation supporting regulation is an on-going problem that can undermine confidence in the system. There are known to be different and, sometimes, conflicting implementations of legislation in different countries that undermine the cohesiveness and comprehensive goal of the regulatory approach. Different countries may have very different views on what should be prioritised in terms of regulations such as zero waste or maximum safety. Combined, these barriers create a need for a more robust and better informed approach to regulation on a global scale.

Challenges of a circular economy

Adapting to a circular economy requires a change of mindset not only for organisations but consumers too. Organisations need to embed principles of the circular supply chain into their strategy and operations. Scaling up circular strategies poses some challenges in terms of business change or reorganisation to accommodate recycling, repurposing and reuse of products. Some products exhibit characteristics that make this process easy (lightweight components that are easy to dismantle) whereas others pose some practical challenges (products containing chemicals or toxins). Inevitably, the process of recycling incurs different skills, procedures and safety protocols. There are also issues of cost to be considered. As a basic economic driver, organisations can only justify participation in the circular supply chain if it is cost effective. If the cost of regenerating products is greater than the value created then the incentive for participation diminishes.

From a consumer's perspective, the circular economy may satisfy their sustainability needs but very often they look towards some added value from the recycled products and services to fully meet expectations. Thus, organisations need to deliver on both the positive social and environmental impacts and the wider stakeholder expectations. Indeed, the social dimension is often overlooked in the process of developing the circular supply chain as the emphasis has traditionally been on fulfilling positive environmental impacts. To address the imbalance between environmental, social and economic factors requires organisations to develop business models around the circular supply chain that offer a viable economic incentive as well as a deeper understanding of how their sustainability practices along the supply chain impact communities and societies in many different contexts.

Perhaps one of the biggest barriers to the development of the circular supply chain is the lack of a comprehensive and generic set of guidelines on how to implement it. The range of different business and practices across a multitude of different industry sectors makes this problematic. More commonly, circular supply chains have been designed in bespoke fashion for the needs of organisations delivering products and services in distinct parts of the economy. This goes some way to explaining the lack of an international standard of performance linked to circular performance.

Mini case 7.3: Ford and McDonald's, USA

Niladri Palit and Angela Sutherland (Glasgow Caledonian University)

The well-known saying 'One man's trash is another man's treasure' applies to Ford Motor Corporation's sustainability initiatives. Towards the end of 2019, Ford and the fast-food chain McDonald's in the USA teamed up together to use the chaffs of McDonald's' coffee beans in the production of headlamps for Ford's cars. It is expected that the resultant products will be 20% lighter in weight, requiring 25% less energy consumption during the moulding process (Ford, 2019; Genovese, 2019). In March 2021, Ford teamed up with Hewlett Packard to reuse spent 3D printed powders and parts, closing the loop and turning them into injection moulded vehicle parts. These materials are being used in Super Duty F-250 trucks. It is expected that these parts will be 7% lighter in weight and 10% less in cost (Ford, 2021). Sustainability is not a new concept for the Ford Motor Corporation. It has a renowned environmental commitment known as the Partnership for a Cleaner Environment (PACE). As part of PACE, the organisation shares best practice and monitoring tools to help its suppliers track and achieve their own sustainability goals. In 2017, the organisation expanded this initiative to include waste and carbon emission reduction practices, and water and energy conservation (Allen, 2017). Ford encourages commitment towards sustainable initiatives across the supply chain. According to the company, it encourages its suppliers to manage sustainability issues and risks in all operations and supply chains. However, it is also difficult for Ford to exercise control to improve sustainability performance beyond its immediate suppliers. For example, McDonald's has received a fair share of criticism when it comes to reputational issues in addressing supply chain transparency and sustainability. One such notable case being the well-documented 1997 McLibel trial (New, 2015) when McDonald's lost an English lawsuit filed against environmental campaigners who had produced a critical factsheet of the company's record on animal rights, environmental policies and nutritional value of its food. While criticisms and debates on sustainability initiatives are likely to continue, the question remains as to how Ford

(Continued)

---

can manage the risk associated with establishing and maintaining supply chain relationships with high-profile suppliers such as McDonald's.

Questions and task

1. What are the risks associated with Ford partnering with McDonald's for the purpose of circularly closing the supply chain loop?
2. What are the main motivators for Ford to use spare parts or waste from other industries?
3. Give two other examples of companies from different industries partnering to create positive environmental or social impacts.

GREEN MANUFACTURING

Sustainability is a key feature of operations and supply chain management in the modern era and permeates all activities where such practices can be introduced. Manufacturing is one area where there is significant potential for incorporating sustainability practice and this has given rise to the term 'green manufacturing' where the production relies on fewer natural resources and where reduced waste and pollution, recycling, reuse of materials and remanufacturing are embedded in the process. These comprise the four 'Rs' of green manufacturing as illustrated in Figure 7.6.

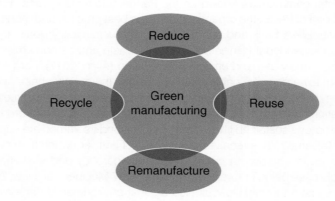

FIGURE 7.6   *The four Rs of green manufacturing*

Reduce refers to the lowering of the level of consumption of resources such as energy and emission of waste. Reuse requires the reusing of products or components of products with the goal of prolonging their lifespan and achieving reduced carbon emissions and waste by extending the time period between purchases. Recycling enables the transformation of products into new or existing products. The former requires component parts to be disassembled and transformed into new products whereas the latter revitalises the product to restore value so it can be resold again. Remanufacture refers to the process of rebuilding a product to specifications of the original manufactured product using a combination of reused, repaired and new parts. This can be achieved by repairing or replacing worn out or obsolete components.

Organisations that are committed to green manufacturing are proactively engaged in research and development of the technologies and processes that support these characteristics with the aim of reducing environmental impacts. The motivation for managers pursuing 'green' solutions to the manufacturing process comes from a number of sources including governments who seek to ensure that industry plays a role in meeting zero carbon targets, pressure groups who aim to hold business accountable for their environmental impact, suppliers who seek partnerships with organisations that share their commitment to sustainability, and consumers who have demonstrated a desire to engage with companies who deliver eco-friendly products and services. Regulators also have a vested interest in ensuring compliance with industry standards that support good sustainability practices across a range of different sectors.

Although there are numerous advantages associated with green manufacturing, the conservation of energy is one of the key ones. This important aim is achieved primarily by reducing or removing hazardous material by-products from the manufacturing process. The green manufacturing process can link either to the delivery of eco-friendly products for consumers, or to delivering traditional products in ways that reduce the environmental impact of manufacture. Green manufacturing principles can be implemented across a wide range of activities such as the processing of raw materials in a manner that does not harm the environment. For some industries this presents a significant challenge due to the nature of the materials acquired. For example, the chemicals industry has to devise means by which hazardous materials can be procured, processed, stored and transported in ways that do not risk polluting the environment or harming people. The fashion industry relies heavily on the production of materials for clothes manufacturing that relies on huge amounts of water, and the use of dyes and other chemicals. Consequently, green manufacturing requires organisations to introduce safe and environmentally friendly ways of handling materials but also their waste management and recycling. These are important ways to reduce reliance on harmful landfill sites for dumping waste and reducing the risk of dangerous chemicals entering the water supply or escaping into the air.

There are also energy conservation activities as part of green manufacturing that reduce demand for scarce and unsustainable materials such as steel and plastic. Recycling or repurposing these materials demands less energy than acquiring new supplies. The economic benefits are also evident as the lower demand for new energy reduces production costs and makes organisations more efficient and competitive. Investment in alternative energy saving facilities ('alternative' refers to non-fossil fuel sources), such as biomass (plant or animal material used as fuel), geothermal, hydropower, wind or solar power or recycling energy sources from municipal solid waste, can all support green manufacturing. Waste can also be used as an effective energy source. US brewers Coors work in partnership with Merrick & Co engineers to use waste beer and turn it into ethanol that is then sold and distributed to gas stations. Whatever the source, workers become specialised in using the technologies that deliver sustainable energy to the manufacturing process.

GREEN TECHNOLOGY

Technology underpins so many of the green manufacturing innovations that drive value in organisations and support sustainability strategies. Each of the four 'Rs' highlighted above features technological inputs that help support their contribution to sustainability. Five core technologies can be identified for this purpose and these are illustrated in Figure 7.7. Green production technology supports a business strategy that focuses on profitability through low environmental impact production and operating processes that includes both inputs (raw materials) and outputs (products). These can link to reusable or renewable energy in the productive process including wind power, solar, or biomass.

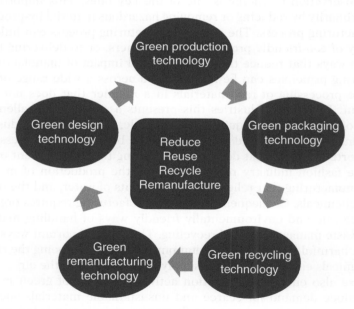

FIGURE 7.7   *Core technologies to support the four 'Rs'*

Transforming waste to energy that powers the productive process is another example of effective green production technology. Towards the sources of supply (raw materials) the green production technology can help reduce the dependence on non-renewable resources. It can also support the exploitation of renewable resources (such as forests) to help mitigate the environmental cost of materials acquisition. For example, radio frequency identification (RFID) can be used to track the movement of trees from their original location to the consumer thereby helping to tackle illegal logging and the impact that it has on sustainability of forests.

Green production technology has to integrate all the other processes that comprise the supply chain, most of which will have green technology support too. The technology needs to support green production in a way that integrates product and process design, planning, control, storage, distribution, logistics, consumption, recycling and reuse in a way that regulates the flow of goods throughout the system in a way that minimises the environmental impact.

Green packaging technology uses sustainable and biodegradable materials for packaging to reduce carbon emissions and aid recycling. As consumers migrate to online shopping as the norm, they have become more aware of the packaging of products in terms of ease of access, recycling and sustainability. This is especially the case with the use of harmful packaging such as plastics. Consequently, there has been an upsurge in innovation and engineering by organisations seeking to demonstrate their 'green credentials' in the packaging of products. In particular, materials science has contributed numerous eco-friendly solutions to packaging that involves lighter, recyclable and sustainable boxes. For example, sports brand Puma worked in partnership with innovator Yves Behar to develop a lightweight shoebox that reduces the use of cardboard by 65% leading to a lowering of carbon emissions by 10,000 tonnes per annum. Plant-based and biodegradable materials have been developed to support sustainability and help reduce carbon emissions. However, it is worth noting that transitioning to green packaging will only be adopted if there is an economic benefit to organisations too. If it proves costly then few organisations will adopt new technologies. Thus, one of the challenges of green designers is to produce solutions that consider the economic element of the process. Ultimately, managers will make rational decisions that are partly informed by the cost of adopting new technologies set against the benefits derived and the comparison with single-use packaging. Set against this is the increasing demand by consumers for organisations to lower the use of plastics, design eco-friendly packaging for recycling, and reduce the carbon footprint associated with this part of the supply chain.

Green recycling technology assists in the process of recycling and makes it easy to embed within organisations to support efforts to lower carbon emissions. Different technologies can be deployed to recycle different types of products based on the materials used, such as electronics, cables, plastic, glass and so on. Plastic forms one of the most challenging waste products with many oceans, rivers and the countryside blighted by the wholesale dumping of this man-made material. Modern thinking around dealing with plastic is to transition towards categorising the material as a renewable rather than waste. New technologies are being developed that enable recycling and reuse of plastic to break the traditional and unsustainable practice of 'make-take-dispose'. For example, at consumer goods giant Proctor & Gamble, the creation of PureCycle Technologies has delivered solutions that remove colour, odour and other contaminants from polypropylene plastic waste and turns them into a resin that forms the basis of new plastic products. With less than 10% of all plastic products recycled, this technology provides an opportunity to reduce the dumping of plastic waste in fragile environments.

Green manufacturing technology enables organisations to be more efficient, cost effective, competitive and environmentally friendly. Technology can support smart factories for example whereby electronic and digital solutions can connect all systems to create an integrated and knowledge-based system that is flexible and capable of self-optimising across the network of activities. The smart factory is capable of adapting to changing conditions in real-time without human intervention. BEA Systems is an international company specialising in aerospace and defence electronics who operate fully connected digital factories using robotics, artificial intelligence and 3D printing, among others, to build new capabilities and transform the way of working. This autonomy is supported by artificial intelligence (AI – intelligence demonstrated by machines), the Internet of Things (IoT – physical objects embedded with software and sensors that connect to other devices) and Big Data (analytical capability for large and complex datasets) that help to automatically run and regulate the entire production process to optimal effect. Importantly, this system is capable of identifying waste so that remedial action can be taken. Appliance manufacturer Whirlpool uses a data analytics platform to determine where and how much waste their manufacturing plants generate on a global scale. This data contributes to better understanding their sustainability performance and informs managers of the appropriate actions required to achieve sustainability strategic aims.

Green design technology supports the creation of designs that take into account life cycle, recycling potential and the environmental impact by reducing them and making them sustainable. Examples of green design include the development of microbial fuel cells using innovative bio-electro-chemical processes that produce electricity using electrons from biochemical reactions catalysed by bacteria. Here, there is an element of biomimicry at play as the process mimics the bacterial interactions that proliferate in the natural world. This concept is developing quickly around the world. For example, the mini case study of the Glengoyne whisky distillery in Scotland in Chapter 1 highlighted the constructed wetland system that mimics the treatment that occurs in their natural wetland surroundings by using a combination of naturally occurring biological, chemical and physical processes. Nanotechnology is another green design innovation and involves the creation or building of 'things' from atoms and molecules so small they are measured in scales of one billionth of a metre. Normal rules of physics do not apply at this level and, therefore, nanotechnology opens up immense opportunities for reconstituting the materials that comprise products. For example, using nanotechnology it is possible to create carbon nanotubes that are over 100 times stronger and six times lighter than steel ones produced at the macro scale. This is just one of many hundreds of applications that have sustainability enhancing properties that can be exploited to reduce environmental impacts. Green design technology will play an increasingly important role in sustainability strategies in future and will form the locus of much innovation and creativity for improving efficiencies, creating competitive advantage and tackling environmental challenges on a global scale.

SUSTAINABLE LOGISTICS

Logistics refers to those parts of the supply chain management that plan, implement and control the efficient and effective forward and reverse flow, and storage of goods and services between their point of origin and point of consumption. Note that logistics is only concerned with that activity in one organisation whereas supply chain management includes numerous activities across a network of organisations. Effective logistics management integrates functions, and coordinates and optimises all logistics activities including inventory, warehousing, outsourcing, production planning, packaging, transport management and recycling. Traditionally, the main aim was to meet customer expectations at lowest possible cost. Whilst this remains true, doing so with the lowest environmental and social impact has become an integral part of modern sustainable logistics management.

The main aim of sustainable logistics is to reduce the carbon footprint of the process of bringing goods and services to consumers. This invariably focuses on issues of pollution, carbon emissions, noise, toxic waste, errors and faults, land use, air quality, water quality, and other climate change contributors. The social imperative of sustainable logistics refers to issues of health and safety, workers' rights, equality and fairness. Organisations also need to be sensitive to changes in consumer demand as the awareness of environmental and social issues informs public discourse on these important issues. These should be tackled within the economic aims of increasing competitiveness and generating profit and growth. Some typical examples of green logistics include ensuring best fit for products when packaging, reuse of packaging, replace existing transport fleet with electric vehicles, use renewable energy such as biomass or ethanol, reduce waste by identifying optimal efficiencies, source materials and parts locally, source only from partners with minimum sustainability performance results, undertake reverse logistics by reselling, refurbishing, readapting, reconstituting, recycling, repurposing, and remanufacturing, and ensure fit-for-purpose products to minimise returns.

The opportunities that green logistics present for making a significant contribution to sustainability are broad ranging and entirely achievable. However, challenges persist and some are proving difficult for organisations and consumers to overcome. For example, there remains a stubborn dependence on fossil fuel demand by both business and the ordinary consumer that the emergence of alternatives, such as electric cars, has yet to penetrate. The transition of consumers to online shopping has created a huge fleet of distribution vehicles many of which operate on fossil fuel. Many distributors operate at less than optimal efficiency in load volume thereby increasing their relative carbon emission levels. To the consumer, logistics is an unseen and relatively unknown activity in the supply chain and this gives rise to expectations on delivery times that often cannot be matched by the organisation within demanding economic, social or environmental targets. There is also a lag in some sectors of industry in building the infrastructure that can truly incorporate sustainability practices that make a significant contribution to tackling issues such as climate change. Regulation in the form of local authority emissions limits may force the issue in some sectors but there is a need to apply such standards across all sectors and that is some way off. The marginal returns on many logistics and distribution activities is another reason for the relatively low level of investment in infrastructure that persists across industries.

The need to pursue sustainable logistics is evident and there are expectations from stakeholders that organisations meet the challenges it presents. The competitive advantages that green logistics can contribute provide the economic incentive alongside that of meeting stakeholder expectations and the moral duty of contributing to tackling climate change. To effect this managers need to take an integrated approach to implementing 'green' solutions throughout operations and along the supply chain. As such it needs to be a strategic issue and one that is suitably managed and resourced. Sustainable operations and supply chains need to be incorporated as a core principle and feature as part of the mission and vision of an organisation.

CASE STUDY

Maersk, Denmark

Ocean freight follows a well understood supply chain with goods packaged and housed in shipping containers. A freight forwarder or broker is responsible for the transport of goods and will book space for the goods in the container via a shipping agent. The legal responsibilities of freight forwarders is not consistent or clear as the goods pass through multiple jurisdictions before landing at the destination port. Hence, mandatory regimes need to be established for shipments. The containers are then transported to port before passing through customs at their point of origin. Due to the international nature of freight shipping, the safety is regulated through various United Nations bodies, principally the International Maritime Organisation (IMO). The International Convention for the Prevention of Pollution from Ships (MARPOL) is the regulatory body set up to protect the sea and air environment linked to shipping operations.

Sea-going shipping has traditionally been associated with practices that damage the environment and contribute to climate change. Cargo ships and other vessels have been known to leave a trail of fuel and waste effluence in their wake; they facilitate the transfer of harmful bacteria and animal life to fragile eco-systems, pollute the air quality by burning fossil fuel, and create ocean noise that disturbs the natural wildlife on their routes. These are just some of the examples of the high cost of globalisation and the insatiable demand for goods and services that has been the key driver of the exponential rise in sea-going freight. According to Josephs (2021), the shipping industry accounts for around 2% of global carbon emissions. If it were a country, it would rank sixth in the world behind Germany. To meet the expectations of stakeholders and to prevent further regulatory intervention, shipping companies have been proactive in creating sustainability strategies to address the social and environmental challenges linked to sea freight operations. Established in the early twentieth century, the Danish company Maersk is the world's biggest container shipping line and one of the leaders in developing systems of oversight, safety and environmental protection in the industry.

The three main pillars of the sustainability plan for Maersk are strategy, governance and partnership. At the strategic level, the company has a global integrated set of priorities for embedding sustainability throughout the wide range of business activities. In particular, this involves taking the lead in the industry on decarbonising logistics. This is in accordance with commitments made to support the Paris Agreement but also to demonstrate the improvements in efficiencies and reduced costs through less waste that combine to meet stakeholder expectations. Necessarily, this strategic priority means achieving and maintaining superior sustainability performance against rival firms, an ambitious target but one that underpins the status of Maersk within the global shipping and logistics industry. To this end the company is committed to net zero carbon emissions by 2050. Milestone targets have been set towards this including a 60% relative reduction in carbon emissions by 2030 from a 2008 baseline due to the 20–25-year lifetime of vessels. An important means by which this can be achieved is to ensure the scale and scope of the strategy supports end-to-end

sustainability in what the company can offer to clients including supply chain risk.

The second element of the strategy is focused on responsible business practices across all operations. This includes governance, accountability and transparency so that stakeholders can scrutinise sustainability performance across multiple different activities the company undertakes. In fact, such is the high priority the company places on governance that it features as a key part of the overall strategic aim. By way of emphasis the structure of the organisation has been designed to ensure compliance and direction of travel for sustainability with a Board of Directors and an Executive Leadership team taking control of the oversight of sustainability practices and policies, aims and targets, and determining how these will be implemented. Fundamentally, the Maersk sustainability strategy is designed to mitigate risk to negative environmental and social impacts and to support responsible business practices. These are demonstrated in a number of different ways including proactively supporting regulation on caps to sulphur content in fuel to reduce air pollution, improve the safety record of ship recycling, supporting industry and third-party agencies in improving ocean health, integrating responsible procurement into company policy, and implementing policies that support diversity and inclusion within the company.

The third element of the integrated sustainability strategy is the development of partnerships. In line with the Paris Agreement on climate change, Maersk is one of numerous companies that have signed up to adopting new roles that address critical solutions beyond that of applying their business model. This is evidence of a developing trend of

▶

companies using their resources, knowledge and influence to effect positive change to support efforts to meet the challenges of the climate emergency. For Maersk, the development of partnerships is key to the success of this initiative. The company has LEAD Participant status on the UN Global Compact initiative that commits to continuous improvements in sustainability performance by implementing the ten principles into their strategy and operations and then meeting advanced level reporting standards. The company also partners with Kuwait-based logistics company Agility and global distribution carriers UPS to form the Logistics Emergency Teams (LET) to ensure emergency support in the event of natural disasters on a global scale. In the industry, Maersk is a partner in the maritime Anti-Corruption Network (MACN) that promotes good practice in the shipping industry, the Trident Alliance that is a coalition of shipping owners with common interests in enforcing maritime regulation, and the Forum for the Future's Sustainable Shipping Initiative (SSI) that aims to develop initiatives to support the profitability and sustainability of the industry by 2040. Other partnerships include initiatives to support clean cargo, extractive industry transparency, and global logistics emissions.

The sustainability strategy has been formulated and implemented during a time of significant change in the industry with new technologies, such as blockchain (Maersk has partnered with tech giant IBM to implement digital solutions), being integrated across operations. The economic environment within which these sustainability targets have been set has also been characteristically volatile with higher fuel prices and unpredictable changes to container freight rates. Added to these pressures is the on-going friction between the company and the International Maritime Organisation regarding the strategy for climate change which Maersk management believe is not in alignment with what the industry can deliver. In particular, Maersk management argue that it cost $4 billion for fuel costs in 2020 but that this would double to meet net zero carbon targets by 2050 and that would mean a 20% rise in prices for customers. The company points to their efforts to tackle climate change through innovation as evidence of their commitment such as the plan to launch the first carbon-neutral liner vessel in 2023 that runs on renewable ethanol fuel. Achieving sustainability targets is not cheap and the company expects that some of the cost of investment across the range of activities that support their strategy will have to be passed on to consumers.

Questions and task

1. What are the three pillars of the Maersk integrated global sustainability plan?

2. Give an example of how Maersk addresses each one of the three pillars.

3. What are the main sustainability challenges facing the container shipping industry?

SUMMARY

This chapter on sustainable operations and supply chain management provided clear definitions of what each of these concepts means and how the sustainability aspect has been incorporated into activities that support them. The discussion around sustainability used the product life cycle and the stages of the life cycle as means by which an understanding of how sustainability can be a feature of these functions within organisations can play out and the different forms of sustainability practices that can be linked to different stages of the process. The discussion on sustainable supply chains featured practical ways in which sustainability can be introduced to the process and used examples of how just-in-time, lean production, redesign and architecture can support efforts to improve sustainable practices. Understanding the concept of the sustainable supply chain was helped by the use of a theoretical framework that highlighted the links to environmental, social and economic factors and how a sustainable supply chain can work towards an optimal position where these three factors merge. The discussion was framed within the parameters of strategy, risk, organisational culture and transparency. This was followed by a critical discussion of the development of the circular supply chain including the efforts to encourage participation through regulation and the challenges associated with its implementation. Three other areas of importance were also featured including the four 'Rs' of green manufacturing, the influence of green technology and the concept of sustainable logistics.

REVIEW QUESTION AND TASKS

1. Give a definition of sustainable supply chain management.
2. Explain what is meant by 'goals and scope' in a life cycle assessment.
3. What are the four 'Rs' of green manufacturing? Give an example of each.

FURTHER READING

Achillas, C., Bochtis, D.D., Aidonis, D. and Folinas, D. (2018) *Green Supply Chain Management*. Abingdon: Routledge.

This book is a well-crafted and lucid strategic overview of supply chain management and calls on theoretical underpinnings and key principles to address various relevant themes such as the benefits and impact of green supply chain management, enablers and barriers on supply chain operations, inbound and outbound logistics, and production and packaging. The authors highlight the challenges associated with incorporating sustainability into these activities and provide a roadmap for supporting decision-making in that quest.

Belvedere, V. and Grando, A. (2017) *Sustainable Operations and Supply Chain Management*. New York, NY: Wiley.

This book provides a useful insight into sustainable operations and supply chain management by using a step-by-step guide for supporting management decisions linked to effective product life cycles. The comprehensive guide includes product design, sourcing, manufacturing, packaging, distribution, reverse logistics and recovery.

Bouchery, Y., Corbett, C.J., Fransoo, J.C. and Tan, T. (2016) *Sustainable Supply Chains: A Research-Based Textbook on Operations and Strategy*. London: Springer.

This research-based textbook addresses attempts to find effective solutions to creating more sustainable supply chains and provides insight into how to tackle some of the most salient questions around this central theme based on academic research.

8

ETHICS AND CORPORATE SOCIAL RESPONSIBILITY

LEARNING OUTCOMES

- Understand the concepts of ethics and corporate social responsibility in the context of sustainability.
- Critically assess the philosophical approaches to ethics in the context of global sustainability management.
- Critically assess global sustainability management for ethical practice and corporate social responsibility.
- Understand the role of corporate social responsibility in the mission and sustainability goals of organisations.

INTRODUCTION

The global financial meltdown of 2008 was one of the most compelling catalysts for change in consumers' and citizens' attitudes towards business organisations in general and financial institutions in particular. A significant development from this has been the rising profile and importance of ethics in business and corporate social responsibility (CSR). These issues have become important themes in the public narrative around the behaviour of the business community, government, regulators and wider civil society. Central to the debate has been the perceived ability or willingness of corporate bodies to balance the need to achieve growth and profits with the wider responsibilities towards people and the environment. Higher expectations of stakeholders has resulted in corporate bodies being placed under unprecedented levels of scrutiny when it comes to their ethical behaviours and social responsibilities. The so-called 'credit crunch' of 2008 can be viewed as a tipping point in the relationship between society and business in the aftermath of some reckless and irresponsible behaviour by financial institutions as part of their obsession with achieving growth and profit. The result was a greatly reduced level of public confidence and trust in business organisations to manage their affairs in a manner that takes into account the welfare of citizens and consumers alongside their own performance targets.

There are numerous examples of poor corporate social responsibility and unethical behaviour in the business world with some gaining notoriety. Perhaps the most high-profile failures are American companies Enron and Union Carbide. The case of Enron proved so catastrophic to public confidence in business that it acted as a catalyst for wholesale changes to the way corporations report and audit their finances. The unique aspect of the case was that both the company management and the auditors, whose job it was to verify the corporate finances, were in corrupt collaboration to falsify the records (overstating the share price) and allow certain executive managers to gain from the discrepancies. This almost unprecedented scenario led to a radical overhaul of corporate governance procedures in the USA. The Union Carbide case of 1984 was a human and environmental disaster. To take advantage of lax health and safety rules, the company set up a chemical plant in Bhopal, India that eventually leaked toxic gas into the surrounding area killing many thousands of civilians and poisoning the land in a large area round the plant. Although the company claimed to have provided monetary and medical assistance at the time, responsibility for the disaster was argued through various courts for decades afterwards. The fact that Union Carbide had been acquired by US chemical giant Dow Chemical further complicated matters. In 2017 Dow Chemical merged with another US giant of the chemical industry DuPont, further reducing hopes that the victims' families will ever receive compensation for their suffering and loss.

By way of contrast, there are companies that embed corporate social responsibility into their mission and strategies. For example, in the UK the Cooperative Bank has a long-standing commitment to only supporting ethical investments. The challenge in this instance is to determine what 'ethical' is, given that it is subject to wide interpretations based on different attitudes, beliefs and cultural norms around 'ethical' practices. Despite this caveat, the bank has been able to derive additional reputational capital from its commitment to business ethics. UK cosmetics retailer Lush has built a reputation for producing a range of products from natural resources and engaging in ethical and responsible practices that underpin a commitment to sustainability and protection of the environment. Sustainability has become a key feature of the company strategy and involves minimising packaging, accessing sustainable raw materials (the company abandoned the use of palm oil for more sustainable oils for their soap products), maximising products made from waste and recycled materials, committing to reducing energy consumption and innovating to reduce water consumption in the manufacturing process. The company has also an established policy of non-animal testing for their range of products. In an industry that has struggled to meet the increasing demands for sustainable practices, Lush has demonstrated a commitment to addressing many of the concerns of consumers and other stakeholders as part of their corporate social responsibility agenda.

> **Definition: Ethics** refers to moral principles that underpin modes of behaviour. Corporate social responsibility (CSR) refers to the commitment shown by business to behave in an ethical manner.

Business ethics and corporate social responsibility in the context of global sustainability management forms the content of this chapter. Initially, the chapter provides an introduction to some chosen philosophical approaches linked to ethics that have emerged since the advent of industrialisation in the eighteenth century. Starting with moral principles, the section highlights the key characteristics of utilitarianism, human rights and the role of the individual. These philosophical approaches have influenced the way societies have developed and how the fabric of society is woven. Key differences between corporate sustainability and corporate social responsibility are presented before the key benefits that derive from engaging with ethical business practices and CSR in the context of sustainability are discussed. The chapter features discussion on global sustainable management for ethical practice and CSR and the associated advantages at both organisational and societal levels. There follows analysis of the implementation of global sustainable management and CSR activities that support sustainability before the discussion turns to the incorporation of ethics and CSR in mission statements and organisational goals featuring sustainability.

PHILOSOPHICAL APPROACHES TO ETHICS

No single, dominant ethical or moral code has been universally accepted. Instead, many different interpretations and perceptions of ethics exist in different cultures and societies (and even within those societies) on a global scale. Although significant differences are exhibited by different individuals, groups and communities, there have been attempts to formalise ethical codes around philosophical stances down the centuries. By using some of the most highly recognised ones to have been developed, it is possible to contextualise their characteristics and effects around the issue of sustainability in the modern era. The main philosophical approaches to ethics are outlined in Figure 8.1.

Moral principles

The moral principles approach is when an ethical dilemma is presented. Here, decisions are made on the basis of a recognised moral code or accepted mode of behaviour which has gained consensus by members of society such that they act as guides to what is considered right and wrong. The understanding of moral principles is often universally accepted (such as the understanding that murder

FIGURE 8.1 *Philosophical approaches to ethics*

is wrong) but each has a contextual basis (it is not considered wrong to kill an enemy during wartime). Moral principles also extend to the business environment as there is a recognised requirement for personnel to follow accepted modes of behaviour in the workplace. For example, the manager/subordinate relationship is based not only on mutual respect, but also an accepted understanding that the manager has the right to issue instructions. Although the style of management is relevant, the relationship depends on the extent to which an understanding of the unwritten moral principles are understood and acted upon by staff.

> **Definition: Moral principles** are fundamental principles that underpin understanding and knowledge of what is right and wrong.

Central to the moral principles approach is the universality of their justification. As Fisher and Lovell (2006) note, these principles are universal irrespective of their consequences. This universal principle can be applied to the environmental element of the Triple Bottom Line consisting of economic, social and environmental factors. In particular, there is broad consensus that the ecological and environmental welfare and health of the planet is diminishing rapidly to the point where a 'climate emergency' has been declared by many governments concerned with the impact this has on the societies they represent. Despite some dissenting voices, there has emerged in the last decade a consensus in support of moral and ethical principles that underpins the responsibility that humankind has for creating this calamity. This acceptance informs global managers' decision-making such that the issue of sustainability features as a priority alongside the social and economic factors. The social aspect of sustainability is almost as diverse in nature as the environmental with issues of diversity, human rights, inclusive societies, mobility and opportunity providing just some of the plethora of factors featuring as narratives across many different parts of civil society on a global basis. Even at the economic level, the focus on sustainability has informed much of the dominant thinking since the turn of the millennium. In particular, the use of technology as an economic tool has combined with myriad different forms of innovation to find solutions to the problems of unsustainable growth through the exploitation of resources. In the modern era there is a distinct shift towards moral principles underpinning a rationalisation of resources and a more balanced approach to the Triple Bottom Line of economic, social and environmental factors.

Utilitarianism

The utilitarian approach to ethics is based on the consequences of decisions and action and relies on the pursuit of maximising utility (or a favourable outcome) for the greatest number of people. English philosopher John Stuart Mill (1861) coined the term 'consequentialism' as a means of defining the essence of utilitarianism. That is, the moral value of any course of action is determined by the result of the outcome. Thus, the morality of an action can only be determined once all the relevant consequences are known. The guiding principle of this approach is that an outcome should lead to advantages for the majority. This feature of utilitarianism necessarily involves a tolerance of a certain number of losers if the majority of people are winners. This characteristic has often been deemed to be flawed and proved to be a catalyst for adopting a human rights approach where issues of equality inform the philosophical underpinning. That said, in a business context there are many examples of managers making decisions based on the notion that the outcome will benefit the majority but not all. There is also the concept of 'satisficing' whereby managers will accept a sub-optimal outcome motivated by a range of factors such as compromise, negotiation, progress or necessity.

Despite its limitations, the utilitarian approach does exhibit an emphasis on social welfare by reference to the 'quality of life' for society as a whole. As O'Connor (1997) notes, 'the preferences of individuals in comparison to those of the society are not formed in isolation but rather through reciprocal influence and socialization'. Interventions such as the United Nations Sustainable Development Goals, represent examples of institutions attempting to standardise quality of life. From the perspective of sustainability, it is evident that these types of interventions are required to close the gap that exists between different societies. For example, the relatively affluent western democracies provide the world's greatest consumers, whereas the emerging nations are predominantly the locus of production and supply. The utilitarian perspective assumes a tolerance of this imbalance that is at odds with the modern understanding of human rights and equality. Of course, the Earth perceived no such boundaries whether economic, political or geographical and, therefore, the impact of the imbalance is felt across the global, albeit to differing levels of intensity. It is clear in the twenty-first century that the planet cannot sustain the prevailing level of resource consumption without risking catastrophic consequences. The utilitarian perspective of tolerance for the few who lose out is, of itself, unsustainable. Global managers have a role to play in the change required to balance the economic, social and environmental factors in a way that places sustainability at the heart of their strategic agendas.

Mini case 8.1: US Forest Service

The US Forest Service is an agency of the Department of Agriculture that administers the country's 154 national forests and 20 grasslands. The mission of the service is to sustain the health, diversity and productivity of the Nation's forests and grasslands to meet the needs of present and future generations (fs.usda.gov/about-agency). Gifford Pinchot was the first appointed Director of the service in 1910. Responding to a question regarding the fundamental purpose of the service, Pinchot replied that it was to deliver 'the greatest good to the greatest number of people for the longest time' (Pinchot, 1998; Miller, 2013). Although the context was land conservation, the link to modern ideas of sustainable development can be discerned and contrasted. Pinchot's quote is an example of utilitarian thinking around ethics that informs practising the morally correct thing to do in any given situation. The process necessarily involves identifying various courses of action, determining and evaluating the advantages and consequences of each option, and then choosing the option that derives the greatest benefit and least harm to people. In the modern context, the environmental element would be added to this framework whereby issues of bio-diversity, animal protection and habitat conservation among others would be woven into the evaluation. Even if this more complete framework were to be designed, the efficacy of the utilitarian approach in the modern context remains incongruous set against the prevailing human rights philosophy. Also, the utilitarian approach requires some form of calculation of the positive and negative outcomes of an action prior to its implementation. Determining a value based on human factors is complex and unpredictable but adding the non-human elements makes it an impossible task. Also, if the outcome of actions resulted in the greatest good for humans at the expense of animal species (or vice versa), would that be considered ethically and morally acceptable? Although Pinchot's quote speaks to another age and can be viewed with a measure of sympathy around the intention being conveyed, it reveals the limitations of the utilitarian approach in the context of modern thinking.

Questions and task

1. Access the US Forest Service website and identify the four actions that support the mission and purpose of the organisation.
2. Is the utilitarian approach suitable for meeting the aims and objectives of the organisation?
3. What moral philosophy do you think best applies to the work of the US Forest Service? Explain your choice.

INTRODUCTION TO GLOBAL SUSTAINABLE MANAGEMENT

Social justice and human rights

The social justice and human rights approach is based on widely held beliefs and consensus on how decisions and actions are made in support of social justice and how they affect the human rights of individuals or groups. Protecting human rights and the principle of equality emerged as the dominant approach in the wake of the horrors witnessed and experienced by many during World War II. These principles underpinned attempts to shape a new world order and part of this process included the creation of global institutions such as the United Nations and its subsidiaries, the International Monetary Fund, NATO and, what was to become the European Union. Foremost among these was the United Nations, an intergovernmental organisation created to maintain international peace and security and achieve international cooperation among nations. In 1948 the United Nations delivered the Declaration on Human Rights which the majority of countries are signatories to. This milestone document set out fundamental human rights to be universally protected.

Part of the motivation for taking a human rights approach was to enshrine in law the basic principle that every citizen of the globe should be afforded a minimum right to life, freedom of speech and movement. Human rights underpin many of the employment laws that govern the way organisations deal with workers. However, the application of human rights varies markedly not just between different organisations but between different regions and cultures around the globe. This has led to the establishment of various monitoring organisations such as Human Rights Watch which seeks to identify, record and rectify cases of human rights abuses under the principle of fairness and of social justice whereby the equal distribution of opportunity as well as hardship is observed. Essentially, the social justice approach maintains the principle that all individuals should be treated equally and that justice can only be observed when all people have equal access to society's opportunities and bear an equal share of its burdens (Rawls, 1971; Boatright, 2007). The same can be said for communities, societies and nations around the world. Of course, as history has shown, the divergence from equality has been stark across all these dimensions. Nowhere has this been more evident than in the unequal distribution of wealth as well as the unequal exploitation of wealth. The charity Oxfam reports that the world's richest 1% have more than twice as much wealth as 6.9 billion people on Earth. Billionaires have more wealth than 60% of the world's population (Oxfam, 2014). Of course this is nothing new. The legacy of colonialism dating back centuries is the story of the hegemony of political and economic power used to exploit the resources of developing countries to widen the gulf in opportunity. It can be seen that the most glaring examples of unsustainable business practices lie in the relationship between powerful Western companies and their relationship with developing countries and the exploitation of their resources.

Virtue ethics

Virtue ethics relates to decisions based on ethical integrity and character. This approach is taken by individuals who view and evaluate the environment in terms of the effect it has on them as individuals. Actions are deemed to be right if they serve an individual's self-interest. This philosophy was the basis behind the work of economist and philosopher Adam Smith (1776) who argued that if each individual concentrated on their own self-interest then society as a whole would benefit. In a business context the philosophy determines that risk takers and entrepreneurs should only act in their own self-interest and that by doing so they would benefit others. Chicago school economist Milton Friedman (1962) was one of the proponents of this approach. Indeed, he viewed the role of business as being separate from that of the wider society by emphasising that the reasons commercial organisations exist is to maximise returns for shareholders. If they can do this without causing harm to others, then Friedman viewed that position as fulfilling their *raison d'être*. This approach found some support in the 1980s when the credo of 'greed is good' informed much of the business philosophy of the era, especially in the financial and stockbroking sectors. In the UK the government under Prime Minister Margaret Thatcher (1979–1990) implemented free market principles that encouraged individual aspiration, the profit motive and the role of the entrepreneur. Critics, such as former Prime Minister Gordon Brown (2007–2010), accused her of betraying the wider needs of society by this narrowly focused lens on monetary gain (Brown, 1989). Although the emphasis on individualism has waned in the intervening years, there remains a significant number of people in the business community who adopt this approach. Whether or not they look beyond self-interest as a motivator is open to debate.

Although this chapter focuses on ethics and corporate responsibility at the organisational level, it is as well to remember that these stem from decisions made by individuals or groups within organisations. Ultimately, global sustainable managers and workers have to make their own judgements and decisions regarding the manner in which they carry out their duties in accordance with accepted modes of behaviour. Clearly, it is vital that managers lead by example and this requires the demonstration of integrity. Managers who lack integrity are more likely to commit or tolerate unethical acts (Koehn, 2005; Audi and Murphy, 2015). No matter what short term gains may be derived from this, the ultimate effects are a loss of reputation and goodwill amongst stakeholders, mistrustful employees, and poor motivation and morale. Integrity lies at the heart of knowing what is right and wrong and then transforming that understanding into actions. Fundamentally it underpins ideals of honesty, fairness, character and conduct. In the context of sustainability this requires managers to demonstrate commitment by following through on agreed actions supporting waste reduction, lowering carbon emissions by increasing energy efficiency, implementing recycling policies, sourcing sustainable materials by closely evaluating the practices of supply chain partners and only participating in ethical supply chains, undertaking responsible marketing and promotion, upholding workers' rights by implementing fair and equal pay and safe environments, and engaging meaningfully with stakeholders. These are just a few examples where global sustainable managers can demonstrate virtue ethics alongside open, honest and transparent reporting of the outcomes of their actions.

INTRODUCTION TO GLOBAL SUSTAINABLE MANAGEMENT

CORPORATE SUSTAINABILITY AND CORPORATE SOCIAL RESPONSIBILITY

Before discussing the advantages of global sustainability management linked to ethical practice and CSR, it is useful to set the scene by highlighting the similarities and dissimilarities of the key concepts of CSR and corporate sustainability. It is clear that organisations around the world are placing greater emphasis on the issue of sustainability and the motivations for doing so are multifaceted and often nuanced (Abad-Segura et al., 2019; Schaltegger and Burritt, 2015). In some instances there is a clear commitment to contributing actions that support sustainability for entirely altruistic reasons. That is, the management of organisations believe in the mission to support sustainable practices for the good of the planet and humanity with some companies, such as Ben & Jerry's, Patagonia and Cisco Systems, building the actions into their strategies. Others are motivated for reputational purposes that has both social, environmental and economic benefits. In other cases, organisations engage with the rhetoric of sustainability but fail to follow through significantly in terms of actions that support it. Furthermore, there may be cost advantages associated with the technologies that link to sustainability that make firms more efficient and competitive. Thus, there is a wide spectrum of engagement with the concept and, consequently, the scale and type of management interventions.

Whatever the motivation, it is evident that sustainability has become a key part of the business agenda and has given rise to the term 'corporate sustainability'. This refers to a corporate management model that emphasises growth and profitability through business practices in support of the Triple Bottom Line (TBL) of economic, social and environment factors. As explained in Chapter 4, the goal of corporate sustainability is to provide long-term value to stakeholders without compromising any of the three factors that comprise the TBL.

Corporate Social Responsibility (CSR) is a broader concept than corporate sustainability as it refers to the means by which organisations can be socially accountable to stakeholders. Global sustainable managers can implement actions that enhance society by engaging with CSR in an on-going and dynamic manner, rather than one-off interventions. In other words, it is a strategic issue that requires resourcing, management and set aims and objectives. Due to the multifaceted nature of CSR not all organisations can invest in it to the same level but all can invest to some level. The common feature of corporate sustainability and CSR is that they both allow companies to be ethically profitable. Nevertheless, there are some key differences between them too as illustrated in Figure 8.2. Firstly, CSR tends to be reflective and looks back on what an organisation has done to create social value. Corporate sustainability tends to look forward by developing strategies for the future. Also, it is often the case that CSR targets those stakeholders with influential voices such as the media, pressure groups or those with political leverage. Corporate sustainability, on the other hand, targets the whole of the value chain from end-customers to other stakeholder groups.

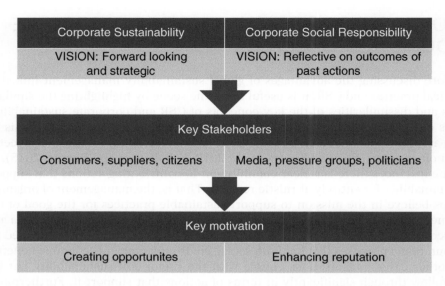

Corporate Sustainability	Corporate Social Responsibility
VISION: Forward looking and strategic	VISION: Reflective on outcomes of past actions

Key Stakeholders	
Consumers, suppliers, citizens	Media, pressure groups, politicians

Key motivation	
Creating opportunites	Enhancing reputation

FIGURE 8.2 *Differences between corporate sustainability and corporate social responsibility*

ADVANTAGES OF GLOBAL SUSTAINABLE MANAGEMENT FOR ETHICAL PRACTICE AND CSR

Ethical business practice and corporate social responsibility around sustainability have a number of distinct advantages both for the organisation and the wider society. These include economic advantages including the achievement of competitive advantage based on brand loyalty of consumers who recognise and support the sustainability credentials of firms, enhanced image and reputation, improved stakeholder relationships, increased lobbying power, accreditation, safer products and processes, and environmental benefits of sustainable business practices. Table 8.1 highlights some of the key advantages of global sustainable management for ethical practice and CSR.

For global sustainable managers there are numerous advantages associated with ethical business practice and the adoption of corporate social responsibility principles that extend beyond the notion that it is the 'correct thing to do'. One of the most compelling factors is the potentially positive effect they have on performance as consumer awareness of the impact of the exploitation and use of resources on the environment can build brand loyalty to those firms that demonstrate actions that support CSR, and sustainability in particular. Antonetti and Maklan (2014) highlight the role of feelings of guilt and pride play in convincing consumers of the effectiveness of sustainable choices. One consequence of this raised awareness is the increasing concern for future generations that has become part of the discourse in civil societies across the globe. Thus, sustainability as a

TABLE 8.1 *Advantages of global sustainable management*

ORGANISATION	SOCIETY
Brand loyalty	Environmental
Reputational capital	Social value
Stakeholder relationships	Economic security
Influence and lobbying power	Lower waste
Industry accreditation	Lower carbon emissions
Health and safety standards	Sustainable futures
Cost savings	Recycling
Innovation	Workers' rights
Employee satisfaction	Human rights
Talent acquisition	Poverty reduction
Competitiveness and profitability	Health improvements

concept is closely linked to how consumers perceive organisations in relation to sourcing materials, managing their supply chains and the environmental effects of producing their goods and services among others. Harrison et al. (2005) present evidence to suggest that the ability to attract and retain customers is lower for companies associated with practices that do damage to the environment or deplete resources in an unsustainable manner. The consequences invariably have negative implications for company performance as well as reputation. However, there is debate as to the extent to which customers alter buying behaviour as a direct consequence of company behaviour. Although there is evidence to suggest that customers are more aware and more knowledgeable of the environmental impacts of business activity, the response in terms of changes to buying behaviour remains marginal (Carrigan and Attalla, 2001; Devinney et al., 2010).

Another key advantage is the manner in which workers' rights are observed and supported within organisations. Failure to recognise this aspect of sustainable business practice can have long-lasting consequences for firms. The negative publicity afforded Nike following the exposure of poor working conditions and practices in their manufacturing plants in developing countries led to a complete reworking of their human resource strategy. In various plants across south east Asia the company banned child labour, created educational opportunities for locals, set up healthcare facilities and improved working conditions. The oil giant Shell has been the focus of online petitions seeking reparations for the environmental damage caused by exploration activity in the Nigerian delta region. In particular, the oil drilling and pipeline activities in the tribal lands of the Ogoni people have been at a devastating environmental and human cost. Their rivals BP paid out billions of dollars in compensation and fines after the Deepwater Horizon blowout in the Gulf of Mexico (Lustgarten, 2012). Management incompetence and poor safety practices were among a raft of failings identified by the official enquiry.

In some instances, the way in which organisations engage with consumers can have unintended consequences. For example, many financial institutions have had to compensate customers for mis-selling pension protection products. These, and other examples have forced many companies to reassess their business practices. Consequently, CSR has gained in importance and features as a key strategic issue for building reputational capital and seeking a competitive advantage. Often, it can be seen that global managers are increasingly required to balance the economic with the social and environmental pressures. In an important article, the link between CSR and competitive advantage is the focus of attention of Porter and Kramer (2006). Their argument promotes the need for managers to take a proactive approach to planning for implementing effective CSR policies and actions that enhance brand loyalty, bolster the organisation's image and reputation, and support strategies for gaining and sustaining competitive advantage. For a more in-depth understanding of this process, Saeidi et al. (2015) provide evidence to support a positive relationship between CSR and the financial performance of firms through the mediating factors of competitive advantage, reputation and customer satisfaction.

Global managers who demonstrably implement sustainability practices can improve the image and reputation of the organisation. These are valuable assets when building brand loyalty that increases market share and, ultimately, can help to create a competitive advantage. However, the primary motivation should be driven by a commitment to contribute to the social and environmental welfare of the planet and not the pursuit of economic gain. Increasingly, organisations are sensitive to the way they are perceived by stakeholders, particularly customers, and come under a great deal of scrutiny regarding their trading practices and impact on the environment. Building knowledge of the sustainability needs and expectations of different stakeholders helps global managers better understand the way the organisation should behave. Research has shown that an endorsement of social responsibility can have a positive response from the market (Bird et al., 2007; Doh et al., 2010; Partalidou et al., 2020). In the last two decades the 'green' credentials of organisations has become a litmus test of how they impact the environment and acts as a check on how they manage their operations in line with heightened expectations regarding respect for the environment (Combe, 2014). This is evident in the mission statements of many modern organisations where references to their commitment to sustainability are more prevalent and detailed. Although some commit to rigorous scrutiny and audits (the Action Platform of the UN Sustainability Development Goals is one means by which companies can commit to having their reported actions measured and monitored on a voluntary basis), many others display a high level of rhetoric and are not necessarily followed through with actions. This can take the form of so-called 'greenwashing' whereby firms convey a false impression or give misleading information on the environmental impact of their products.

Mini case 8.2: Sézane, France

The fashion industry has struggled with a reputation for high environmental impacts and poor workers' rights across supply chains. Much of the reputation is well founded with the industry accounting for around 10% of global carbon emissions and nearly 20% of wastewater. In particular, fast fashion (relatively cheap clothing produced quickly by mass market retailers) has been criticised for the 'throw away' consumer culture that drives that part of the industry. The environmental footprint of the fashion industry is enormous as it requires huge amounts of energy and water resources, uses toxic dyes and other chemicals, and produces billions of tonnes of non-biodegradable microplastics. The poor conditions many workers endure in mainly low-cost countries is another concern, the deaths of some 1134 garment workers at the Rana Plaza factory in Bangladesh in 2013 being one of the most tragic consequences of this form of exploitation. In many ways, this incident has proved to be a turning point in attitudes within the sector. Increasingly, companies across the supply chain are introducing strategies to address issues of child labour, low wages, workplace safety, employees' health and the impact on the environment. In design and production there has been a significant shift towards sustainability in the processes of dying, printing, finishing, manufacture and transport. New technologies are helping to create new and sustainable fabrics with demand for organic fashion on the rise. Some fashion houses have now firmly embedded sustainability into their strategies and the Paris-based Sézane is one example of this.

Founded by Morgane Sezalory, Sézane was one of the first French labels to set up as an e-commerce only site selling vintage clothes from eBay. In 2016 the company set up its first physical store in Paris called L'Appartement. The label specialises in easy-to-wear, vintage-inspired floral skirts, silk shirts and t-shirts. However, alongside the fashion statement, Morgane Sezalory was committed to pursuing high sustainability ideals for the company. Among the actions that support a sustainable business model at Sézane is a production model that leaves no items unsold, recycling of fabrics and no waste, use of vegetable tanning methods for leather goods, manufacturing in Europe to minimise the carbon footprint, and extensive use of eco-friendly materials such as organic cotton, recycled polyester and linen. The company has also switched to 100% recycled cardboard packaging. There is also a philanthropic arm to the business called Demain that channels revenue to charities. Initiatives that support this include releasing new designs, sales of recycled items at their hub Paris boutique, and the voluntary time commitment to charity work by Sézane employees. The company has demonstrated actions to support their claims of being a sustainable brand by delivering on social sustainability (ethical working conditions and fair pay), environmental sustainability (using natural and recycled materials and reducing the use of chemicals), slowing

(Continued)

production (reducing the volume of output), and circular practices (encouraging returns of used garments from customers).

Questions and task

1. Check your own fashion carbon footprint using fashionfootprint.org
2. Why does the fashion industry have a poor reputation for sustainability?
3. What four criteria are used to determine the sustainability of a fashion house?

The right to compete in an industry can be another reason for companies engaging in sustainable business practices or demonstrating corporate social responsibility. Accreditation or standards criteria are mandatory across many industry sectors with compliance allowing organisations to carry out their operations and activities safely and to a minimal standard of quality. For example, car manufacturing companies operating within the European Union have to meet stringent standards for carbon emissions before being given a licence to produce. This makes the violation by Volkswagen all the more remarkable. In 2016 the company was found guilty in a US court of violations to the Clean Air Act including three counts of conspiracy, obstruction of justice and introducing products into the US by means of false statements. The US Environmental Protection Agency (EPA) had discovered 'defeat device' software in Volkswagen cars that could detect when they were being tested. This allowed them to change the performance to improve results (Ameen, 2020). The outcome was costly to the company not just in terms of finance but also the loss of trust with consumers and the wider public. This example is one of several that has contributed to the accreditation and monitoring process becoming an industry in itself. Some industries draw up a code of conduct themselves to ensure a closer system of monitoring of managers' and employees' behaviour.

As has been noted previously, the influence that stakeholders wield on organisations can affect performance, strategy, and consumer and public opinion. It is important for organisations to understand the relative power and influence that each stakeholder group has and to engage in dialogue with them to prevent negative publicity. Very often this may require organisations to communicate with groups who are fundamentally opposed to their activities. There is value in forming some communication channel with rival stakeholders so that the perspective of the organisation is heard. For example, there is a close dialogue between representatives of the farming community and the pressure group Compassion in World Farming. Whilst the latter opposes many of the practices seen in modern agricultural business, the channel of communication is a positive and constructive means of airing different views and seeking solutions to difficult problems. The farming industry benefits from being seen to be actively engaged in problem solving some of the ethical issues related to their practices, and the pressure group gets access to the key decision-makers in the industry. Constructive engagement is a focus of academic attention as well as activists and business practitioners. For example, Argenti (2004) outlined the strategy of Starbucks in entering constructive collaboration with non-governmental organisation activists Global Exchange. Stung by the negative publicity of the storming of their annual conference, Starbucks avoided reprisals (such as calls for boycotts of their products) by engaging with the activists and addressing their concerns linked to low pay for coffee farmers and adopting 'Fairtrade' practices in the buying of coffee beans. Simultaneously, there is also a trend within the NGO activist community to switch tactics away from high profile 'shaming' stunts to closer and more subtle forms of engagement in many sectors including nuclear, palm oil, animal welfare and others. Other movements, such as climate change activists Extinction Rebellion, remain firmly adversarial in their approach.

Pressure from stakeholders can force organisations to act ethically or adopt a corporate social responsibility stance. This can manifest itself in changes to the way products are produced (exposing the exploitation of cheap labour in Third World countries by leading Western brands such as GAP, Next and Nike), packaged (imported goods to the USA are rigorously checked for safety), advertised (products aimed at children are banned from advertising on television in Sweden) and consumed (smoking in public places has been banned in many countries around the world). Some stakeholders form formal organisations to pursue their agenda. For example, Fairtrade is a charity established in London to support and empower poor and marginalised producers of crops around the world. The group has had some success in influencing organisations to adopt fairer and more equitable buying policies to help the economic and social development of subsistence farmers and labourers. Developments in information and communications technologies have helped stakeholder groups coordinate strategies on a global scale to lobby corporate bodies over a wide range of issues including sustainability, workers' rights and environmental protection.

> **Definition: Corporate governance** is a system of control over the actions and practices of managers in organisations through an agreed set of relationships between a company's management, board, shareholders and other stakeholders.

GLOBAL SUSTAINABLE MANAGEMENT AND CORPORATE SOCIAL RESPONSIBILITY

Corporate social responsibility refers to the duty of global sustainable managers to nurture, protect and enhance the welfare of stakeholders (Blowfield and Murray, 2008). There are several ways managers respond to this duty as illustrated in Figure 8.3.

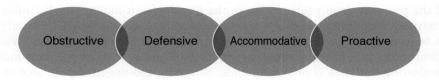

FIGURE 8.3 *Management approaches to CSR*

Obstructionist response: managers choose not to be socially responsible.

Defensive response: managers stay within the law but make no attempt to exercise additional social responsibility.

Accommodative response: managers realise the need for social responsibility.

Proactive response: managers actively embrace social responsibility. Managers accrue benefits by being responsible.

Different approaches adopted by different organisations reflect differences in factors such as the competitive position, industry, country, environmental and ecological pressures, and so on. A CSR approach can manifest itself in many different ways within an organisation or through the way the organisation interacts with external stakeholders. For example, marketers have attempted to incorporate a CSR element into their activities by developing the so-called '4e' principles. These include guiding principles that:

 (i) make it **easy** for the consumer to be green
 (ii) **empower** consumers with solutions
 (iii) **enlist** the support of the consumer
 (iv) **establish** credibility with the wider public.

Some critics have questioned the motivation of managers who seek to gain value from adopting a CSR stance or overtly extolling the virtues of their organisation's ethical credentials. Those who seek added value from such claims cannot be considered global sustainable managers. Asongu (2007) offers some insight into this phenomenon. However, to demonstrate commitment, organisations can be proactive in incorporating CSR into their performance targets that include social and environmental value. Some may undertake a social audit for this purpose whereby managers specifically take ethics and business into account when making decisions on performance targets. A social audit attempts to measure a company's actual social performance against the social objectives it has set for itself. A social audit may be conducted by the company itself, although one conducted by an outside consultant will more likely impose minimal biases and may prove more beneficial to the organisation. Once the social audit is complete it can be distributed internally or externally (or both), depending on the organisation's goals and situation. Some organisations include a section in their annual report devoted to corporate social responsibility activities; others publish a separate periodic report on their social responsiveness. The social audit may be used for more than simply monitoring and evaluating the organisation's social performance. Managers also use social audits to scan the external environment, determine firm vulnerabilities, and institutionalise CSR within the culture of the organisation.

> **Definition:** a **social audit** is a process that enables an organisation to assess and demonstrate its social, economic and environmental benefits and limitations. It is a measure of the extent to which an organisation matches its actions with actual commitment to agreed shared values and objectives.

Mini case 8.3: Patagonia, USA

In 1965 avid rock climber Yvon Chouinard partnered with his friend Tom Frost to create Chouinard Equipment, a company with a mission to manufacture innovative climbing equipment to a growing market. By 1973 they were an established company trading as Patagonia and have remained a family-run business led by Yvon and Malinda Chouinard. Alongside a commitment to produce top-quality outdoor apparel using the latest technologies, the company has been dedicated to sustainability and socially responsible business practices. The commitment to CSR is underpinned by a series of actions that demonstrate ethical business practice including donating 1% of their annual sales to environmental charities. Rather than viewing such actions as acts of philanthropy, the company has a culture management that sees such contributions as a standard cost of doing business. The commitment to sustainability also extends beyond the organisation by including those who they do business with along the supply chain as well as rivals. In 2010 the company founded the Sustainable Apparel Coalition whereby 30 companies from the clothing and footwear industry commit to measuring their environmental impact across their supply chains, benchmark their performance against the other member companies, and publish their results. The process helps global managers engage with sustainable practices when sourcing materials and developing new products.

Patagonia has a reputation for taking innovative approaches to demonstrating their CSR credentials including advertisements with the slogan 'Don't Buy our Jackets' as a means of putting the brakes on the excessive consumption linked to Black Friday in many retail stores. At the strategic level, the company also created some interest by disbanding their Sustainability Department. Originally viewed by some as a lessening of the commitment to the sustainability cause, in fact, the opposite was the case. The rationale put forward by managers was that the ethos

(Continued)

of sustainability had to permeate throughout every department and individual within the organisation and not be seen as the preserve of a stand-alone functional entity of it. Thus, it is deemed fundamental to the core values of the organisation that each and every employee integrates innovative sustainability thinking into their everyday working lives. These and a raft of other actions to support ethical business and sustainability have garnered a whole new generation of customers who value the principles that Patagonia exhibit. It is also worth noting that the company has been valued at over one billion dollars and registered some $800 million in profits in 2019. Clearly, for this company the old adage of 'doing well by doing good' stands true.

Questions and task

1. What are the benefits of the measurement tools that the Sustainable Apparel Coalition use to assess their environmental and social impacts?
2. What are the four core values of Patagonia?
3. In 2011 Patagonia rolled out their 'Don't Buy our Jackets' advertisement. Undertake research to discover if their sales revenue increased in the following year.

THE ROLE OF CSR AND SUSTAINABILITY IN MISSION AND GOALS

Whether an organisation is developing a new business or reformulating the direction for an on-going business, it must determine the basic goals and philosophies that will shape its strategic posture. This company mission is defined as the fundamental purpose that sets an organisation apart from others of its type and identifies the scope of operations in product and market terms. Essentially, a mission statement embodies the overriding philosophy of the firm's strategic decision-makers, implies the image the organisation seeks to project, reflects its self-concept, and indicates the principal product or service areas and the primary customer or stakeholder needs the organisation will attempt to satisfy. No external body requires that the company mission be defined, but rather it is a statement of attitude, outlook and orientation. The objectives of mission statements are multifarious but may include:

- To ensure unanimity of purpose within the organisation.
- To provide a basis for motivating the use of the organisation's resources.
- To develop a basis, or standard, for allocating organisational resources.
- To establish a general tone or organisation climate.
- To serve as a focal point for those who can identify with the organisation's purpose and direction.

- To facilitate the translation of objectives and goals into a work structure involving the assignment of tasks to responsible elements within the organisation.
- To specify organisational purposes and the translation of these purposes into goals in such a way that cost, time and performance parameters can be assessed and controlled.

THE ROLE OF CSR IN MISSION FORMULATION

Three indispensable components of the mission statement are specification of the basic product or service, specification of the primary market, and specification of the principal technology for production or delivery. Often the most referenced public statement of an organisation's selected products and markets appears prominently in the mission statement. Three economic goals guide the strategic direction of almost every business organisation. Whether the mission statement explicitly states these goals, it reflects the organisation's intention to secure survival through growth and profitability. In the public sector, organisational goals are different and tend to reflect issues related to accountability, transparency and best value.

The statement of an organisation's philosophy usually accompanies or appears within the mission statement. It reflects or specifies the basic beliefs, values, aspirations, and philosophical priorities to which strategic decision-makers are committed in managing the company. Fortunately, the philosophies vary little from one firm to another. Despite the similarity of these statements, the intentions of the strategic managers in developing them do not warrant cynicism as company executives attempt to provide a distinctive and accurate picture of the firm's managerial outlook. Mission statements should reflect the public's expectations since this makes achievement of the firm's goals more likely. A negative public image often prompts firms to reemphasise the beneficial aspects of their mission. Firms seldom address the question of their public image in an intermittent fashion. A major determinant of an organisation's success is the extent to which the firm can relate functionally to its external environment. To assess its proper place in a competitive situation, the organisation must realistically evaluate its competitive strengths and weaknesses. Both individuals and organisations have a crucial need to know themselves. The ability of either to survive in a dynamic and highly competitive environment would be severely limited if they did not understand their impact on others or of others on them. The characteristics of the corporate self-concept have been summarised as follows:

- It is based on management's perception of the way in which others (society) will respond to the company.
- It directs the behaviour of people employed by the company.

- It is determined partly by the response of others to the company.
- It is incorporated into mission statements that are communicated to individuals inside and outside the company. Ordinarily, descriptions of the company self-concept per se do not appear in mission statements. Yet such statements often provide strong impressions of the company self-concept.

CSR and sustainability goals

A goal, according to Etzioni (1964), is 'a future state of affairs that an organisation attempts to realise'. This definition can be applied to all organisations. Stated goals exist to provide a focus for the activities of internal stakeholders. In most organisations, goals incorporate a general statement of organisational purpose or 'mission' and a set of more detailed aims and objectives that guide strategic and operational decision-making. Figure 8.4 illustrates five categories of organisational goals.

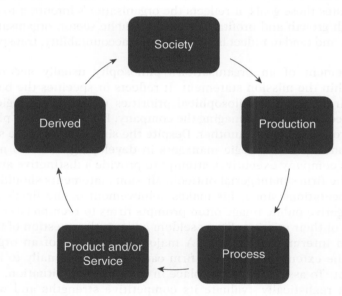

FIGURE 8.4 *Categories of organisational goals*

Society: goals as perceived by the wider society such as the standard of health and safety of products, carbon emission levels, welfare rights of workers, etc.

Production: output targets over a set period of time.

Process: goals relating to the process stage of organisational activity such as production rates, system failure rates, etc.

Product and/or service: relate to the characteristics of the output and may be expressed in terms of quantity, quality or availability.

Derived: goals that may not be formally stated in the organisation's mission statement but are pursued by organisational activity. Examples include lobbying activity to exert political influence, active involvement in charitable concerns or forms of community engagement.

In the context of ethics and corporate social responsibility it can be seen that each of the types of goals set out above can be the focus of attention. Clearly, the societal and derived goals feature most commonly in the action of organisations in support of CSR or wider ethical goals. Nevertheless, it is possible to discern examples of these in the productive processes of firms, procurement activities regarding access to raw materials, advertising campaigns, workers' welfare and in a host of other activities undertaken by organisations. In fact, the emphasis on CSR and ethics has been subject to change over time as attitudes, beliefs and values in the wider society change. Consequently, it is inevitable that the goals of organisations change over time for reasons not just to do with economic returns, but also to reflect the expectations of customers and other stakeholders. In modern businesses the goal of profit maximisation has often been subject to goal displacement as new goals are developed which entirely change or go counter to previous goals. This has been evident in the trend towards incorporating a more socially responsible aspect to the activities of organisations, improving internal corporate governance, and better engagement with the wider society. In some circumstances CSR is a focus of goal succession where new or modified goals are incorporated into existing ones in such a way that the broad organisational focus remains the same.

Perhaps the most important characteristic of CSR is an understanding of the society in which organisations operate and particularly how government, business, educational institutions, security and control organisations, and civil society support organisations operate. An appreciation of how economic and social structures are created and organised underpins knowledge of how to operate within those structures. It is from this knowledge and understanding that a sense of an organisation's role and responsibilities within them starts to emerge. Very often organisations do not create and implement strategies in support of CSR in isolation but, rather, they seek suitable partnerships to help them achieve their objectives. Building capacity for delivering on strategic plans that incorporate CSR is an important aspect of management whereby networking skills are the catalyst for creating external partnerships, strategic alliances or at least channels of communication. For example, where once power generation companies were in direct opposition with ecology protection groups such as Greenpeace, there is now effective dialogue and consultation between the two camps.

Another characteristic underpinning effective CSR includes questioning of the status quo or 'business-as-usual' approach to addressing some of the most pressing global issues such as climate change, structures of economies, social welfare, political reform and so on. Testing times require sometimes radical new ideas and innovative methods of problem solving. In terms of CSR, it can be seen that more and more organisations are adopting a proactive approach to dealing with their responsibilities to the wider society by adopting new forms of doing business (such as public service partnerships, or partnerships with social enterprises). Part of this process is to have better and more effective relationships with stakeholders that may include giving them a platform or channel of communication that informs change within organisations. All these characteristics need to be part of a strategy that includes CSR. This requires organisations to not only take a strategic view of the business environment, but to build in a strategic view of how their activities can be undertaken without harming the wider environment or the people that inhabit it.

In a globalised economy, effective CSR can only be achieved through embracing diversity and adjusting the lens through which managers view the world around them. Understanding and harnessing diversity is a pre-requisite for dispensing CSR in the modern global economy. The framework can be extended to incorporate indications of levels of CSR attainment. The aim is to transform the characteristics of effective CSR activities along a trajectory from awareness of the need for CSR through to embedding it into the leadership of an organisation. Figure 8.5 illustrates the components of the CSR attainment levels.

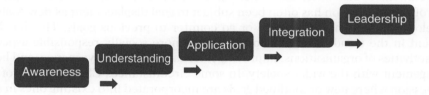

FIGURE 8.5   *The process of CSR attainment*

Awareness refers to the level of appreciation of the key CSR characteristics and the extent to which they inform and influence decision-making in the organisation. The level of understanding links to the knowledge and comprehension of the key issues affecting the formation of CSR as a concept. Here, there is some implied notion of competence in transferring the knowledge into applied actions that support CSR. Integration is a level of understanding that is more focused, detailed and in-depth that transforms comprehension and knowledge into specific expertise in embedding CSR into the decision-making process in the organisation. Effective leadership is achieved when those at the executive and strategic decision-making level support managers for fully integrating CSR activities across the organisation.

Although there is a general consensus that CSR is a force for good within organisations and for the welfare of the wider society, it is not without its critics. Some, such as Doane (2005) point to the fact that very often CSR initiatives become obscured by wider corporate interests. For example, some CSR initiatives have been designed to ensure a greater community engagement from organisations. This may benefit a minority of the population but the main advantage resides with the organisation in the form of enhanced reputation and goodwill among stakeholders. So, for a minimal investment, organisations can derive significant marketing economies at low risk. In some cases the public can only benefit if they actually purchase products. Organisations that have delivered benefits such as sportswear to youth clubs or computers to schools can link the 'benevolence' to sales. This can be done through setting targets for returns of product wrappers for instance. Critics argue that this type of approach is a cynical exploitation of a market demographic that has little understanding of sophisticated marketing techniques. Also, the nature and scope of such initiatives have only marginal effect on societal change. Again, critics point to the fact that the majority of CSR related initiatives fail to really address the major issues of the day such as climate change, social transformation, universal healthcare, economic reform and so on.

CASE STUDY

Mining in Chile

Antonio Cecchi Fyfe (Lecturer, University of Santiago, Chile)

In 2020 BHP were forced to suspend operations at the Cerro Colorado copper mine in northern Chile after the Supreme Court upheld a complaint from local indigenous communities relating to the company's excessive extraction of water resources that had an environmental impact on local wetlands. Previously, BHP had an environmental project approved but the ruling overturned that ruling. The company was forced to embark on an entirely new environmental plan for the mine. The setback placed the viability of the mine in doubt along with several hundred jobs in the area. The outcome may not have come as a surprise to managers at BHP having previously been charged by the regulator for similar water misuse in the world's largest copper mine at Escondida in the country's Atacama Desert. In that instance, the company was found to have caused a sufficiently serious drop in the water table to merit suspension along with the threat of closure. However, it is possible to discern a shift in emphasis at the company as the pressure to operate more sustainable practices starts to take effect. For example, the company signed four contracts in 2019 to switch from coal-fired power to renewable energy at two of its copper mines, including the one at Escondida. It is expected that the two sites will be entirely powered by renewable energy by the mid-2020s and lead to an overall reduction of 3 million tonnes of carbon emissions. Energy users are also expected to benefit by an expected 20% reduction in

►

energy prices. The move is seen as a positive development in addressing economic (increased efficiency), social (economic security for local communities through job retention) and environmental (lower carbon emissions, less dust, preserved water supplies and less noise) impacts.

Copper mining is one of the key industries in Chile with huge revenues being generated on the back of a product that is in high global demand. However, companies such as BHP have to consider the social and environmental factors alongside that of economic drivers. Here, the relationships with stakeholders is key with communities, wildlife activists, environmental campaigners, shareholders and government at all levels all contributing to the pressure to develop into a sustainable business. To this end, BHP produce an annual Sustainability Plan that details their actions designed to manage the transition to sustainability. Of interest is the attitude of shareholders to the development of a sustainability strategy. In 2019 around 20% of shareholders backed a resolution calling for the company to relinquish relationships with any industry association that did not support the principles of the Paris agreement on climate change. As one of the world's largest carbon emitters, BHP have a long journey ahead to meet stakeholders' expectations ahead of the 'net zero' target of 2050.

Mining activity comprises the attainment of legal licenses, development of infrastructure, exploration, excavation, transportation and ore selling activities. These actions generally involve positive and negative effects on people and the environment (Carvalho, 2017). The industry creates positive effects on the local economy and public infrastructure modernisation. However, negative effects such as contamination and depletion of water resources have been seen to significantly affect communities' wellbeing (Irina and Stuckelberger, 2013; Aboka et al., 2018; Entwistle et al., 2019). These can trigger rejection by communities of mining operations and mining companies in the form of protests, court legal actions and blockades (Meesters and Behagel, 2017), resulting in the cancellation or suspension of mining activities, such as in the case of BHP. This has raised the level of debate regarding the role of societal approval in the process of granting a Social Licence to Operate (SLO) that permits operations of mining companies in Chile.

In recent decades, mining companies in Chile and around the world have been operating under a higher level of public scrutiny regarding their ethical actions that impact the environment and local communities. This has resulted in a range of measures designed to allay the fears of opponents of mining and local communities. Consequently, mining companies produce sustainability reports and develop CSR frameworks as a basis for self-regulating operations (Araya et al., 2019). Thus, gaining an understanding of how people perceive mining operations can be linked to the sustainability performance and the achievement of stated targets as part of CSR frameworks.

There is a wide agreement that the implementation of CSR in developing countries has barriers due to weak institutional systems, bureaucratic inconsistency and corruption problems. These issues obstruct the implementation of CSR actions oriented to improve housing, education, and the healthcare and social needs of mining communities (Amos, 2018). The raft of social problems in mining communities (isolation, alcoholism, mental health, etc.) also reflects a lack of governmental capabilities to improve living conditions. There is an expectation by government that mining companies should bridge the gap in social welfare provision (Deloitte, 2019). There is some evidence to suggest that mining companies leverage advantage by trading economic and social benefits in exchange for the right to operate unhindered by local protest. This approach has the potential for exacerbating the social problems and widening the economic disparities between communities (Perez-Rocha and Moore, 2019). In the case of Chile, mining communities generally live with a wide range of unsolved social problems. For instance, 32% of inhabitants do not have access to utilities and 12% of households live in crowded conditions (INE, 2017). Also, social inequality issues are well documented in rural areas of Chile where mining operations take place. To lend context to this, it is revealing that the annual educational budget of local councils in Chile averages less than 1% of mining companies' annual investment budgets.

Tasks

1. Identify six social and environmental impacts associated with the mining industry.

2. The Communities and Sustainability Report 2018–2022 of BHP identifies health, environment, safety and education as the key main target areas. Give an example from each.

3. Identify the competing social, economic and environmental factors that shape the perceptions of the public in Chile towards the activities of mining companies.

SUMMARY

This chapter started with definitions of ethics and CSR before discussing relevant philosophical approaches to the concept of ethics from a sustainability perspective. This part highlighted the transition to the human-rights approach and the importance of equality as a basic human right. The differences between corporate sustainability and corporate social responsibility were highlighted before the discussion focused on the key advantages of global sustainable management in ethical practice and CSR. Here, the work set out chosen economic, strategic, social and environmental reasons that drive this type of management. Examples of good and bad practices set the context of the discussion and issues of contention were also raised to balance the arguments presented. In the final section the work then turned attention to management approaches to CSR before setting out how it features in the formulation of company mission statements and sustainability goals.

FURTHER READING

Horrigan, B. (2010) *Corporate Social Responsibility in the 21st Century: Debates, Models and Practices*. Cheltenham: Edward Elgar Publishing.

This inter-disciplinary and cross-jurisdictional analysis includes debates on governance, practical guidelines for responsible businesses and government roles in supporting CSR. With an international focus, the author introduces a range of controversial issues from around the world. The content delivers a useful insight into ethical issues in business from different cultural and legal perspectives.

Reed, B. (2020) *Communicating Social and Environmental Issues Effectively*. Bingley: Emerald Publishing.

The author designed Scotland's national recycling campaign and has worked with a range of large corporations on sustainability strategies. The book explores how environmental and social issues can be effectively communicated to target audiences. The discussion provides examples of innovative and creative means of engaging with sustainability through different approaches to communicating ideas and concepts.

Trevino, L.K. and Nelson, K.A. (2017) *Managing Business Ethics: Straight Talk about How to do it Right* (7th edn). Chichester: John Wiley & Sons.

In this book the discussion evolves from the individual to the managerial level before turning the focus to organisational contexts. The clarity of the narrative provides an effective guide to readers engaged in the process of understanding the complexities of human behaviour that underpin the development of business ethics. There are compelling chapters reflecting on the financial crash of 2008 and the motivations and challenges of being ethical.

9

SUSTAINABILITY CULTURE

INTRODUCTION

Alongside the output of human resources, the achievement of strategic aims, or the effectiveness of change, organisational culture is a key factor that determines the performance of an organisation. However, although it makes a significant contribution, the issue of organisational culture needs to be treated with some caution as it is a dynamic, changeable and sometimes difficult to identify phenomenon. Although there is no consensus on a precise definition of organisational culture, it is necessary for managers to determine what it means in order to operationalise it in some form that contributes value to the organisation. For the purposes of this discussion the definition of organisational culture is a system of shared beliefs and values held by workers that form a dominant culture that is unique to the organisation. Although this definition is relatively easy to comprehend, its characteristics create challenges for managers as they seek to influence the formation of a positive organisational culture. This is further complicated by incorporating a specific conceptual aim such as that of sustainability. Organisational culture is an intangible phenomenon subject to change and, therefore, managers need some guidance on how to identify, influence and manage the formation of a positive organisational culture around the issue of sustainability.

There are a range of different perspectives that can be used when analysing organisational culture. For example, Deal and Kennedy (1982) noted that strong cultures have a predominantly positive effect on organisational performance and that they tend to emerge as a result of close links between the organisation and its external environment and underpinned by shared values and well-defined behaviours. Peters and Waterman (1982) also adopted this view and used it to set out the means by which managers could motivate workers through the development of a positive organisational culture. There is some consensus that, fundamentally, organisational culture does not operate in isolation from other culture-forming influences. For example, the social culture around which it forms has a bearing on the development of a dominant organisational culture. Similarly, the internal environment can also act as a major influence.

> **Definition: Organisational culture** is a system of shared beliefs and values held by workers that form a dominant culture that is unique to the organisation.

When discussing organisational culture, two extreme perspectives emerge as first identified by Burrell and Morgan (1979). The authors set out two camps split between those who view culture as something an organisation *is*, as compared to the alternate view that culture is something an organisation *has*. Whereas the former views the concept of culture as inseparable from the organisation (that is, it exists and is a given) and cannot be controlled, the latter perspective presents managers with a powerful organisational tool that can influence behaviour, promote a sense of identity among members, and help to establish the accepted 'ground rules' for decision-making (Ogbonna, 1992). Both views are prescient contributions to the argument but for the purposes of explanation and discourse in this chapter, the perspective of organisational culture as a tool that can be used to influence behaviour underpins the discussion. This approach aligns to the development of sustainability as a cultural phenomenon dependent on human interaction and activity. For example, 40 years ago few workers or managers were aware of sustainability as part of their ordinary working lives, whereas, in the modern era the concept is better understood and influences behaviour and with it the emergence of a distinct or even dominant organisational culture or sub-culture. Schein (1984) effectively articulates this process by highlighting that organisational culture is a process that can be learned and unlearned. That is, the behaviours, attitudes and beliefs that supported its aims in one period may give way to new ones as the situation or environment changes, and it has to adapt accordingly.

This chapter starts by presenting a formal definition and types of organisational culture, and the key elements of sustainability culture. This leads on to a discussion of the different approaches that managers can take to influence and shape the formation of a dominant organisational culture around sustainability practices and a critical evaluation of the means by which managers can position sustainability as part of a positive organisational culture. A theoretical framework of organisational culture contextualised around sustainability is then used to form the basis of a deeper understanding of how a sustainability culture can be formulated and developed.

ORGANISATIONAL CULTURE AND SUSTAINABILITY CULTURE

Organisations can be viewed as ordered and purposeful groups of people who collaborate to deliver goals and objectives within an organisation. The organisational culture plays a significant role in determining the achievement of stated goals and objectives. The dominant culture within an organisation emerges from shared values and beliefs that are based on consensus and implicit assumptions held by group members that inform behaviour. Importantly, these factors determine how workers perceive and react to changes within the organisation and manifest themselves in the formation of norms of behaviour that can have either positive or negative consequences. Inevitably, organisations seek to influence the formation of a positive culture as that is most conducive to achieving stated aims and objectives. New recruits in an organisation will be exposed to these values, beliefs and norms of behaviour in both explicit and subtle ways as part of their initiation into the fold. Acceptance within the organisation will be largely dependent on how quickly and how well newcomers adapt their behaviour to fit into the dominant culture (Combe, 2014). This form of socialisation underpins the dominance of the culture and helps it to endure. Every organisation has a unique culture and although some have tried to mimic successful ones, there is no prospect of entirely replicating an organisational culture. Both individual and group behaviour reflect the accepted norms, beliefs and values with reinforcing outcomes that ensure the maintenance of the dominant culture. These can be underpinned by formal codes of conduct or informal signals around behavioural expectations. Sometimes a dominant culture emerges, or a series of sub-cultures. They are changeable and dynamic in nature. However, the main types were highlighted by celebrated management writer Charles Handy (1993) and these are set out in Figure 9.1.

Power culture

A power culture is one characterised by the relationship between workers and the individual upon whom power is bestowed. How this power is applied is key to determining the effectiveness of a power culture. Reactions of workers will vary depending on the ways in which power is exercised by the individual or

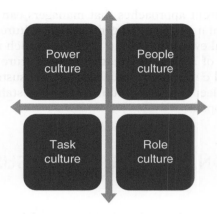

FIGURE 9.1 *Types of organisational culture*

individuals who wield the power. The way in which this dynamic plays out has a significant influence on the efficiency and performance of an organisation. This type of culture has longevity when workers believe in and follow the leadership of the individual with power. Effective leadership requires followers to legitimise the leadership power. Only when those with power lose the trust, and with it the following, of workers will there be a shift in the power culture towards an alternative, or a new lead who can re-establish trust with workers. There are a number of other factors that can destabilise and undermine a power culture within an organisation such as the size of the organisation (the power dissipates as managing complexity and scale becomes more problematic) or when the leader leaves. The power culture may coalesce around the style, personality or charisma of an individual and when that individual leaves the power culture may be eroded as a consequence leading to the emergence of a new dominant culture. That is, it may not be possible to replicate the characteristics and attributes of the individual who previously wielded the power in terms of attitude, trust, management style, communications, respect among peers, or influence in the industry or at political level. In some cases the personality of the individual with power is inextricably linked to the brand or what the organisation stands for. For example, Elon Musk is not only the owner of Tesla but his persona permeates all aspects of the organisational culture.

People culture

The formation of a people culture requires the coordination of activities and attitudes, beliefs and values by a group of workers that combine to create a sense of purpose and mutual benefits to the group members. This may involve a sub-group within an organisation such as a special interest group or research group, or it may be a group formed for a specific purpose such as supporting a specific cause

INTRODUCTION TO GLOBAL SUSTAINABLE MANAGEMENT

or objective. These groups are defined by a shared common interest and aim that binds them together and helps maintain the people culture. Organisations that champion the cause of sustainability often exhibit characteristics of a people culture where the passion for the cause forms the basis for the collective. The Tauranga Carbon Reduction Group in New Zealand is an organisation set up to bring together stakeholders to inform and knowledge-share on ways to reduce greenhouse gas emissions. The culture of the organisation is people centred whereby ideas can be transformed into practical measures to contribute to the organisation's aims.

Task culture

Task cultures are linked to activities carried out within organisations such as sales, marketing, production, customer service, logistics and so on. Specific tasks are assigned to groups of workers who often specialise in value adding activities that help achieve stated outputs or aims. The development of a task culture depends on a flexible and dynamic set of relationships from different parts of the organisation that combine to apply skills and experience to achieve specified outcomes. An example is project management whereby a task culture combines different staff skills and expertise to complete set tasks. In many modern sustainable organisations this is essential for driving innovation for the development of sustainable products and services that add value to customers whilst creating positive environmental impacts and reducing carbon footprints. The task defines the culture and informs the attitudes and behaviours of workers operating within the groups.

Role culture

The range of different activities undertaken in an organisation determines the types of roles that need to be carried out by individuals or groups. These roles may be well established and offer a level of stability and efficiency to the activities in an organisation based on the assigned and specialised roles given to individuals and groups of workers. The factory setting is one whereby the role culture is most obvious as each member of staff is assigned a role and work activity. It is also prevalent in bureaucratic or administrative types of work environments. Hierarchical organisational structures that assign authority and a span of control are typical characteristics of a role culture. This enables organisations to spread the tasks among their workers and avoid duplication of effort.

Handy's framework sets the scene for identifying possible determinants for the formation of an organisational culture. However, it is built upon assumptions that place limitations on its effect. For example, the assumptions may only reflect the ideology of management rather than support greater clarity or insight into organisational culture. The assumption that managers can undertake forms of 'social engineering' to influence and shape a positive culture is contentious. Although some influence may be evident, the formation of a distinct organisational culture that aligns directly to organisational aims and objectives is often elusive. The complex nature of organisational culture makes this type of management intervention problematic. The sub-cultures are often the source of tension and conflict and are often working against each other. That is, organisational culture rarely, if ever, comprises a single and unified entity. Nevertheless, managers do seek to exert some influence on the formation of a positive culture and it is worth exploring this in more detail in the context of the development of a sustainability culture.

Sustainability culture

Sustainability culture refers to sustainability development based on cultural beliefs, values and norms of behaviour that affect social, environmental and economic impacts of an organisation. Sustainability becomes embedded within an organisational culture when it informs decision-making, behaviours, attitudes and practices of the workers and management. The dominant culture of an organisation is often linked to the vision first put in place by the founders of the business and will reflect their aspirations and how they view the business growing over time. Core values are established and a clear understanding of what the organisation stands for is set out. However, over time this may be subject to change as the environment changes and priorities need to be revised. For example, organisations that now have a strong sustainability culture may not have started out with that concept featuring as part of their vision.

> **Definition: Sustainability culture** is a set of beliefs, values and norms of behaviour that support and drive economic, environmental and social development without doing harm to people or the planet.

Sustainability has developed into a key strategic issue across multiple industry sectors and has required a transition to embrace the concept and ideas that support it. This has had the effect of realigning organisational cultures around the principles of sustainability to varying degrees. In other words, a sustainability culture has required a whole new form of socialisation of group members to embed the new and evolving values and beliefs around the concept. Over time, an organisation that aspires to develop a sustainability culture will identify and select workers who demonstrably support this ethos and who share the values expected by the organisation. This helps to maintain the sustainability culture and works in tandem with top management who are the principal architects of the values, beliefs and norms of behaviour that support and maintain the sustainability culture. Sustainability can be addressed differently in different organisations, with some exhibiting a selective approach to practice and in others a more integrative or holistic approach is taken (Gerner, 2019). Determining these factors is important for organisations committed to embedding sustainability practices as part of their strategic aims and objectives as it helps to represent a source of the organisation's identity, values, creativity, environmental impact, social responsibility, and economic growth. Sustainable management practice is a vital component of this process and plays a key role in developing and maintaining a positive culture based on sustainability principles.

Mini case 9.1: Cascades, Canada

For many organisations the rising profile of sustainability has encouraged closer engagement with the concept and practices over a period of time. Different organisations transition towards building a sustainability culture at variable rates of change. In some instances, organisations have had a long-standing commitment to sustainability and this has helped them to develop distinct cultural formations around the concept. One such is example is the Canadian packaging and hygiene experts Cascades, ranked 17th for best practice in sustainability by the Global 100 index in 2020.

Cascades was founded in 1964 and now employs over 11,000 people in dozens of production units across North America and Europe. The organisation has built a reputation for sustainable, innovative and value-added solutions to packaging that has been based on good quality products and services, effective research and development for continuous improvement and a participatory management approach that has lent impetus to the formation of a positive sustainability culture. The organisation now benefits from its long engagement with practices that support economic growth, protection of the planet and respect for workers. This engagement stretches back to the 1960s when Cascades adopted sustainable practices that made them pioneers in the field. The vast array of learning, knowledge and experience garnered through practice and research in the intervening years has elevated the company to global leadership status when it comes to sustainability best practice around recycling for the circular economy.

One of the important advantages that Cascades possesses is the ability to tap into the positive sustainability culture that is a central feature of the workforce and management. Recycling was introduced into the company long before it became a widely accepted practice and new recruits are trained in the practice as soon as they arrive onsite, thereby quickly ensuring it becomes part of the everyday working culture. The organisation has used this key asset to set out an ambitious sustainability plan called 'Driving Positive Change' featuring 15 defined targets for 2025 and 2030. Four main pillars of the plan include Respect for the Planet, Solutions Driven, Community Minded, and People Focused. Although the organisation has already reduced its greenhouse gas emissions by 50% since 1990, the new plan sets targets for further reductions and has a commitment to having 100% of packaging manufactured and sold being recyclable, compostable and re-usable by 2030. Although the development and use of technology will play a role in achieving the raft of sustainability targets set out in the plan, the key to success lies in the

(Continued)

organisational culture that has sustainability at the heart of business relationships, business practice and processes, and the quest for gaining knowledge and experience.

Questions and task

1. Access the Cascades sustainability action plan 'Driving Positive Change' (2021) and identify the 15 targets set for 2025 and 2030.
2. What UN Sustainable Development Goals does the plan align to?
3. What community minded goals has Cascades set as part of the sustainability action plan?

MANAGEMENT INFLUENCE ON SUSTAINABILITY CULTURE

As sustainability culture can support effective internal and external relationships, improved efficiency, acceptance of change, and improved performance, it is evident that managers have a vested interest in how best to exert an influence that helps to create a positive culture around the concept of sustainability. Where strong cultures reveal the values and beliefs firmly held among workers in one setting, another may only exhibit a tenuous link between these. The relative strength or weakness of a sustainability culture will have a bearing on the level of behavioural control that is exerted by management on workers. Various prescribed actions, monitoring and evaluation are examples of this. A strong sustainability culture will feature characteristics of shared beliefs that manifest themselves in the form of commitment and unity of purpose around sustainability attitudes and practices. Sustainability culture may also be influenced by individual values and beliefs too (Kiesnere and Baumgartner, 2019). Weak sustainability culture will exhibit more fragmented attitudes towards sustainability by workers and no real sense of common purpose around sustainability that binds workers together.

The elevation of sustainability as a strategic issue in many organisations has intensified efforts by managers to influence the creation of a strong and positive sustainability culture. Keys to the effectiveness of this include being able to communicate a clear vision of how sustainability fits within the strategic aim of the organisation. This requires 'buy in' by workers who share the vision and, crucially, how their role supports the attainment of strategic aims that underpin the vision. Consequently, managers must clearly and precisely communicate their vision for the sustainability strategy that is both understandable and attractive to workers. Millar et al. (2012) provide a useful insight into how sustainability is a catalyst for organisational change and transformational vision. A distinct sustainability strategy that workers perceive as coherent and achievable also acts as a means of building a strong and positive sustainability culture. Necessarily, this requires acceptance of change, and different approaches to undertaking activities internally, all of which present challenges to the workforce, some of whom may prefer the status quo. In strong and positive cultures, the workforce may be open to change and accept it as a necessary part of their working environment. In weak cultures the response may be negative and lead to resistance.

Managers can influence a positive sustainability culture by delegating more responsibility and power to workers, leading to higher commitment and engagement in sustainability practices. This can be an effective means of demonstrating stakeholder value as it offers an opportunity to create a vested interest in the welfare of both the organisation and the wider society. However, managers need to be aware that these influencing factors can generate different responses with no guarantee that workers seek or thrive in situations where greater power is bestowed upon them. Caution is required when making generalisations or assumptions regarding the appropriateness or effectiveness of any particular influencing factor.

Managers can influence the creation of a positive sustainability culture by introducing opportunities for workers to bond more closely as a unit around specific sustainability projects. For example, they may be given the task of identifying carbon reduction opportunities throughout the organisation, initiate waste management processes, or facilitate recycling practices. Incentives may link to enhanced sustainability performance through group collaboration and cooperation and often include economic rewards, promotion, access to further sustainability skills training, or increased decision-making power for individuals or the group. Of these incentives, economic rewards exhibit the most limited effect as the reward for performance quickly becomes the norm. Worker 'buy-in' to the ethos of sustainability has to include a genuine belief in the value of the concept beyond what it can deliver to the individual. Rather, the main incentives need to align to the contribution that participation in the sustainability strategy can deliver in more subtle and 'care' orientated forms. Thus, influencing a sustainability culture may involve allowing workers more freedom and opportunities to make decisions that affect their role within the organisation, introducing opportunities for extending their skills through changes to the job design that encourages multi-skilling and multi-tasking around sustainability practices, organising knowledge sharing opportunities (both formal and informal) or introducing peer reward schemes where the attainment of qualifications, skills standards or other attributes that support sustainability practices are formally recognised. Research by Farooq et al. (2019) points to employees with a high level of organisational identity being able to influence the sustainability strategy through the participation process.

Another important influencing factor that managers rely on is trust. Trust can be defined as a positive set of attitudes, values and behaviours that can be the catalyst for superior performance. Essentially, trust can be viewed as a psychological 'contract', an unwritten understanding between employer and employee-based factors such as goodwill, 'buy-in' to the shared vision, and a willingness to go above and beyond the formal employment contract agreement. This informal understanding often emerges most powerfully in organisations that have a vision and mission with higher ideals and aims that workers have an emotional affiliation to. For example, environmental organisations such as Greenpeace or Friends of the Earth attract workers who are committed to the ethos of the organisation. NASA scientists perceive a value that benefits all of humanity in their work. Medics with Medicin sans Frontiers are motivated to bring healthcare to those usually marginalised from such services. In the commercial sector, many organisations have concentrated on re-establishing trust with the wider consumer base in the wake of the 2009 financial crisis that so seriously eroded the relationship. Trust is a vital component in efforts to reinvigorate enterprises by enhancing the quality of relationships with stakeholders. The increased awareness and desire for action on sustainability has offered a pathway for organisations to demonstrate their corporate social responsibility in ways that help to build back that trust. There is also a well-recognised correlation between levels of trust and business performance that makes managing the re-emergence of trust a catalyst for renewal and growth across economies even more important. Adonis (2006) notes that part of the influence that managers can wield is to be proactive in re-establishing a culture of trust, forming relationships by using effective communications, openness and transparency with workers, suppliers, customers, clients and other stakeholders.

SUPPORTING A SUSTAINABILITY CULTURE

There are numerous ways in which a sustainability culture can be nurtured, managed and influenced and each will have their own distinct effect. Three of the most important ways of supporting efforts to create a sustainability culture are the formation of an appropriate organisational structure, building mechanisms for knowledge sharing and learning, and being proactive in managing the changes needed to incorporate improvements in sustainability practices and processes in the organisation. Although these can be discussed as individual factors, it can be seen that they are inter-linked and have a high level of cross-reliance to effect the added value they bring to developing a positive sustainability culture. Figure 9.2 illustrates the close interaction of these three key factors that support the development of a sustainability culture.

Organisational structure

The prevalence of knowledge sharing within organisations in the modern era has led to the dismantling of traditional, hierarchical structures of organisations and replacing them with flatter, more democratic forms of structures that facilitate sharing. Autocratic and controlling forms of management have been replaced by

FIGURE 9.2 *Organisational support mechanisms for sustainability culture*

styles that reflect the egalitarian and trust-based relationships that characterise many modern businesses. This form of structure is most conducive to supporting sustainability processes and practices. Even before the emergence of the Covid-19 pandemic, many workers were located away from the physical premises of their employers. Thus, organisations need a structure that is flexible, agile and based on effective knowledge sharing, mostly via the use of information technology. Knowledge sharing within an agile organisation is an attribute that underpins sustainability strategies and is one of the keys to creating a positive sustainability culture.

The organisational structure evident within organisations gives some indication of the priority that sustainability is afforded. Organisations that are fully committed to sustainability reflect this in the formation of roles at the executive level whereby specific areas of responsibility are demarcated, such as that of a Chief Sustainability Manager who has a seat on the board and is empowered to manage the environmental and social corporate responsibilities of the organisation. It is also a position that reflects the distinct sustainability culture that is appropriate for the organisation, what it stands for and what its core values are. Organisations that do not support sustainability with representation at the highest level are normally unable to set a coherent strategic pathway to developing an effective sustainability culture as the lower-level managers and workers do not perceive any formal leadership permeating throughout the organisation based on sustainability practices and processes. There are usually a series of practical measures that are implemented that underpin a commitment to sustainability that emerge from a structure that is conducive to shaping and designing them. Thus, sustainability aims and objectives, policies, regulations, codes of conduct, sustainability audits, and reporting mechanisms are just some of the means by which sustainability practices and processes can be initiated by managers empowered to drive forward the sustainability strategy. All of these have an influence on the development of a sustainability culture as it becomes part of everyday business at all levels within the organisational structure. However, it is worth noting that the implementation of any specific type of organisational structure does not guarantee advances in sustainability performance. Soderstrom and Weber (2019) provide useful insights from research into corporate sustainability efforts linked to organisational structure and reveal significant variations in outcomes.

Mini case 9.2: Storebrand, Norway

The Norwegian finance, insurance and asset management company Storebrand was established in the mid-eighteenth century and is one of the country's best known brands in the financial services sector. The company has a long association with sustainable finance and investments and has extended this concept throughout their portfolio of services. This has led to the development of a sustainability culture in the organisation that has been developed and nurtured over a long period of time. For example, Storebrand has systematically identified future managerial candidates based on gender equality criteria. This links to the company's management development in areas of strategy, communications and change. The aim of the human resource initiative is to ensure that the company's future sustainability management needs are met whilst, simultaneously, practising equality and diversity principles that reflect the changing needs of the society they serve. This has filtered through to the emergence of a dominant culture within the organisation based on those principles and values. This also reflects the belief of managers that stakeholders' values are based on trust-forming relationships with the company and that sustainability is also a key driver of corporate value and performance. Consequently, the environmental, social and economic impacts play a key role in decision-making throughout the organisation.

The drive towards a positive sustainability culture requires the appropriate structure to be put in place that supports the range of activities where sustainability practices are evident. At Storebrand this has taken the form of two dedicated in-house ESG Teams (environmental, social and governance) who work with investment analysts to ensure that ESG factors are incorporated into investment decisions. These two teams consist of the Risk and Ownership team and the Solutions team. Each is a reflection of the development of a sustainability culture that has a direct and meaningful influence on the way that the company evaluates the Triple Bottom Line factors in their investment decisions. This is especially evident in the exclusions policies that underpin the 'Storebrand Standard', a mechanism for setting minimum thresholds linked to ESG criteria that help their analysts decide whether or not to proceed with investment management services for individual companies.

INTRODUCTION TO GLOBAL SUSTAINABLE MANAGEMENT

The criteria used relate to the proposed client company's position in global trends linked to use of resources, the company's sustainable business practices, and their financial robustness. Also, the structure of Storebrand means that a number of departmental heads have been put in place to oversee this process including those for sustainable investment, human rights, anti-corruption and climate change. The Solutions team is responsible for investment analysis and fund-managing companies with sustainable solutions to the challenges presented by the UN Sustainable Development Goals.

The development of a sustainability culture at Storebrand has been supported by a distinct and effective organisational structure that reflects the importance that sustainability has for the reputation and competitive position of the company. The organisation sees sustainability as a key strategic issue that merits representation at the highest level of decision-making and this priority sets in train the values and beliefs around sustainability practices that permeate throughout the organisation and influences the way workers view and work with sustainability issues. The company's reputation for supporting sustainability has been widely recognised by clients and partners leading to the award of the world's most sustainable insurance company in 2020 by the Global 100 index at the World Economic Forum in Davos, Switzerland.

Questions

1. What role does a sustainability analyst at Storebrand undertake?
2. Why have management-level sustainability roles been established at Storebrand?
3. How does the organisational structure at Storebrand support the development of a sustainability culture?

Knowledge sharing and learning

The creation of a knowledge-sharing culture has become an increasingly important goal for managers since the emergence of digital and information technology. One of the reasons for this is that knowledge sharing has become an effective means of driving sustainability innovation and creativity that adds value to products and services. It also improves the efficiency of internal processes and can coordinate closer relationships with stakeholders. Formal and informal mechanisms can be created for workers to share knowledge internally such as interest groups for specialist sustainability practices or functions that comprise workers from different departments using video conferencing, dedicated web pages, workshops, publications and others. It should be noted that providing the mechanisms through which knowledge sharing is enabled is not sufficient to create a knowledge-sharing culture. In some instances, workers may protect knowledge for their own security or goals at the expense of others. In highly politicised working environments, the dominant culture may be one of knowledge protection which would require a significant cultural shift to gain knowledge-sharing advantages. Nevertheless, in the context of sustainability, culture plays an important role in determining how well knowledge is shared. Much depends on how culture influences assumptions about what knowledge is important. It also determines the relationship between different levels of knowledge, such as what knowledge belongs to the organisation and what belongs to the individual. Managers need to exert some influence on the creation of a dominant culture that is appropriate to their activities and stated goals. That is, managing knowledge sharing will require different approaches depending on the level of cooperation or competition that characterises the dominant culture in an organisation. Research by Oxenswardh (2019) confirms the prerequisite of understanding the drivers and barriers to knowledge sharing about and for sustainability.

The organisational structure should facilitate knowledge sharing and the knowledge should stem from a culture of learning. For successful organisations that are fully committed to sustainability, there is no need for managers to push hard-to-get workers involved as they already have 'buy-in' to the ethos of sustainability. Where real added value stems from is how a sustainability culture delivers new and innovative solutions to practices and processes. The organisational learning process plays a key role in exploiting the experience and knowledge created in the organisation at all levels and ensuring that these intellectual assets are identified, recorded, shared, and used to effect future improvements. To achieve this requires managers to support the learning by making it part of everyday activities, so that it becomes part of the norms of behaviours and attitudes that permeate the organisation.

Practical ways of supporting learning around sustainability practices include debriefing after important events and meetings, analysis of feedback from all involved in the process, and undertaking performance reviews. It is also important for managers to demonstrate that the most valuable learning and feedback can be transformed into action and implemented. This ensures that the exercise of learning is not merely an abstract concept but can be leveraged to gain added value. By applying effective communications throughout the process, managers can highlight examples of how new ideas can transition to implementation. This can act as a motivator for those involved in the process and should be supported by an inclusive approach featuring all workers and managers as well as other stakeholders external to the organisation such as suppliers and consumers. The effective development of a sustainability culture requires leadership, and this is discussed in more detail in Chapter 10. However, it is worth noting that all the means of influencing and driving forward a positive sustainability culture outlined above require leadership that is visionary, open to new ideas, inclusive, and fully committed to the ethos of sustainability.

Managing change

Perhaps the most important of all factors that support the development of a sustainability culture is that of managing change. There is almost universal consensus among the business community that change is necessary to address the most pressing challenges of our times, such as climate change, loss of habitats, and ocean pollution among others. Although sceptics remain in some pockets of industry, the overwhelming majority of business managers and workers recognise the need for change and support efforts to address sustainability, such as the Paris Agreement on carbon reduction targets by 2050. However, the extent to which these efforts play out in reality is variable with some organisations seemingly either slow to change or paralysed by a form of organisational inertia that acts as a barrier to change (Narayan and Adams, 2017). Unless there is a willingness to change that informs the development of a sustainability culture, then no amount of policies, regulations or change initiatives will be sufficient to make a difference. Although operating sustainably has become a prevalent feature in management thinking, the effectiveness of it is dependent on how the changes required to embed this ethos into business practice inform the development of a dominant, or at least positive, sustainability culture. Added to this is the effect of external pressure as stakeholders also demand changes to the way businesses operate to better reflect their changing values and expectations.

The changes required by business to achieve net zero carbon can be considered transformational in scale and scope. This presents significant challenges for many organisations used to small-scale, manageable and low risk forms of change that tend to feature alterations to existing ways of operating. Transformational change necessarily involves risk, large-scale investment and, crucially, a new way of thinking that is reflected in the emergence of a new culture around sustainability. Apart from the scale and scope of change, managers have to contend with the reality that embedding a sustainability culture in an organisation is a permanent and on-going commitment that requires a continuous process of innovation, creativity and radical solutions to overcome the challenges presented by the drive towards sustainability. Simply abiding by the laws or rules set out by regulators will never, in themselves, be sufficient for ensuring that business transitions towards sustainability. Cultural change is a vital component to this process and one that takes a commitment over a long period of time before the results start to emerge. Meanwhile, other pressures are likely to exert themselves such as changes to the trading environment (Brexit for example), external threats (the impact of Covid-19 on performance), shareholder expectations (investors are still predominantly motivated by returns on investment), or political influences (tensions between trading nations threaten the free movement of goods and services). The impact of the myriad external pressures can have the effect of organisations becoming more risk averse and rolling back on the commitment to sustainability, making it less of a priority and diluting its influence on the development of a sustainability culture. However, as has been discussed, sustainability is not an issue that can be visited only occasionally; it has to be a long-term, permanent and meaningful commitment that brings transformational change. The level of business commitment varies between different national cultures too. Some countries are almost hard-wired to seek and accept business change, such as Japan and Taiwan, whereas others are more conservative and risk-averse, such as Portugal and Germany (Burton, 2015; Fietz and Gunther, 2021).

To fully embrace sustainability, it is clear that organisations need to transition towards it by adopting a radical new approach to operations and practices, including the types of relationships built with stakeholders. This requires a cultural shift away from risk-averse and static models towards transformational and dynamic ones. The litmus test of how well they manage this change will be the evident shift in culture towards one where sustainability forms a key, if not dominant, role. This may be perceived as a tall order but is one that is governed by events. Evidence from multiple different and respected scientific institutions informs us of a climate emergency with dangerously high levels of global warming now beginning to visibly affect the lives of citizens and wildlife on a global scale. The size and seriousness of the problem requires radical intervention and change management in organisations around the concept of developing a sustainability culture is a necessary, and urgent, requirement of the business community.

Mini case 9.3: Arcelik, Turkey

The white goods sector (fridges, washing machines, tumble driers, etc.) has faced significant challenges in transitioning to a sustainability future as it has traditionally been associated with poor records in recycling, waste management and greenhouse gas emissions from the wide range of appliances that are manufactured and sold in global markets. The nature of the products poses technical challenges to meet sustainability expectations of customers and, increasingly, the retailers who seek to market and sell the appliances. Some organisations that comprise the sector have taken a proactive stance in addressing sustainability challenges and made efforts to develop a culture that embraces the concept and alter perceptions of the industry.

Headquartered in Istanbul and with 22 production facilities in 8 countries (and sales and marketing offices in 34 countries worldwide), Arcelik manufactures some of the world's best known white goods brands including Beko and Grundig. The company is the second largest in Europe and is one of the leaders in research and development in appliance design. The organisational culture is based on managing change towards durable and sustainable appliances which has contributed to the organisation achieving carbon neutral status in global production plants in 2019. This makes Acerlik a recognised industry leader in sustainability according to the influential Dow Jones Sustainability Index in 2020. This recognition is the result of a very clearly defined strategy for developing a sustainability culture primarily around the design innovations that use cutting-edge technology to deliver durable and sustainable products. The sustainability design includes key elements of durability, energy efficiency along the product life cycle using Energy Management Systems, low carbon emissions, recycling all component parts, and working with supply-chain partners to reduce environmental impacts.

Driving forward the development of the sustainability culture and the actions that support it is the organisation's Sustainability Council with responsibilities for policies, strategies and corporate sustainability principles. The council sets sustainability aims and objectives and communicates to workers how their area of responsibility contributes to achieving these aims. Key Performance Indicators (KPIs) are devised and allocated to working groups to provide clarity regarding expectations around sustainability targets. It is evident that the organisation addresses sustainability challenges using a 'top-down' approach whereby the vision of the executive managers is transformed into a series of actions to support the sustainability culture under the control of designated sustainability working groups. Thus, the culture is defined by conformity to the sustainability principles. Although this approach to managing sustainability differs from the more inclusive approaches that define the culture in many other organisations, it has proven effective in delivering the changes sought by the company and the industry in terms of a sustainable future.

Questions and task

1. Describe the approach to managing sustainability principles at Arcelik.
2. What type of organisational culture is evident at Arcelik?
3. What sustainability characteristics do the designers at Arcelik include in their products?

A FRAMEWORK FOR SUSTAINABILITY CULTURE

Organisations have to build their capacities and capabilities to meet these challenges of change; they need to re-allocate resources to support it, and, crucially, they need to develop a positive culture that reflects the correct attitudes and values that underpin the business principles that support sustainability. For this purpose, it is useful to present a framework to help managers navigate the transition towards a sustainability culture. Bertels et al. (2010) provide an effective systematic review of how to embed sustainability in organisations and the framework applied here is an adapted version used in that important work. The key focus of the discussion is around identifying the practices that best support embedding sustainability in organisational culture. Figure 9.3 illustrates some of the key identified practices for this purpose.

FIGURE 9.3 *Framework for a sustainability culture*

Source: Adapted from Bertels et al. (2010)

This framework has four types of practices that can form the basis for embedding sustainability into the organisational culture including commitment, expectations, managing change and building capabilities. These then link to a series of practices that support the creation of a sustainability culture. Although these can be discussed individually, it is the extent to which managers are able to integrate them that determines the effectiveness of this process.

Commitment

A sustainability culture cannot emerge unless there is full commitment from all levels of management and the workforce within an organisation. Resistance to sustainability change processes will limit the effect of new practices and processes that support it and undermine the vision of management for embedding sustainability into the organisational culture. There are a number of ways that managers can encourage a positive attitude and belief system around sustainability that will manifest in a high level of commitment to the concept. Three ways of building a commitment include the ability to engage, reinforce and communicate as illustrated in Figure 9.4.

Engagement efforts are more effective when undertaken in an informal way rather than through dogma or doctrines that are usually underpinned by policy or rules (even though Mini case 9.3 on Arcelik showed that some traction can be gained from these approaches too). It is important that managers are able to enthuse workers about the benefits of adopting sustainability practices and to set out the means by which engagement can be expressed in practical ways. This may include education and training programmes designed to raise awareness and knowledge around sustainability practices. Sustainability practitioners from other

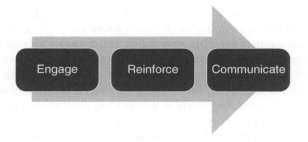

FIGURE 9.4 *Building commitment to sustainability*

fields of expertise can be used to communicate and educate workers as to the benefits. Workers may be able to attend workshops or demonstrations that build their experience and knowledge. As knowledge builds then workers will be in a position to generate ideas around how to improve sustainability practices in their own sphere of influence or workstation. They can also transfer the good practice they learn externally (such as the home, communities or social settings) to the workplace, such as waste management, recycling or energy-saving practices.

Managers need to facilitate the means by which workers can undertake practical solutions to sustainability challenges. This means putting in place the infrastructure to support good practice, removing barriers to participation, and disseminating information around innovations in procedures and processes that support sustainability. Importantly, managers need to build engagement by broadcasting widely the successes that emerge from good practice. Reinforcing the positive outcomes of engagement and communicating them effectively are essential means by which commitment gathers pace. When workers can see the benefits of participation, their engagement levels rise, and they become increasingly motivated to join in the good practices. Over time, this process contributes to the development of a sustainability culture.

Expectations

It is important for the development of a sustainability culture for managers to make clear what the expectations are. At the formal level, these include goal setting, policy development and the means by which practices are operationalised. Goals can be set at all levels of the organisation from individual through to business units and departments. These can incentivise workers as they work to set targets that are formally recognised and, possibly, rewarded. Here, it is important to introduce a measure for each of the sustainability targets so that expectations are clear and manageable and much depends on where the bar is set for each target. It is a fine balance between challenging and motivating workers to extend their capabilities and setting unrealistic targets which can only lead to failure and demotivation. Nevertheless, taking a formal approach also helps managers allocate resources and coordinate activities around sustainability practices.

The formal approach also includes creating policies that guide the behaviour of workers. In many ways, sustainability practices require changes to habits, work processes and relationships. This may be in the form of a code of conduct, an ethical framework, health and safety regulations, quality assurance procedures, or procurement and supplier audits to ensure compliance with set standards. Sustainability issues feature in all of these including the protection of workers, waste management, lowering carbon footprints, recycling practices, partnering with suppliers who comply with organisational and industry standards, and environmental protection. Each of these can be explicitly stated, monitored and recorded. Intervention is possible where practices fall short of expectations. Over time, it would be evident that these practices and attitudes contribute to setting values and modes of behaviour conducive to building a positive sustainability.

The third element of the formal approach is the operationalisation of sustainability practices. This refers to how managers integrate these practices and behaviours into everyday activities of workers. This approach makes it clearer for workers to relate to what the expectations are and what needs to be done to achieve set targets. The presentation of formal procedures and policies helps workers to better understand the concept and translate ideas into actions. The effectiveness of this approach is variable however. Much depends on the context in which this formal approach is enacted. Workers in organisations and industries with a traditionally liberal approach to management and a laissez-faire attitude to working practices (creative industries) may find the formal rules-based approach stifling when it comes to innovation and creativity around the development of sustainability practices. In other settings, the emphasis is on processes and outputs (production line factories) and, therefore, policies, rules and formal procedures are typically an established part of the existing dominant culture.

Building capabilities

Capabilities that support a transition to a sustainability culture require key decision-makers to re-imagine what their organisation stands for, its core values and how sustainability fits into those attributes and characteristics. This requires adopting a holistic perspective by thinking through how sustainability can be a feature across the myriad different activities and processes that comprise the organisation. One technique for developing this concept is 'backcasting' whereby managers identify what the ideal position would be for the organisation at some point in the future and then work backwards to find ways of achieving it. Working backwards from the future vision sets in train the steps required to achieve it and may involve a complete review of products and services, processes, skills and expertise, partnerships, external and internal stakeholder relationships and so on. In the context of sustainability, this technique involves thinking through how practices can be radically altered to infuse sustainability practices throughout the organisation.

To action this requires managers to offer workers a certain latitude in exploring new ideas and solutions. Improvements in sustainability practices often emerge

INTRODUCTION TO GLOBAL SUSTAINABLE MANAGEMENT

as a result of experimentation by workers who have been given the scope to try new approaches or test ideas. Very often, ideas start with workers in specialist and functional areas of the workplace and this grows into self-started projects that include testing new ideas in situ. As noted previously, there should be mechanisms in place to take these initiatives forward and, where real added value can be demonstrated, implemented as part of the sustainability strategy. The extent to which workers are allowed to experiment and initiate ideas plays a significant role in developing a sustainability culture as this process becomes a norm of behaviour among workers throughout the organisation.

Many of the benefits of experimentation, generating new ideas, and taking forward initiatives depend on effective sharing of knowledge and information. Sharing information on all sustainability related developments is another important means of driving forward the strategy and supporting the development of a sustainability culture. Sustainability presents some difficult choices and challenges and the means by which these are addressed often involve internal collaboration or even partnership collaboration outside organisational boundaries. Inevitably, this requires some well-managed and coherent types of communication as well as judgement on what information to share, to whom and when. Ideally, management should work towards an ethos of knowledge sharing, and where possible this is the prevailing approach. However, care needs to be exercised in the manner in which this process is undertaken as there may be a risk to competitiveness if disseminated information reveals details of strategic intent. Nevertheless, sharing knowledge and information is a necessity to ensure that stakeholders are aware of the ideas and initiatives being developed and to gain insights into how they can contribute to new and innovative sustainability practices. Sharing is an important part of raising awareness of sustainability and can be the catalyst for generating new ideas and solutions across different functional areas of organisations. Externally, there may be opportunities to participate in knowledge sharing with other organisations where there are mutual benefits to be gained. This could include discussions on best practice or new initiatives by participating in trade conferences, exhibitions, chambers of commerce events, or industry awards events.

Action

A sustainability culture thrives on the ability of managers and workers to identify opportunities for creating solutions and undertaking actions required to implement them as part of a sustainability strategy. Understanding the level and characteristics of the existing sustainability culture can be ascertained by applying a gap analysis on commitment, expectations and the types of actions that have been implemented to support the development of a sustainability culture. This may involve an audit of each sustainability practice to determine its value, prevalence of use and what added value it delivers. The gap analysis can reveal the practices that best contribute to a sustainability culture and those that only have a marginal or zero influence. Building capabilities also involves supporting chosen practices or projects that exhibit high levels of influence. This is the implementation phase and forms the final part of the process. The capabilities link to each of the sub-sets depicted in Figure 9.3 and managers can decide which ones are most likely to deliver on their goal of developing a sustainability culture. As this process evolves, managers will become more informed of the practices that best contribute to sustainability and the development of a dominant culture around that concept. For those organisations committed to implementing a sustainability strategy, it is essential that the ethos and principles that underpin the goals and objectives include practical ways in which a sustainability culture can be influenced, nurtured and supported. As knowledge and experience build across a multitude of different industry sectors, the understanding of how this process can be managed improves and best practices diffuse throughout different industry sectors. It is already evident that sustainability cultures are emerging in organisations regardless of their different sizes, scope of activities or complexities. The extent to which this is evident remains variable, but the trend is positive and that augers well for meeting the challenges of climate change, social justice and net zero carbon targets that the global business community faces in the years ahead.

CASE STUDY

Sky Studios, UK

The media production industry in the UK is vibrant and world renowned for quality and innovation. The film and television production industry in London is the third busiest in the world behind Los Angeles and New York. Part of the success lies in the history and tradition of leadership in the development of a creative culture. The UK-based production companies have been at the forefront of innovation in the industry and attract talent from all over the world. As a demonstration of how the industry leaders engage with developments in the wider society, the film and television production sector has been proactive in engaging with the concept and practice of sustainability for almost two decades. Across many different

companies that supply services to the sector, a culture of sustainability has emerged that has contributed to efforts to make the industry eco-friendly and attractive to talented workers and consumers.

The industry is represented by the Production Managers Association (PMA) that offers guidance, support and networking opportunities for members involved in all aspects of film and television production. The PMA is actively engaged in a number of sustainability initiatives including the development of their own dedicated sustainability programme called the Green Wing. Other initiatives include Greenshoot, a sustainability management system bespoke for each production, Albert that facilitates collaboration across the industry for addressing environmental and sustainability issues, promoting best practice, and providing certification for sustainability standards, and Scenery Salvage that recycles used scenery and props. The British Academy Film and Television Awards (BAFTA) is also proactive in making sustainability changes to their awards ceremonies and helping the industry to transition towards a net zero carbon future.

One of the most proactive production companies for adopting sustainability practices is Sky Studios, part of the Sky network of companies. Among their portfolio of production outputs are the award winning *Chernobyl* documentary, *The Third Day* starring Jude Law and the BAFTA award winning *Patrick Melrose* starring Benedict Cumberbatch. One of the first media companies in the UK to go carbon neutral, Sky has been at the forefront of driving forward the sustainability agenda in the industry since 2006. Part of this process has been a concerted effort to develop a positive sustainability culture internally and across the sector. In particular, the production side of the business has been the focus of much of the development of practical ways in which workers can implement sustainability practices into their everyday duties as well as contributing to raising awareness and building positive changes to their profession. The commitment to become a net zero carbon organisation by 2030 (the Sky Zero campaign) has further focused minds on ways in which a sustainability culture can be developed, including investing in practical initiatives to support specific environmental causes such as the Sky Ocean Rescue project. Launched in 2017, the project helps raise awareness of plastic pollution in oceans and provides guidance on the practical actions that people can undertake every day to help tackle the problem.

At the production side of the business there have been significant changes implemented to support the development of a sustainability culture that involves practical actions. The 'Planet Test' is an initiative designed to raise awareness of environmental issues and to help editorial staff implement sustainability practices into the productions where possible. Three specified areas form a checklist for proactive editorial consideration around sustainability and each includes key questions around sustainability production values. These include:

1. *Raise the issues*: does the programme help the audience to better understand the world around them and the environmental issues?

2. *Show the actions*: does the programme show positive actions that support the UN's Good Life Goals? (Good Life Goals are personal actions that people around the world can take to support the UN Sustainable Development Goals).

3. *Around content*: how could the production engage viewers outside the programme?

This was one of several initiatives that informed the creation of sustainability principles that help shape the way in which the commissioning and production process is managed. There are six key principles that all producers and promoters at Sky Studios are expected to embed within their business practices including:

1. *Working in partnership* with service providers who align their business practices to achieving net zero carbon targets.

2. *Planning and innovating* to find solutions and mitigate carbon emissions throughout the production process. Each worker is issued with a 'Green Memo' that sets out sustainability guidance for them to follow.

3. *Measuring and tracking* the carbon footprint of each production development stage. Each stage has an 'Albert' carbon action plan that helps managers and workers to track progress throughout the production process.

4. *Applying the 'Planet Test'* to support efforts to create a positive sustainability culture through raising awareness and initiating change.

5. *Learning and sharing* as a means of building knowledge, understanding and expertise in sustainability practices and processes.

The sustainability principles underpin the drive to create a sustainability culture across the whole of Sky businesses, including production. Production managers are expected to take the lead in ensuring the principles are adhered to and are used effectively for ensuring sustainability practices are implemented. Communicating the sustainability goals to production workers (perhaps by holding team meetings, or issuing the 'Green Memo') helps to inform and enthuse workers around the concept and can be the catalyst for changes in the norms of behaviour that raise the profile and status of sustainability practices within the organisation. Here, it is essential that all production workers and managers are able to communicate and share knowledge about best practice or disseminate information on new sustainable ways of working. Many good practices have already been embedded in the production process including use of renewable energy, transport, waste management, recycling, buying ethically sourced supplies, catering using locally produced products, use of LED lighting, no single-use plastic, and many more.

The media industry has traditionally been associated with behaviours that point to excess and wastefulness but there is evidence to suggest that this legacy is being replaced by a more considered and sensitive approach to what the viewing public expects. There has already been a significant shift in cultural values throughout the industry to reflect the values of viewers and consumers. For example, research by Global Action Plan (2020) revealed that 77% of young people in the UK want to see environmental issues included in programmes. Sky Studios has been one of the leaders in initiating a cultural shift to reflect the growing awareness and challenges that sustainability brings to their sector of the media industry.

Question and tasks

1. Identify three initiatives that film and television production workers at Sky Studios can adopt to support the development of a sustainability culture.

2. What sustainability production principles support Sky Studios' commitment to net zero carbon by 2030?

3. Explain what 'The Planet Test' is at Sky Studios.

SUMMARY

This chapter presented different definitions for culture and sustainability culture to set the scene for further discussion around the different types of organisational culture. The work highlighted the power, people, role and task cultures to provide a basis for linking them to sustainability cultures within organisational settings. The work proceeded to offer a means of better understanding the key elements of the formation of sustainability culture and how managers can influence the development of a sustainability culture. Key influencing factors were identified as creating a vision, values and beliefs in the concept of sustainability, achieving workers' 'buy-in' to the vision, and operating an inclusive approach to participation or workers across the entire organisation. The support mechanisms for supporting sustainability were identified as the organisational structure, knowledge and learning, and the process of managing the change to transition towards sustainability. It was noted that these three elements are interrelated and combine to help support the coherence of actions that support the development of a sustainability culture. The chapter then used a theoretical framework as a basis for discussing some of the practical ways managers can influence and support the development of a sustainability culture. Four key pillars of support were identified as commitment, expectations, actions and the building of capabilities with related actions identified and critically assessed. The chapter has used theory, examples and analysis to provide a clear understanding of the importance of organisational culture as a key driver of achieving stated aims and objectives as part of a sustainability strategy in organisations.

REVIEW QUESTIONS AND TASK

1. What factors drive the emergence of a dominant organisational culture?
2. What is sustainability culture and how does it differ from organisational culture?
3. Identify a sustainability culture in a chosen organisation and explain how it is influenced and supported by management.

FURTHER READING

Ehrenfeld, J. (2008) *Sustainability by Design: A Subversive Strategy for Transforming Our Consumer Culture*. Newhaven, CT: Yale University Press.

This enduring work contains discussions on key issues linked to global warming and sustainability. In particular, the author argues that possible remedies such as eco-efficiency, sustainable development and corporate social responsibility are mere 'band-aids' and that the real problem lies in how humans are able to transform behaviours that will ensure mankind's longevity on Earth. The book highlights a number of practical ways that consumers can develop a sustainability mindset.

Pava, N. (2018) *Green Wisdom: A Guide to Anyone to Start, Engage and Energize a Sustainability Team*. Oakland, CA: Allegria Partners.

The author provides some valuable guidance gleaned from cases of business managers forming sustainability teams in their organisations. The discussion helps to better understand the process of incorporating sustainability into other practices that support the corporate business model, how teams are formed, embedded into the organisation and how they can inspire others.

Wirtenberg, J. (2014) *Building a Culture for Sustainability: People, Planet and Profits in a New Green Economy*. Santa Barbara, CA: Praeger.

The book provides a pathway to creating a culture of sustainability that is based on the presentation of 'best practices' identified in a number of well-chosen case studies from a range of different industry sectors including manufacturing, hospitality and telecommunications. The content focuses on the ways in which managers explain their vision for transforming their organisations into ones capable of meeting the challenges of sustainability and how this process can be the source of business opportunity.

10

SUSTAINABILITY LEADERSHIP

LEARNING OUTCOMES

- Understand and contextualise sustainability leadership behaviours.
- Understand the difference between leadership and management.
- Relate theories of leadership to their application for sustainability.
- Assess and apply a sustainability leadership model.
- Critically assess types of responsible leadership.

INTRODUCTION

Effective leadership is essential when organisations transition towards a business model which embraces, supports and promotes sustainability. Leadership acts as an enabler in shifting organisational culture based on a management structure, operational model and day-to-day activities which support positive impacts on the environment and takes steps to protect and preserve the planet for future generations. Leadership is an integrated part of an organisation and is normally associated with the need to identify a sense of direction for workers. This sense of direction contributes to the feeling of purpose, security and collectiveness as workers look for guidance, support and solutions to sustainability problems. Followers look to leaders for inspiration of ideas, motivation and guidance and expect certain qualities to be evident in the character of leaders such as confidence, judgement and persuasiveness.

Individuals who take on the role of leadership need to provide a guiding vision, drive and strategy around a common goal. They also need to capitalise on the organisational energy that delivers added value from tangible and intangible resources, competences and assets (Cole et al., 2005). By mobilising assets, synergies are developed which act as enablers of competitive advantage. However, in the context of sustainability there is more to leadership than meeting economic performance targets. Sustainability leaders and their teams acting within a sustainable business ethos aim to use the organisational energy as a vehicle to develop a responsible business model designed to meet stakeholder expectations. Organisational energy drives employee motivation and involvement. Effective leaders in organisations with a sustainability strategy succeed in motivating their employees by instilling a sense of responsibility towards the natural environment and contribution to their local community. Leaders play an important role in maintaining high levels of motivation amongst their staff by seeking sources of organisational energy to be directed towards awareness and positive emotions around environmental and social aspects of sustainability. Thus, followers expect their leaders to develop and foster a working environment which respects the natural environment as well as social dimensions such as gender, colour and ethnic diversity.

This gives rise to the concept of responsible leadership whereby a heightened sensitivity to these factors prevails in the attitudes, beliefs and actions of leaders. Responsible leaders aim to develop a working environment which respects the organisation's employees, embraces diversity, and puts systems in place which ensure the wellbeing of staff. This, ultimately, can also improve economic performance. Inceoglu et al. (2018) have documented the impact of leadership behaviour and employee wellbeing and how positive leadership drives higher productivity levels. Individuals who take on the role of leaders need to be aware of the responsibility and accountability of their position. The role of a leader comes with appreciation of influence, decision-making power and impact on the beliefs and actions of the workers.

This chapter begins with an overview of the concept and definition of leadership in general and sustainability leadership in particular. The model of leadership expert John Adair is presented and discussed in the context of sustainability. The main characteristics of sustainability leadership behaviours are set out and discussed. There then follows an explanation of the key differences between leadership and management before going on to present and critically review different types of theories that have been developed to better understand leadership. A sustainability leadership framework is used for this purpose. The discussion highlights different styles of leadership and their characteristics in the context of supporting sustainability practices and processes. The chapter concludes by turning attention to what constitutes responsible leadership in the context of sustainability practices and processes.

THE CONCEPT AND DEFINITION OF LEADERSHIP

Leadership requires a following to be considered valid. Only when people 'buy into' the influencing power of a leader does it become an effective tool. Leadership is the ability to influence others to behave in ways that are conducive to achieving the aims and objectives set by the leader. In a business setting, leaders create the vision and mission of an organisation and determine its strategic direction and goals. To achieve these requires the workforce to respond positively to the direction given by the leader. Thus, leadership consists of a mix of different skills and attributes such as communication skills, analytical abilities, strategic thinking, inspirational and motivational personal traits, charisma and personality, intelligence and so on. Leaders may specialise in just one of these and still be effective, or they may possess a mix of them that proves sufficient to create a following.

> **Definition: Leadership** is the ability to influence a group in the attainment of goals or objectives.

Organisations are a collective of people working towards a shared vision, mission and a set of business objectives. The common sense of direction sets the organisation's resources towards a path of development and ultimately growth whether this is measured financially or in non-profit oriented key performance indicators. In addition, the organisation is influenced by its stakeholders' expectations, and their interests and power in influencing executive decisions. It is the responsibly of the organisation's leadership and management teams to ensure the organisation navigates the increasingly complex, dynamic and turbulent business environment in a sustainable and responsible way.

Leadership is present in all types of human activity from politics to private enterprise, from public sector organisations to sports teams. It typically involves an individual or a small team setting a direction and pathway for a majority of followers with clear aims and objectives. For leadership to be effective, authentic and to make an impact requires a collection of certain attributes which the leader or leadership team should possess and these are explored in more detail later in this chapter. It is important to distinguish between leadership and management. Leaders have a different role to that of managers. Managers are responsible for the operational effectiveness of the organisation at functional, business or corporate level. Managers are tasked with ensuring that the day-to-day operations run smoothly: supplies to the manufacturing process arrive on time and in good order; inputs are transformed into finished goods or services within the quality management parameters; customers receive their orders on time and are satisfied with their experience and aftersales provision. Managers also ensure resources are available to the required level and that the added value created from supporting identified activities in the organisation's value chain are developed to ensure continuous improvement.

By contrast, leaders are less concerned with day-to-day operational issues but, rather, concentrate on strategic issues, bringing stakeholders together, setting the vision, mission and strategic direction of the organisation. This vision, mission and strategic direction will impact across all levels of the organisation and engage all internal stakeholders. Throughout this process, leaders need to be able to project their personality to the workers, be able to think creatively about where the organisation needs to be positioned sometime in the future and how to get it there whilst generating enthusiasm and motivation among the followers. Although there are distinct characteristics that separate leaders from managers, it is possible to discern a cross-over between the two. Effective managers often exhibit leadership behaviour and attributes at different times when carrying out their duties. However, a key difference between leaders and managers is how they engage with the organisation's stakeholders with the former using both formal and informal mechanisms. The informal mechanisms are based on social dimensions and networks which shape and influence the impact of leaders on internal and external stakeholders. This is in contrast with managers who predominantly follow a more formal and structured approach. As Chiu et al. (2017) noted, managers are appointed by the organisation, but leaders are anointed by their followers and achieve results through persuading people to act in ways that support the leader's goals.

John Adair, a leading authority on the subject, developed the theory of action-centred leadership. According to Adair's (1973) construct, leaders build their organisation around three interlocking elements of achieving the task, developing the individual, and building the team. These can be discussed in the context of sustainability.

The first priority is to achieve the task. Organisations made of teams thrive when operating under a mission. Value builds when individuals put their energy, knowledge and skills towards a combined effort that helps achieve synergies towards a given task. Tasks may be located at corporate, business or functional level. Corporate level tasks are of strategic importance and aimed at identifying sources of competitive advantage. Corporate level strategies focus on the alignment of the organisation's business units to promote a common culture, ethos and set of values. The culture and values will, to a large extent, reflect the core beliefs of the leadership team towards sustainability. The leadership team looks for signals towards sustainability and in particular at industry trends, attitudes across the supply chain and the direction and likely impact of government policies. For business level strategies, the task may focus on identifying a new market segment or developing a new product. Such a task will most likely include working with new customers (business-to-business or business-to-consumer) and suppliers, and both of these groups will form new stakeholders. Suppliers need to pass an auditing process to ensure they fit the organisation's sustainability and corporate social responsibility agenda. Finally, at functional level, leaders and managers introduce business practices aimed at lowering the carbon footprint and energy consumption, make customers aware of the sustainability achievement (part of the marketing function), and source funding from sustainable sources (part of the finance function).

The second element is to develop the individual. Adair's interpretation of individual needs linked to Maslow's construct of the 'hierarchy of needs'. Maslow (1943) points to the physiological, safety, belonging, esteem and self-actualisation needs of individuals. Successful leaders pay attention to the individual needs and strive to provide their staff with a safe working environment with opportunities for training and upskilling, promotion, financial and non-financial rewards. Training will first focus on making employees aware of how sustainability enhances the working environment and relationships with external stakeholders. Making staff aware of the benefits of sustainability supports the future vision of the three levels mentioned above – corporate, business and functional. Developing the individual to embrace responsible business may facilitate the emergence of sustainability champions at business unit or functional level. Such initiatives align closely to Maslow's description of the individual's need for feeling a sense of belonging and achievement.

The third element is to build the team. Leaders aim to develop and build teams which are made of highly skilled and motivated individuals who work collectively towards achieving the task. As noted previously, the task may be located at corporate, business or functional level and aimed at mobilising a team of employees towards a common sustainability goal. Effective sustainability strategies require teamwork and a collective endeavour by workers. The type of leadership that supports this requires an understanding of how to form groups that possess the correct mix of skills, experience, motivations and personalities that combine to create value and achieve stated goals. This can prove problematic as human factors tend to be dynamic, changeable and often difficult to predict. The chemistry that binds one group effectively may be entirely missing in another. It is for leaders to make judgements about the composition of workers that comprise a team.

SUSTAINABILITY LEADERSHIP

Sustainability leadership exhibits many of the characteristics and attributes of general leadership but is distinctive in the form of the core motivation around environmental, social and economic factors. It is inextricably linked to responsible leadership whereby actions and communications are designed to affect a wider stakeholder group. Sustainability leadership entails taking a holistic vision of the organisation, devising a mission to support that vision, thinking strategically over the long-term, and setting goals and objectives that can be monitored, measured and evaluated. Sustainability leaders need to be accountable to the wider citizenship and be open to scrutiny around the decisions they take.

> **Definition: Sustainability leadership** is when leaders in organisations manage the organisation with positive environmental, social and economic sustainability goals in mind.

Sustainability leadership entails long-term thinking about where the organisation needs to be positioned sometime in the future to achieve sustainability strategic goals and objectives. Effective sustainability leaders need to exhibit a range of different behaviours to support this role with many of them coalescing around the building and nurturing of effective relationships with internal and external stakeholders that involve an understanding and sensitivity to their needs and expectations. Sustainability practices and processes can create value for stakeholder groups if leaders are able to engage with them in ways that demonstrate emotional intelligence and the type of behaviours that foster cooperation and collaboration. Some of the key behaviours expected of sustainability leaders are illustrated in Figure 10.1.

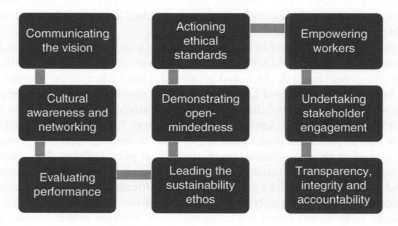

FIGURE 10.1 *Sustainability leadership behaviours*

There are a great many types and forms of behaviour that align to leadership but it would be quite impossible to list them all. Some are subtle and nuanced forms of behaviour, whereas others exhibit gregarious and charismatic actions that are both visual and impactful. Ex-Unilever CEO Paul Polman comes under the latter category with charisma, high energy and a communication style that is both confrontational and impactful. Under his charge, Unilever was able to demonstrate that it is possible to effect growth whilst being sustainable. In fact, the persuasive skills and vision of Polman proved to be a key factor in transforming attitudes of managers and shareholders to the view that sustainability was a real business opportunity. One fundamental aspect of leadership is the ideal of communicating a vision that the leader not only intrinsically believes in, but is proactive in championing through various communications behaviours. The vision is the basis of the sustainability strategy and needs to be crafted in a way that achieves both understanding and 'buy-in' from followers. To gain 'buy-in' requires leaders to be authentic, reliable and consistent. Much of this depends on the ethical stance they demonstrate as this sets the tone and ethos of the organisation that then determines the standards for followers. Emmanuel Faber, CEO of French food company Danone, achieved this by articulating his commitment to a 'multi-stakeholder' model whereby social and environmental priorities became embedded in the company strategy. In 2020, he won shareholder approval to change the legal status of Danone to one of a social enterprise. Here, it can be seen that the vision and ethical stance of the leader was transformed into actions that helped 'buy-in' from workers and other stakeholders. Sometimes ethical stances are transformed into formal ethical standards and codes of conduct that followers can use as reference guides to moderate their own behaviour. This can work by setting parameters around behavioural norms that support sustainability actions. Leaders can benefit from the 'buy-in' from workers by empowering them and bringing them into the decision-making process. Delegation and empowerment are useful tools that effective leaders have in their desire to influence, persuade and enable workers to follow their vision. Workers who feel part of what the organisation is trying to achieve will thrive in an environment whereby their input is recognised as important.

Workers are just one of a number of stakeholder groups that leaders need to communicate effectively with. This need informs many of the behaviours they exhibit including networking, engaging with audiences using different media channels, influencing the way their industry supports sustainability, driving forward the agenda in support of the vision, and using their personality to champion the cause of sustainability. This will often require a higher level of cultural awareness as it is likely that stakeholders will emerge from vastly different backgrounds with a range of different, and sometimes competing, expectations. This requires leaders to exhibit behaviours that are understanding, diplomatic, inclusive and sensitive. For example, Helena Helmersson, Chief Sustainability Officer at H&M in Sweden, had a formidable challenge creating a sustainability strategy for the fast-fashion company in an industry sector with a poor reputation in the field. Helmersson introduced a range of practical measures including more transparency in the supply chain and a recycling process. However, it was her ability to reach out to partners and policy makers in different countries that made the difference when introducing new systems for supporting sustainability that work locally. Active support for a culture of knowledge sharing is key, alongside putting in place systems that facilitate it. These skills support balanced relationships and encourage reciprocal commitment from stakeholders. Simultaneously, leaders have to be determined, candid, tough and open-minded, as well as being capable of standing firm under pressure. These forms of behaviour need to be expressed at appropriate times and in appropriate contexts.

Effective leaders become adept at judging their audience and their expectations and moderate their behaviour to gain favourable outcomes from engaging with different stakeholders. This can be enhanced if leaders are considered authentic and this often depends on the level of transparency and integrity that stakeholders assign to the leader. High levels of these attributes encourage trust and 'buy-in' by followers which can then be used to influence support for sustainability practices and processes. Leaders who are seen to be accountable for their actions, and who take responsibility for outcomes, build trust and benefit from the goodwill of stakeholders that leverages a greater following. The issue of sustainability has gained a higher profile in recent decades and has presented an opportunity and a challenge for modern leaders to emerge and exhibit the range of behaviours that elevate that profile to one that forms a new and dominant culture internally as well as influencing attitudes and behaviours external to the organisations they represent. Effective leaders in this context will be highly adept in the way they support the ethos of sustainability. This can be bolstered by measuring, reporting and acting on performance across a range of criteria that determines how the form of leadership is playing out in achieving stated aims and objectives. Effective leadership also involves holding others to account for performance and taking all necessary action to ensure that targets, goals and objectives are achieved. The combination of these attributes and behaviours give a glimpse into the possible ways in which leaders can build a following and persuade and influence people to support the vision around which the sustainability strategy has been created.

Mini case 10.1: Michael Mann, USA

One of the key sustainability leadership behaviours is to lead the sustainability ethos. This may sound like a relatively simple task if a person passionately believes in the value of sustainability for effecting the protection of the planet for future generations. An increasing number of people around the world subscribe to the ideals and principles of sustainability and there is science-based evidence on climate change that lends credibility to those who support change for a sustainable future. Alternatively, there are those in positions of power who deny the existence (or at least the negative environmental impacts) of climate change. Most infamously, ex-President Donald Trump believed climate change to be a hoax, and his former Secretary of State Rex Tillerson (ex CEO of oil giant Exxon Mobil) was similarly sceptical. Some scientists and entrepreneurs have also poured scorn over claims that human intervention is seriously affecting the climate and putting at risk the future viability of the planet. Moreover, the climate change deniers are not passive in their beliefs but, rather, they seek to influence opinion and wield their power to challenge efforts to implement sustainability practices into the business strategies of companies. In most cases, the impact of this change on the profits, growth and economic power of large corporations informs the mindset of the sceptics.

Taking a leadership role within the sustainability and climate change eco-system requires the protagonists to exhibit many of the behaviours previously discussed. One other key factor in the personality make-up of those who champion the sustainability cause is that of courage. Those with a vested interest in undermining the case for sustainability have been proactive in challenging the views and actions of supportive leaders. One case in point is that of geophysicist and climatologist Michael Mann who contributed science-based evidence from research into climate change over a 1000-year period. His seminal work of 1998 included a 'hockey stick' diagram that illustrated the exponential increase in global temperatures since 1900, caused predominantly by the burning of fossil fuels. The revelation brought an onslaught from climate change deniers leading to everything from a concerted media campaign to discredit his work to death threats. None of these attacks dissuaded Mann from changing any of his findings or continuing to champion the cause and he has defended his research ever since, winning several awards and gaining recognition for his work. The prestigious National Academy of Sciences elected him as a member and he has won numerous court cases against individuals and organisations that have libelled his reputation. The leadership that Michael

Mann has exhibited is determined by a number of different traits and personality characteristics, with courage being a central factor. His determination and meticulous academic research has been the catalyst for raising the profile of climate change in the public discourse and helped citizens to better understand the complexities and nature of the phenomenon.

Questions and task

1. Identify and provide a reference for Michael Mann's historic 1998 paper exposing the extent of climate change.
2. What leadership qualities does Michael Mann exhibit?
3. What does the 'hockey stick' diagram in Michael Mann's paper illustrate?

MANAGEMENT AND LEADERSHIP

Management involves overseeing various functions within an organisation including planning, organising and controlling. Leadership is also considered a function of management as it plays an important part in ensuring the effective running of an organisation. However, the attributes and characteristics of leadership are quite distinct from the other functions. For example, many of the skills required to plan and organise resources and to implement control mechanisms in an organisation can be considered tacit knowledge that can be transformed into written documents or passed on through knowledge sharing, education or training. Management techniques are often based on tried and tested operational guidance that can be learnt and then communicated to others in the form of direction. Leadership as an attribute is an entirely different prospect and cannot easily be passed on in this manner. For example, some managers create a following by the force of their personality or charisma.

Contrary to some of the modern-day thinking around leadership, it is difficult to teach people how to project such a personality unless they already have that innate ability. Many of the traits required to be a leader are in the genes – people are born with character traits that allow them to assume leadership roles. In some instances, leaders emerge because of their technical or competence-based skills. In these cases the following emerges because of the inspirational effect their abilities have on others. For example, Steve Jobs of Apple had a worldwide following due to his strategic and innovative thinking around applications of technology. Nevertheless, he still had to communicate ideas to a broad audience as a means of establishing that following.

Management and leadership are evident in organisations as they are inextricably linked. Kotter (1990) emphasised the order and efficiency that good management brings to an organisation whilst recognising that leadership is necessary to effect change and to provide motivation and inspiration to employees. Most commonly, the manager and leader is one and the same person as it is expected that the manager carries out functional duties whilst simultaneously displaying leadership qualities.

The distinction between management and leadership can best be described as functions that create order and stability and ensure that processes are carried out efficiently (management), and attributes and skills that inspire, motivate and effect change (leadership). Perhaps the most distinguishing feature of leadership is the attendant attribute of creating and communicating a vision for the organisation that inspires followers to want to contribute to its achievement.

LEADERSHIP THEORIES AND SUSTAINABILITY

The numerous leadership theoretical models that have been developed over time is a reflection of the interest in this role within organisations. For this chapter, leadership theory is presented and evaluated in the context of sustainability. Theory offers the basis for gaining an insight and better understanding of how pursuing sustainability strategic goals has an influence on different types of leadership. The chosen theoretical models that form the basis of the discussion are illustrated in Figure 10.2.

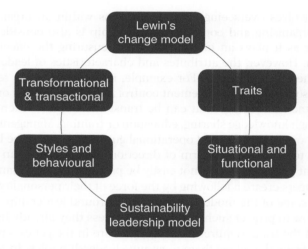

FIGURE 10.2 *Theoretical frameworks for leadership*

LEWIN'S CHANGE MODEL

Leadership behaviour stems from the leader's beliefs and exposure to others' leadership styles and experiences. Leaders arrive at the organisation with their own understanding of what sustainability entails, why it is important and how it can be achieved. Sustainability is a relatively recent milestone in management thought with universities and executive trainers having introduced the discipline in the aftermath of the United Nations Communities of the Parties (COP) 2015 and its subsequent Paris Climate Agreement. Leaders who are fully committed to sustainability are bold in their vision and adept at managing strategic change to realise their sustainability goals. An effective leader will be confident in driving the organisation through change by enthusing its staff and management team, pointing to the strategic advantages of achieving the vision and identifying development and training needs. Strategic change will engage Lewin's (1947) change model of unfreezing–changing–refreezing as set out in Figure 10.3.

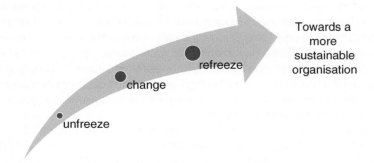

FIGURE 10.3 *Sustainability journey*

The three-stage model by Lewin starts with unlocking the challenges and resistance linked to introducing sustainability into the strategic and operational activities of the organisation. This is followed by the unfreezing stage that requires dissolving the status quo, cultural barriers and operational processes, and identifying the resources required to introduce sustainability practices within the organisation. Change follows a period of disruption and rebuilding new processes, norms and behaviours amongst the members of the organisation. Finally, the refreeze stage embeds sustainability practices into the architecture of the organisation making such practices part of the organisation's value chain.

Mini case 10.2: Gwénaëlle Avice-Huet, France

Undertaking and managing the three-stage model devised by Lewin in a modern, complex and highly competitive organisation is a significant challenge and requires a high level of business acumen and leadership, diplomacy and a vision of the future that followers can commit to over the long-term. Gwénaëlle Avice-Huet was appointed President and CEO of the North American arm of French utilities company Engie in 2019. Under the leadership of Avice-Huet the company has

(Continued)

undertaken a truly transformational shift from fossil-fuel energy to renewables, with around $15 billion of coal assets replaced by clean energy sources in 2020 alone. Previously an advisor to the French Prime Minister's office and the World Bank, Avice-Huet joined Engie in 2010 with the intension of 'unfreezing' the prevailing dominant attitudes and culture around the dependence on fossil fuels as the main energy source. This was a challenge both internally (many managers remained sceptical about the potential of renewables for growth) and externally (the White House and House of Representatives showed little enthusiasm for renewables at that time). Nevertheless, Avice-Huet led from the front with an almost evangelical zeal around her core belief that all industries will eventually transition to renewables and that Engie could steal a march on rivals by progressing this sooner rather than later. In particular, the emphasis was on constant innovation to deliver a mix of technologies that could deliver on the high expectations of client companies (24/7 to affordable and efficient renewable energy) and wider stakeholder groups (positive social and environmental benefits.

The changes introduced by Avice-Huet were radical but clearly thought through with some designed to facilitate process changes (recycling, better targeted procurement, adoption of new technologies such as bio-gas and green hydrogen, etc.) and others designed to change the organisational culture (an emphasis on innovation, new technologies, digitalisation and decarbonisation). The strategy was designed to amalgamate these two management approaches to deliver practical solutions to the need for change whilst simultaneously influencing behaviours and attitudes towards support for that change. Although there was resistance from managers, the long-term approach has started to pay off as the trend towards renewables started to gather pace across the energy sector. The change required further impetus and Avice-Huet set about reorganising and restructuring the company to decentralise control, delegate responsibility throughout the organisation, and empower people to make the innovative changes necessary to realise the vision. In an interview with sustainability support non-profit organisation GreentownLabs, in 2021, Avici-Huet noted that 'The company today is so different from what it was five years ago – and that is exactly what we wanted. Our focus on climate brings together the company, the employees, the clients and the shareholders. It shows that it's possible to reconcile economic performance with a positive impact on the planet'. Impressed by what Engie could deliver in the evolving renewables energy space, many companies sought partnerships or became clients of the company. For example, Microsoft agreed a deal to purchase renewables to support its wind and solar power projects in Texas. The attraction of such high-profile clients and the revenues they help to deliver vindicate the risk taking, visionary and entrepreneurial leadership style of Avice-Huet and has helped to set the company on a new strategic pathway that more closely aligns to stakeholder expectations of the future.

INTRODUCTION TO GLOBAL SUSTAINABLE MANAGEMENT

Questions

1. Does the case of Engie, under the leadership of Gwénaëlle Avice-Huet, closely align to Lewin's change model?
2. What leadership behaviours were evident in Gwénaëlle Avice-Huet during her time at Engie?
3. What process changes did Gwénaëlle Avice-Huet introduce at Engie to effect the shift towards renewables?

SUSTAINABILITY LEADERSHIP MODEL

Visser and Courtice (2011) developed the Sustainability Leadership Model and this has been adapted and presented in Figure 10.4. The model has three sections dedicated to leadership context, leadership traits and styles, and leadership actions. The leadership context relates to the internal and external environment and refers to the ecological, economic, political, cultural and community influences on the way in which sustainability leadership manifests itself and how it is exhibited based on the varying types of pressures that each exerts on leadership behaviour. For example, sustainability has become an increasingly politicised issue in recent years as contentious consequences become more pressing such as climate justice (the effect on one nation's welfare and resources as a result of actions by other nations' actions), or the pace and delivery of changes to support net zero carbon and the relative effects they have on citizens' work, life, health and so on. Internal organisational pressures also exert influence on leadership behaviours linked to sustainability and many of these have been discussed elsewhere in this book including the impact on different industry sectors, the organisational reach and culture, the governance measures put in place to ensure minimum standards of practice, reporting and measuring sustainability practices are observed, as well as the distinct role that leaders play within organisations.

Leadership actions are also linked to the type of leadership exhibited. These can be viewed as a set of actions that are applied internally and externally. The actions that link to internal processes involve key decision-making attributes that have fundamental impacts on the sustainability strategic goals. These decisions are predicated on a superior knowledge of the organisational resources and capabilities, the capacity for achieving set targets, an understanding of sustainability issues at industry level, an appreciation of the political environment in which decisions are taken and the ability to exploit knowledge gained from learning and experience to support new innovations that support sustainability practices. In many instances the leader will delegate or empower others to make decisions

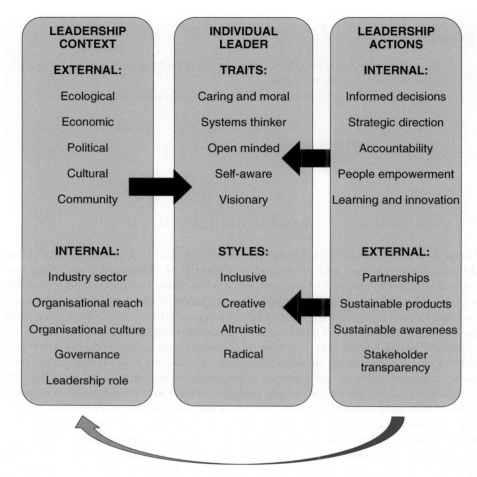

LEADERSHIP CONTEXT	INDIVIDUAL LEADER	LEADERSHIP ACTIONS
EXTERNAL:	**TRAITS:**	**INTERNAL:**
Ecological	Caring and moral	Informed decisions
Economic	Systems thinker	Strategic direction
Political	Open minded	Accountability
Cultural	Self-aware	People empowerment
Community	Visionary	Learning and innovation
INTERNAL:	**STYLES:**	**EXTERNAL:**
Industry sector	Inclusive	Partnerships
Organisational reach	Creative	Sustainable products
Organisational culture	Altruistic	Sustainable awareness
Governance	Radical	Stakeholder transparency
Leadership role		

FIGURE 10.4 *Sustainability leadership model*

Source: Adapted from Visser and Courtice (2011)

and the timing, scale and scope of this process depends on good leadership judgement. It should be noted, however, that engaging with sustainability challenges often entails dealing with paradox, contradictions and complexity. Very often there is no one right solution or optimal way of achieving aims. Setting targets in this environment can be fraught with difficulties and good leaders need to recognise these limitations and parameters.

All these attributes are exhibited and actioned within a business ethos based on high levels of accountability and integrity. External factors also influence sustainability leadership including building effective partnerships with suppliers, customers, regulators, government agencies, trade bodies, and even competitors. These are important when driving forward the sustainability ethos across the industry and beyond. Here, effective leadership skills involve networking, exerting

INTRODUCTION TO GLOBAL SUSTAINABLE MANAGEMENT

influence, promoting the development of sustainable products, raising awareness and persuading stakeholders to support the drive towards sustainability. These relationships need to be based on honesty and transparency to build the goodwill that is so vital to making progress in the sustainability eco-system. Leaders need to be proactive in creating opportunities for people to collaborate and generate solutions as a collective. Although directing people plays a part in leadership, the ethos around sustainability is more aligned to developing and implementing actions in collaboration with others. These attributes of leadership are shaped by the philosophy that underpins much of the efforts to support sustainability whereby no individual action exists in isolation but, rather, is part of a holistic view of the organisation and its environment where everything in the eco-system is related and interconnected, just as it is in the natural world.

TRAITS THEORY

A trait is an aspect of personality that influences behaviour in a particular direction. Personality traits are innumerable and often defined by complexity as they invariably involve wide-ranging innate characteristics formed by a mix of genetics, cognitive thinking, personality, intelligence, culture, education, upbringing, values and beliefs, morals and so on. Traits theory is founded on the idea that there exists some quality in certain individuals which distinguishes them from others and marks them out as leaders. The related 'Great Men' version of trait theory sees these characteristics as links to key attributes of innate qualities such as courage, determination, open-mindedness, knowledge and integrity. In the sustainability leadership model, key traits are identified as caring and moral (with the proviso that morals vary markedly between different settings and cultures), systems thinking, open-mindedness, self-aware and visionary. Many of these have been discussed previously but it is also worth adding a few more factors that underline effective sustainability leadership. These include intelligence (particularly good at solving complex and abstract problems), initiative (independence and inventiveness, and with the capacity to perceive a need for action and the urge to do it), self-assurance (self-confidence, high self-ratings on competence and aspiration level), and the helicopter factor (the ability to rise above the particulars of a situation and perceive it in relation to the overall environment).

Another trait often linked to effective leadership is that of extraversion. This personality trait aligns to those leaders who thrive in social situations, often exhibiting dominance or assertiveness. It can be seen that the force of personality is as significant as any leadership attribute such as knowledge and experience. Other traits are similarly evident such as emotional balance and resilience. These traits are often conducive to leading and effecting change. Contemporary perspectives of traits theory have less emphasis on innate characteristics and more on ideas linked to traits that are socially acquired. Importantly, the assumption that leadership as an attribute can be learned through education or training of managers is highly contentious. Even so, the number of proponents of this perception has increased markedly in recent decades and accounts for the exponential growth in training consultancies, commercial training agencies, and others who design their programmes on the basis that leaders can be created. This perception has also gained in currency among human resource departments whereby leadership traits form the basis of selection for certain positions.

A comprehensive list of traits has proved problematic with attempts at identifying common factors having variable value. A key limitation of research into leadership is the differences that exist in determining the qualities that make a leader in one organisational setting compared to another. In some industries, such as engineering, leadership qualities are often linked to technical aptitude, whereas in the creative industries it is more often the force of personality and inter-personal skills that define effective leadership. In many cases it is the situation that defines an effective leader. For example, the qualities that make Sir David Attenborough a prime candidate for being a 'great leader' and champion of sustainability are linked to the climate emergency that has been emerging in the last few decades. That situation requires leadership to communicate the seriousness of the position and to galvanise responses to it. Those, such as Attenborough, demonstrate a reputation for knowledge, insight, commitment and persuasiveness that the situation demands.

STYLES AND BEHAVIOURAL THEORIES

The styles approach to leadership is characterised by the need to include followers in any effective analysis. One of the ways in which effective leadership can be discerned is the ability to adapt in order to appeal to different types of followers and this becomes evident in the style of leadership displayed. Leadership style plays an important role in determining the level of organisational performance and accounts for its prominence among style theorists as they seek the most appropriate one for different situations. The styles approach outlined in Figure 10.4 relates to inclusiveness (being proactive in engaging with all stakeholders), creativity (problem solving), altruism (thinking of benefits beyond the self, or the organisation to include the wider community) and radical thinking (informed risk taking). These leadership styles require attributes of courage, understanding, sensitivity, knowledge, toughness, resilience, intellectual abilities, charisma, emotional balance and many more. This may explain why the very best leaders are a rarity and highly sought after. The traits and styles theories of leadership help to provide some useful insights into the characteristics that effective leaders exhibit and the effects they can have on followers.

SITUATIONAL AND FUNCTIONAL THEORY

Whereas proponents of trait theory posit that 'great men' (note the gender specific title points to a different age) are almost pre-destined to find their place in history through effective leadership, social scientists take a contrasting view. Leadership in this case results from the situations that emerge and where leaders take command to achieve goals and objectives. Thus, situational theory is based on the assumption that different situations require different types of personality or traits and that, by consequence, there is no one type that is dominant. The work of Hersey and Blanchard (1977) is an example of situational theory of leadership based on four leadership styles (from highly directive to laissez-faire) and four levels of followers (able, willing, unable and unwilling). For effectiveness, Hershey and Blanchard assert that the leadership style must match the appropriate level of followership development. Thus, leadership behaviour becomes a function not only of the characteristics of the leader, but of the characteristics of followers as well.

Functional theory offers a useful insight into leadership by focusing attention on specific leader behaviours that are expected to deliver organisational effectiveness. Early work by McGrath (1962) and later Hackman and Walton (1986) emphasises the key role of the leader as one of facilitating the needs of workers to complete tasks. According to this view, leadership effectiveness is determined by the extent to which the leader has contributed to group effectiveness and group cohesion (Fleishman et al., 1991; Hackman and Wageman, 2005). Functional theory is flexible and can be applied not only to group leadership but also at the organisational leadership level (Zacarro et al., 2001). Klein et al. (2006) highlight five main functions of leadership for promoting group effectiveness. These can be viewed in the context of sustainability leadership and include:

- Environmental monitoring
- Organising subordinate activities around identified sustainability practices
- Teaching and coaching subordinates on how to undertake sustainability practices
- Motivating others to adopt sustainability practices within and external to the organisation
- Intervening actively in the work of the group to ensure sustainability practices are observed and actioned.

TRANSFORMATIONAL AND TRANSACTIONAL LEADERSHIP

The main theoretical models presented in the previous discussion in this chapter have featured forms of transactional leadership where the individual leader directs, motivates and influences followers to act in ways conducive to achieving stated goals and objectives. Here, the leader communicates the nature of the task(s) and the role(s) required to undertake them to the followers. There are a number of factors that characterise this form of leadership. First, there is normally a reward system in place that is underpinned by a formal contract. This is necessary to ensure that followers are suitably rewarded for their performance. The reward system may extend beyond economic rewards to include promotion, increased decision-making powers, greater freedom to explore new ideas, leadership of a project team and so on. Second, the style of management may include intervention when actions or outcomes deviate from a previously agreed standard or pathway.

The type of intervention will depend on the leadership style; some may be passive (only intervenes when there is evidence of deviation) or active (seeks evidence of deviation). However, it is worth noting that transactional forms of leadership can include the laissez-faire approach whereby the leader takes an inactive, passive and non-interventionist stance. It can be argued that this barely constitutes leadership at all but much depends on the organisational culture and the reaction of workers to the environment that this style creates. Transactional forms of leadership rarely gain traction in building effective relationships that support sustainability practices. Monetary rewards, for example, are limited in the effect they have on workers over the long-term as the reward system becomes the norm and behaviours revert to type. To drive forward the sustainability agenda requires a form of leadership that is inspirational and capable of motivating in ways that becomes part of the organisational culture.

Transformational leadership is in stark contrast to transactional leadership. Fundamentally, it is more reliant on the force of personality and communications skills of the leader to inspire followers to undertake actions that are primarily in the interests of the organisation's sustainability strategic aims and objectives. In transformational leadership, self-interest takes a subordinate position to the achievement of the goal(s). Transformational leaders usually have a profound and powerful effect on those followers whose actions they seek to influence. Once followers 'buy-into' the goal or objective of the leader they become highly self-motivated in the tasks that help in the pursuit of the goal or objective. In the movement to tackle climate change, for example, Greta Thunberg has become a globally recognised transformational leader who has gathered a following in the pursuit of the goal of effecting social and political change to save the planet for future generations. Activist Malala Yousafzai has similarly created a following by championing the cause of equal rights for girls first in her native Pakistan and then, as the following grew, to a global audience.

In the sustainability business environment, transformational leaders inspire followers to seek new and better ways of producing, marketing and selling products and services in sustainable ways. Alternatively, they motivate people to perform beyond their current capabilities by encouraging them to engage in developmental activities or improving their skillsets that support sustainability practices. The key to transformational leadership in sustainable business is to influence stakeholders in ways that make them want to contribute to the organisation's sustainability strategic goals. This is achieved by instilling a sense of greater purpose in the followers, perhaps by giving a sense of pride to be part of something bigger and more rewarding than simply undertaking an agreed set of tasks for a specified reward. Sustainability as a concept and an ideal has characteristics that are conducive to eliciting those emotions among stakeholders. This is due to the future-oriented nature of the concept whereby the welfare and security of future generations are at stake. This emotional engagement is something that transformational leaders can tap into and use as leverage to communicate their sustainability vision.

Transformational leaders need to be able to communicate ideals and a vision that encourages followers to raise their performance and seek new and innovative ways of contributing to the organisation's goals and objectives. This may be expressed in a myriad of different ways including intellectual (such as problem solving), creative (new designs for products), innovative (new and better ways of producing the product) or emotional inputs (mentoring subordinates) that contribute to the achievement of sustainability strategic goals and objectives. The key characteristic of transformational leadership is that followers willingly undertake actions that add value and contribute to the goal achievement as a result of the respect, trust and admiration they have for the leader and the ideals he or she promotes. Consequently, transformational leaders tend to instil a greater ambition in the minds of followers.

Mini case 10.3: Jacinda Ardern, New Zealand

It is not only the business community that exerts leadership traits and style for the development of sustainability. Political leaders wield the power to make huge differences and drive forward the sustainability agenda. Some political leaders step up to the plate more readily than others. Some are ideologically or politically stuck in another age and seem impervious to the impact of climate change on the very citizens they purport to protect. In other cases, political leaders have taken proactive, and in some instances, radical approaches to using their power to further the cause of sustainability. One such case is that of New Zealand Prime Minister Jacinda Ardern.

Elected in 2017, New Zealand's Prime Minister has a very distinctive and effective leadership style that is based on her engaging personality, inclusive belief system and underpinned by authenticity of compassion and care. In the often cynical world of politics this has come as a refreshing change for many of her followers both at home and internationally. There is also a steely determination aspect to her personality that ensures she does not shrink from some of the big challenges that have marked her premiership. In particular, her tenure has coincided with an earthquake in Christchurch, a terror attack in the same city, and the emergence

(Continued)

of the Covid-19 pandemic. Part of her effectiveness as a leader has been the swift and decisive action she undertakes when a course of action has been determined. She implemented tighter gun laws in the aftermath of the terror attack on mosques in Christchurch. Her communications style is consistent, direct and concise. This helps her constituents clearly understand the message. She is also adept at displaying the softer side of her personality by reaching out to people (she thanked her 'team' of 5 million 'Kiwis' for their resolute response to her Covid-19 strategy) and showing the types of emotions that ordinary citizens display in challenging situations. Many voters around the world are weary of the adversarial and aggressive posturing of many politicians and the gentler, kinder and more empathetic approach of Ardern has won many followers.

Ardern is also a passionate supporter of efforts to tackle climate change and the development of sustainability practices. She has used her powers to effect changes that are both relatively small scale and radical in scope. For example, she initiated the plan to ban single-use plastics in New Zealand. However, perhaps her boldest move to date has been to drop Gross Domestic Product (GDP) as the main measure of economic performance for the country. The new measure includes economic, social and environmental factors thereby better reflecting the range of issues that most concern citizens. Significantly, the shift in mindset towards including social factors influenced the decision-making process in the early onset of the Covid-19 pandemic with the Prime Minister unhesitatingly locking down the entire country before a single death was reported. The quick and decisive leadership proved pivotal in New Zealand avoiding the high casualty rates recorded in countries where lockdowns were delayed.

Question and tasks

1. Identify three leadership behaviours of Jacinda Ardern that help to support sustainability practices in New Zealand.
2. Why did Jacinda Ardern remove GDP as the measure of economic performance for New Zealand?
3. Research and explain a policy introduced by Jacinda Ardern's government that supports sustainability in New Zealand.

RESPONSIBLE LEADERSHIP

Leaders and senior management teams dedicate their time, effort and energy in empowering their resources. The empowerment of resources (human resources and other tangible/intangible resources) aims to achieve a common vision and set of objectives. A degree of alignment in the beliefs, behaviours and norms when operationalising resources is typical when empowerment is required. Within a sustainability-driven organisation leaders respect, evaluate and utilise the diversity of their employees and by doing so support creativity and innovation across their organisation.

Drath et al. (2008) describe leadership as the task to promote and fulfil the commitment of the members of a collective (i.e. organisation) to 'subsume their own interest and benefit within the collective interest'. In order for the collective interest to materialise, a responsible leader in collaboration with their management team seek to create synergies in the interests, benefits and power of the organisational stakeholders. Synergies require alignment of stakeholder and organisational objectives. A dialogue will be required therefore amongst all the players to agree on compromises and ensure an ethical decision-making process has been implemented. The ethical decision-making process offers an equal opportunity to all voices within the collective to be heard to ensure a balanced decision which reflects the collective interest and benefit. This ethical decision-making process is, in essence, a dialogue which empowers and motivates the diverse members of the collective. Leaders with their organisational seniority play a very important role in driving motivation by displaying responsible leadership.

One of the competencies of responsible leaders is the ability to engage with learning, reflection and personal continuous improvement. Leaders of either a small functional team or leaders at the top of the executive ladder feel the responsibility and the impact of their decisions across internal and external stakeholders. Recognising their influential role across individuals and groups requires ongoing learning and reflection of past success, challenges and mistakes. A responsible leader seeks feedback from their peers and stakeholders by engaging in detailed and meaningful conversations and setting in motion a personal continuous improvement cycle that includes learning, feedback and reflection. In addition, responsible leaders recognise the importance of engaging with others to build their own management experiences. Leadership requires critical self-reflection and commitment to self-development. These two self-centred approaches expect the leader to be a good listener and to be able to learn from others. These help to form what could be considered as the responsible leader where attributes of honesty, integrity and trust are key.

Finally, responsible leadership can be exerted effectively for the development of sustainability within organisations. For example, at the social level, leaders must recognise the benefit of a diverse workforce. Diversity recognises and values differences in human resources including different backgrounds, knowledge, experiences and skills. Diversity is linked to equality and inclusion. Leaders who realise the value of diversity and equality have a strong belief in the notion that no one individual or group should be treated differently or less favourably. At the same time, effective sustainability leaders recognise that a diverse and inclusive culture is a source of competitive advantage and attracts and retains talent in the long term. A diverse talent pool is often more creative and capable of deriving the types of solutions required to meet sustainability challenges.

Ilham Kadri, Solvay, Belgium

Moroccan born Ilham Kadri is the Chief Executive Officer (CEO) of Belgian chemicals giant Solvay. Founded in 1863, the company employs over 25,000 people in 53 countries around the world. Specialising in the production of chemicals and plastics alongside other advanced materials, the company has built a formidable presence in the chemicals industry with revenues of over €10 billion registered in 2020.

The chemicals industry has traditionally struggled with a reputation for negative environmental impacts due to the nature of the products and the processes of manufacturing them. Generally considered to be hazardous to humans and the environment, the industry has faced major challenges in managing the transition to a more sustainable future. Consequently, the company has sought leadership that can drive the transition towards sustainability across its multiple value chains, build cooperation and collaboration with partners and competitors across the industry, and engage with stakeholders more closely. The appointment of Ilham Kadri to CEO in 2019 was a significant moment for the company, not only because she became Solvay's first female CEO, but also because it ushered in an era where social and environmental factors would be considered as equally important as economic growth in the strategic priorities of the company.

Kadri is especially committed to diversity and inclusion through creating a culture of mentoring for young women across the industry and promoting female leadership. Her leadership skills in driving forward the sustainability agenda has been evident in many of the posts she has held including those at Dow Chemical and Royal Dutch Shell. Her business acumen was demonstrated in the turnaround of the struggling Diversay Care company, the cleaning and hygiene arm of Sealed Air Corporation. Notably, Kadri led the technological innovation strategy at the company and helped launch the first global range of cleaning robots that now proliferate across many different industry sectors. This is in keeping with the attributes that she has demonstrated throughout her career whereby openness to new ideas, visionary, inclusiveness and entrepreneurial elements feature. When Diversay Care was acquired by Bain Capital in 2017 she became CEO of the newly formed Diversay company. The turnaround of the company involved a rebranding based on the newly acquired independence of the company and emphasised the ethical dimension to keeping customers safe when using the company products and a commitment to sustainability. Kadri saw the company as pioneers in their industry when it came to embracing sustainability practices. By 2019 she had attracted the attention of Solvay who sought a leader who could manage the economic growth ambitions of the company alongside the commitment to social and environmental protection. On her appointment in 2019, Kadri initiated the strategy G.R.O.W., the Solvay One Planet sustainability plan.

The Solvay One Planet sustainability plan was an opportunity for Kadri to bring together her leadership attributes. For example, the plan was ambitious in scope and entailed a significant amount of risk as the company was venturing into territory in which it had relatively little experience. Leadership qualities exhibited by Kadri aligned to her vision of what the plan should deliver for the organisation, and many of them link to the sustainability leadership model outlined in Figure 10.4. This included a bolder set of objectives (risk taking), a distinct pathway towards achieving stated social and environmental goals (strategic direction), meeting challenges through science and innovation (learning and innovation), and sustainability awareness (the plan was inspired by the UN Sustainability Development Goals). Kadri also exhibited traits conducive to pushing forward with her vision including open-mindedness (responsive to new ideas), self-awareness (she understood exactly what she could contribute to driving forward the plan in a determined, focused and values-based manner), and ethical awareness (caring and moral attributes that set the standard for all followers). Styles approaches to her leadership included a radical approach to problem solving, inclusivity and empowerment (encouraging all others throughout the organisation and beyond to generate ideas and innovations in support of the sustainability plan), and creativity (new ways of demonstrating sustainability practices). Another important aspect to the leadership qualities of Kadri was her ability to reach out and engage with others who shared her vision. Collaboration was a key mindset that helped forge important and valuable relationships and led to Kadri being appointed as vice chair of the World Business Council for Sustainable Development (WBCSD).

The WBCSD is a global, Chief Executive Officer (CEO) led organisation comprising over 200 companies and around 60 national and regional business councils and partner organisations. The purpose and aim of the organisation is to support the efforts of their members in the quest to become both successful and sustainable by finding ways to maximise the positive impact for shareholders, the environment and communities around the world. Kadri brings a wealth of experience and leadership skills to the organisation and aligns to her commitment to collaboration to solve some of the world's most pressing social and environmental challenges. In particular, Kadri is passionate about the circular economy and how good practices can be implemented across a wide range of industry sectors including the one she represents, the chemicals industry. Much of the knowledge acquired through collaboration can be introduced into the practices of Solvay for positive environmental impacts. For example, the company is working with energy giants Veolia to develop a recycling capability for car batteries that contain precious metals such as cobalt and lithium.

The leadership skills of Ilham Kadri are based on a mix of genetics, background experiences (raised in humble surroundings in Casablanca), relationships (business and social), knowledge (a science-based education), experience (building a career across different industry sectors) and personality (determined, principled, strategic and moral). She has used her leadership skills to transform perceptions of the chemicals industry into one where sustainability practices become evident across the sector. She has ensured that sustainability has become embedded in the purpose of Solvay in a way that would not have been previously thought. Three pillars of sustainability underpin the vision including Climate, Resources and a Better Life. The company has now committed to reducing greenhouse gases twice as fast as originally planned in the first sustainability plan. In resource use, the company has committed to doubling its revenues from the circular economy using more renewables and recycled materials. To support the Better Life pillar, the company seeks to reach gender equality in management by 2035. Kadri believes that it is important to 'unlearn' what has been done in the past and 'relearn' and 'rethink' how sustainability practices will develop into the future. Her leadership skills will play a key role in progressing the vision for Solvay and the other partner organisations she works with.

Questions

1. What are the three pillars of the Solvay One Planet sustainability plan?

2. What traits does Ilham Kadri exhibit in her leadership? Give examples of how these support her vision for Solvay.

3. What leadership skills can she use to contribute to the aims of the World Business Council for Sustainable Development in her role as vice chair?

SUMMARY

This chapter has presented a number of different theoretical perspectives as a means of improving our understanding of sustainability leadership. It first set out the key differences that demarcate leadership from management. It has highlighted the differences between general management and leadership by emphasising the unique set of characteristics that underpin leadership such as personality, emotional intelligence, culture, communications skills and so on. While the debate as to whether leaders are 'born' or 'made' is one that will go on into the future, the discussion in this chapter sets out the various types of leadership and associated behaviours in the context of taking forward the sustainability agenda in organisations. Clearly there is a great deal more research required to fully understand the nature of effective sustainability leadership in different organisational contexts, diverse cultural locations, and complex situations. However, the chapter provided a critical evaluation of the key theoretical perspectives of leadership and contextualised the discussion around the concept of sustainability. Just one of the many key challenges facing modern leaders is the extent to which they want to control the environment in which they operate. The trend in recent years has been for managers to delegate authority and decision-making powers to groups of workers or project teams as a means of harnessing the skills and expertise of workers. The form of leadership evident in organisations has reflected this trend with the emphasis being on traits and styles that inspire and motivate rather than ones that focus on the task. Consequently, it was determined that the development of sustainability management is better served by transformational leadership.

FINAL THOUGHTS

Each of the sections that comprise this book highlight key functions and related aspects of management that contribute to an understanding of how, why and where sustainability development can be supported in organisations around the world. However, perhaps the most important aspect is that of leadership. The planet is surely at a tipping point when it comes to the effect that mankind has on climate change and the consequences of that. The emphasis on economic growth has encouraged behaviours over many decades, even centuries, of the reckless exploitation of the world's resources to feed the seemingly insatiable consumption of goods on a global scale. Where once, ignorance of the effects of this phenomenon on the future of the planet may have elicited some sympathy, the overwhelming and compelling evidence generated from credible science now points to a critical juncture in the Earth's evolution as a result of human activity. Now more than ever the world needs leaders who can create a following that galvanises people into changing their consumption patterns, implement strategic changes in organisations that lower carbon emissions, uses only sustainable energy, supports sustainability practices, and influences governments to support the sustainability agenda through effective and targeted policies and strategies. This chapter has highlighted some exemplars from the world of politics, science and business in the quest to deliver on climate change targets set out in the Paris Agreement. More needs to be done. The droughts, fires, floods and other extreme weather events act as a clarion call for all those privileged enough to be in leadership positions to use their influence, knowledge and communications skills to drive forward the global sustainability management agenda that will help to slow, and then reverse, the level of danger the planet faces and to ensure a secure and habitable environment for future generations.

FURTHER READING

Henriksson, H. and Grunewald, E.W. (2020) *Sustainability Leadership: A Swedish Approach to Transforming Your Company, Your Industry and the World*. London: Palgrave Macmillan.

This substantial contribution to understanding sustainability leadership is authored by a former CEO of Swedish truck manufacturer Scania and a former Chief Sustainability Officer at information technology giant Ericsson. The book uses a three-step guide to effective leadership in organisations set on a transformational pathway towards sustainability. The authors provide valuable experienced-based knowledge on the challenges and opportunities that sustainability leadership brings. The work delivers practical insights around three phases of sustainability leadership from establishing solid foundations around purpose, culture values and principles, to integrating sustainability into the core business, and finally executing the vision.

McAteer, P. (2021) *Sustainability is the New Advantage: Leadership, Change, and the Future of Business*. New York, NY: Anthem Press.

In response to the warming planet and polluted oceans, the author has produced a book that addresses the issue of how leadership can affect the changes needed to address sustainability challenges. The author identifies and discusses the skills, best practices and new ideas that contribute to the understanding of effective leadership and the change agenda that is aimed at informing and educating the next generation of managers around the development of sustainable organisations.

Stanwick, P.A. (2020) *Corporate Sustainability Leadership*. London: Routledge.

This book provides a valuable resource for students interested in sustainability leadership at the corporate level by presenting key issues such as stakeholder theory, organisational change, decision-making, ethics and culture, and strategic thinking in organisations with a sustainability vision. The discussion extends to macro issues including the role of government, suppliers, consumers and the natural world. There are a range of insightful case studies including Volkswagen and Shell that illustrate key leadership challenges and practices.

REFERENCES

CHAPTER 1

Akins, R., Bright, B., Brunson, T. and Wortham, W. (2013) Effective leadership for Sustainable Development, *Journal of Organizational Learning*, 11(1): 29–36.

Banjeri, S. and Willoughby, R. (2019) Addressing the human cost of Assam tea: an agenda for change to respect, protect and fulfil human rights on Assam tea plantations, *Oxfam Briefing Paper*, October 2019. Oxford: Oxfam.

Bartlett, C.A. and Ghoshal, S. (1992) What is a global manager? *Harvard Business Review*, 70(5): 124–132.

Cameron, K.S. and Quinn, R.E. (2006) *Diagnosing and Changing Organizational Culture: Based on the Competing Value Framework* (2nd edn). San Francisco: Wiley.

Daft, R.L. and Benson, A. (2016) *Management*. Boston: Thomson Learning.

Drucker, P.F. (2001) *The Essential Drucker*. New York, NY: Harper Business.

Hanke, J.E. and Wichearn, D. (2013) *Business Forecasting* (9th new international edn). Upper Saddle River, NJ: Pearson.

Kiesnere, K. and Baumgartner, R.J. (2019) Sustainability management in practice: Organizational change for sustainability in smaller larger sized companies in Austria, *Sustainability*, 11(572): 1–40.

Kotter, J.P. (1990) *A Force for Change: How Leadership Differs from Management*. New York, NY: The Free Press.

Levitt, T. (1983) The globalisation of markets, *Harvard Business Review*, May/June: 92–94.

Martin, R., Tyler, P., Storper, M., Evenhuis, E. and Glasmeier, A. (2018) Globalization at a critical conjuncture?, *Cambridge Journal of Regions, Economy and Society*, 11(1): 3–16.

Merchant, K.A. (1982) The control function of management, *Sloan Management Review*, Summer: 43–55.

Mintzberg, H. (1989) *Mintzberg on Management*. New York, NY: Free Press.

Porter, M.E. and Kramer, M.R. (2007) Strategy and society: the link between competitive advantage and corporate social responsibility, *Harvard Business Review*, 84(12): 78–92.

Rhinesmith, S.H. (1992) Global mindsets for global managers, *Training and Development*, 46: 63–69.

Weiss, J.W. (2008) *Business Ethics: A Stakeholder and Issues Management Approach* (5th edn). Cincinnati: South Western College.

Websites

Finlays: www.acre.com/job/global-sustainability-manager-1

Finlays Sustainability Report (2018): www.finlays.net/wp-content/themes/Finlays%20V2/docs/Sustainability-Report-2018.pdf

CHAPTER 2

Berman, S.L., Wicks, A.C., Kotha, S. and Jones, T.M. (1999) Does stakeholder orientation matter? The relationship between stakeholder management models and firm financial performance, *Academy of Management Journal*, 42: 488–506.

Bryson, J.M. (2004) What to do when stakeholders matter: stakeholder identification and analysis techniques, *Public Management Review*, 6(1): 21–53.

Eisenhardt, K.M. and Westcott, B.J. (1988) Paradoxical demands and the creation of excellence: the case of just-in-time manufacturing. In R.E. Quinn and K.S. Cameron (eds), *Paradox and Transformation: Toward a Theory of Change in Organization and Management*. Cambridge, MA: Ballinger.

Epstein, M.J. (2009) *Making Sustainability Work: Best Practices in Managing and Measuring Corporate Social, Environmental, and Economic Impacts*. Oakland, CA: Berrett-Koehler Publishers.

Epstein, M. and Wisner, P. (2001) Good neighbours: implementing social and environmental strategies with the BSC. *Balanced Scorecard Report*, May–June, 3.3. Boston, MA: Harvard Business School Publishing.

Farjoun, M. (2010) Beyond dualism: stability and change as a duality, *Academy of Management Review*, 35(2): 202–205.

Figge, F., Hahn, T., Schaltegger, S. and Wagner, M. (2002) The sustainability balanced scorecard – linking sustainability management to business strategy. *Business Strategy and the Environment*, 11(5): 269–284.

Freeman, R.E. (1984) *Strategic Management: A Stakeholder Approach*. Boston, MA: Pitman.

Freeman, R.E. (1999) Divergent stakeholder theory, *Academy of Management Review*, 24(2): 233–236.

Freeman, R.E. and Gilbert, D.R. (1988) *Corporate Strategy and the Search for Ethics*. Englewood Cliffs, NJ: Prentice Hall.

Freeman, R.E., Parmar, B., Harrison, J.S. and Purnell, A.C. (2010) Stakeholder theory: state of the art, *The Academy of Management Annuls*, 3(1): 405–445.

Gilbert, D.U. and Rasche, A. (2008) Opportunities and problems of standardized ethic initiatives: a stakeholder theory perspective, *Journal of Business Ethics*, 82(3): 755–773.

Hahn, T., Figge, F., Pinkse, J. and Preuss, L. (2017) A paradox perspective on corporate sustainability: descriptive, instrumental, and normative aspects, *Journal of Business Ethics*, 148: 235–248.

Hart, S.L. (2005) *Capitalism at the Crossroads: Next Generation Business Strategies for a Post-Crisis World* (3rd edn). Upper Saddle River, NJ: Financial Times/Prentice Hall.

Hart, S.L. and Milstein, M. (2003) Creating sustainable value, *Academy of Management Executive*, 17(3): 56–67.

Horisch, J., Johnson, M.P. and Schaltegger, S. (2014) Implementation of sustainability management and company size: a knowledge-based view, *Business Strategy and the Environment*, 24(9): 765–779.

Jensen, M.C. (2002) Value maximisation, stakeholder theory, and the corporate objective function, *Business Ethics Quarterly*, 12: 235–256.

Johnson, D.S. (1998) Identification and selection of environmental performance indicators: application of the balanced scorecard approach, *Corporate Environmental Strategy*, 5(4): 34–41.

Jones, P. (2011) *Strategy Mapping for Learning Organizations: Building Agility into Your Balanced Scorecard*. Abingdon: Routledge.

Kaplan, R. and Norton, D. (1992) *The Balanced Scorecard*. Boston, MA: Harvard Business School Press.

Laplume, A.O., Sonpar, K. and Litz, R.A. (2008) Stakeholder theory: reviewing a theory that moves us, *Journal of Management*, 34(6): 1152–1189.

Lozano, R., Carpenter, A. and Huisingh, D. (2015) A review of 'theories of the firm' and their contributions to corporate sustainability, *Journal of Clean Production*, 106(4): 30–42.

Mathur, V.N., Price, A.D.F. and Austin, S. (2008) Conceptualizing stakeholder engagement in the context of sustainability and its assessment, *Construction Management and Economics*, 26: 601–609.

Mitchell, R.K., Agle, B.R. and Woods, D.S. (1997) Toward a theory of stakeholder identification and salience: defining the principle of who and what really counts, *Academy of Management Review*, 22(4): 853–886.

Mitroff, I. (1983) *Stakeholders of the Organizational Mind*. San Francisco, CA: Jossey-Bass.

Montiel, I. and Delgado-Ceballos, J. (2014) Defining and measuring corporate sustainability: are we there yet? *Organization & Environment*, 27(2): 113–139.

Morgan, G. (1996) *Images of Organization*. London: Sage.

Nilsson, E. (2001) Balanced Scorecard – a vehicle for the greening of business meetings? A case study of Telia Nara AB and Skanska facilities management AB, Sweden. Masters Thesis 2000–2001, International Institute for Industrial Environmental Economics (IIEE), Lund University, Sweden.

O'Driscoll, A. (2008) Exploring paradox in marketing: managing ambiguity towards synthesis, *Journal of Business and Industrial Marketing*, 23(2): 95–104.

Ozanne, L.K., Phipps, M., Weaver, T., Carrington, M., Luchs, M., Catlin, J., Gupta, S., Santos, N., Scott, K. and Williams, J. (2016) Managing the tensions at the intersection of the triple bottom line: a paradox theory approach to sustainability management, *Journal of Public Policy & Marketing*, 35(2): 249–261.

Quinn, R.E. (1988) *Beyond Rational Management: Mastering the Paradoxes and Competing Demands of High Performance*. San Francisco, CA: Jossey-Bass.

Quinn, R.E. and Rohrbaugh, J. (1983) A spatial model of effectiveness criteria: towards a competing values approach to organizational analysis, *Management Science*, 29(3): 363–377.

Reed, D. (1999) Stakeholder management theory: a critical theory perspective, *Business Ethics Quarterly*, 9: 453–483.

Sangle, S. and Ram Babu, P. (2007) Evaluating sustainability practices in terms of stakeholders' satisfaction, *International Journal of Business Governance and Ethics*, 3(1): 56–76.

Smith, W.K. and Lewis, M.W. (2011) Towards a theory of paradox: a dynamic equilibrium model of organizing, *Academy of Management Review*, 36(2): 381–400.

Starik, M. and Kanashiro, P. (2013) Toward a theory of sustainability management: uncovering and integrating the nearly obvious, *Organization & Environment*, 20(1): 7–30.

Sundaramurthy, C. and Lewis, M.W. (2003) Control and collaboration: paradoxes of governance, *Academy of Management Review*, 28(3): 397–415.

Tushman, M.L. and O'Reilly, C.A. (1996) The ambidextrous organizations: managing evolutionary and revolutionary change, *California Management Review*, 38(4): 8–30.

Wallis, A.M. (2006) Sustainability indicators: is there consensus among stakeholders? *International Journal of Environment and Sustainable Development*, 5(3): 287–296.

Zingales, F.G.G. and Hockerts, K. (2002) Balanced Scorecard and sustainability: examples from literature and practice. In S. Schaltegger and T. Dyllick (eds), *Sustainable Management and the Balanced Scorecard: Concepts and Case Studies*. Wiesbaden: Gabler, pp. 151–166.

Websites

Ibá: https://iba.org/eng/about-us

Ibá Planted Forests in Brazil and the United Nations Strategic Plan for Forests: www.un.org/esa/forests/wp-content/uploads/2020/01/Iba.pdf

Iberdrola Annual Reports, 2019 Annual Report: www.iberdrola.com/shareholders-investors/annual-reports

Iberdrola, Sustainability: leaders in promoting the SDHs and climate change: www.iberdrola.com/wcorp/gc/prod/en_US/corporativos/docs/IB_Sustainability_Report.pdf

Iberdrola, Statement of non-financial information: Sustainability Report, Financial Year 2019: https://www.iberdrola.com/wcorp/gc/prod/en_US/corporativos/docs/gsm20_IA_SustainabilityReport19_Acc.pdf

Iberdrola, Statement of non-financial information: Sustainability Report, Financial Year 2020: https://www.iberdrola.com/wcorp/gc/prod/en_US/corporativos/docs/IB_Sustainability_Report.pdf

Walmart, Environmental Highlights 2020: https://corporate.walmart.com/esgreport/environmental

Walmart Global Responsibility Report 2018: https://corporate.walmart.com/media-library/document/2018-grr-summary/_proxyDocument?id=00000162-e4a5-db25-a97f-f7fd785a0001

CHAPTER 3

Allio, M.K. (2005) A short, practical guide to implementing strategy, *Journal of Business Strategy*, 26(4): 12–21.

Argyris, C. (1992) *On Organizational Learning*. Cambridge, MA: Blackwell.

Baumgartner, R.J. and Ebner, D. (2010) Corporate sustainability strategies: sustainability profiles and maturity levels, *Sustainable Development*, 18(2): 76–89.

Baumgartner, R.J. and Korhonen, J. (2010) Strategic thinking for sustainable development, *Sustainable Development*, 18: 71–75.

Cavaleri, S. and Shabana, K. (2018) Rethinking sustainability strategies, *Journal of Strategy*, 11(1): 2–17.

Combe, C. (2014) *Introduction to Management*. Oxford: Oxford University Press.

De Wit, B. and Meyer, R. (2014) *Strategy: An International Perspective*, Boston, MA, Cengage Learning.

Dobson, P., Starkey, K. and Richards, J. (2011) *Strategic Management: Issues and Cases* (2nd edn). Oxford: Blackwell.

Formisano, V., Fedele, M. and Calabrese, M. (2018) The strategic priorities in the materiality matrix of the banking enterprise, *The TQM Journal*, 30(5): 589–607.

Hart, S.L. and Milstein, M.B. (2003) Creating sustainable value, *The Academy of Management Executive*, 17(2): 56–67.

Kay, J. (2001) *Foundations of Corporate Success: How Business Strategies Add Value* (2nd edn). Oxford: Oxford University Press.

Long, T.B. (2020) Sustainable business strategy. In W.L. Filho, A.M. Azul, L. Brandli, P.G Ozuyar and T. Wall (eds), *Decent Work and Economic Growth: Encyclopedia of the UN Sustainable Development Goals*. Cham: Springer.

Lynch, R. (2018) *Strategic Management* (8th edn). Harlow: Pearson.

Meinel, C. and Leifer, L. (2011) Design thinking research. In C. Meinel, L. Leifer and H. Plattner (eds), *Design Thinking: Understand – Improve – Apply*. Berlin: Springer, pp. 13–21.

Pelard, F. (2020) *How to be Strategic*. London: Penguin Business.

Porter, M.E. (1980) *Competitive Strategy*. New York, NY: The Free Press.

Porter, M.E. (1985) *Competitive Advantage: Gaining and Sustaining Superior Performance*. New York, NY: The Free Press.

Senge, P. (2006) *The Fifth Discipline: The Art and Practice of the Learning Organization* (2nd edn). New York, NY: Random House Business.

Soderstrom, S.B. and Weber, K. (2019) Organizational structure from interaction: evidence from corporate sustainability efforts, *Administrative Science Quarterly*, 65(1): 226–271.

Wheelen, T.L., Hunger, J.D., Hoffman, A. and Bamford, C. (2017) *Strategic Management and Business Policy: Globalization, Innovation and Sustainability* (global edition). Upper Saddle River, NJ: Pearson.

Zotova, A.S., Kandrashina, E.A., Ivliev, A.D. and Charaeva, M.V. (2016) Evaluation methods basis for strategy development effectiveness of the enterprise, *International Journal of Environmental & Science Education*, 11(14): 6715–6725.

Websites

iea (2020) Global EV Outlook 2020: trends and developments in electric vehicle markets: www.iea.org/reports/global-ev-outlook-2021/trends-and-developments-in-electric-vehicle-markets

Nike: https://about.nike.com/

Patagonia Mission and Vision Statements Analysis (2021): https://mission-statement.com/patagonia/

Unilever: https://www.unilever.com/our-company/

CHAPTER 4

Attenborough, D. (2020) *A Life On Our Planet: My Witness Statement and a Vision for the Future*. London: Penguin Random House.

Boulding, K. (1966) The economics of the coming spaceship Earth. In H. Jarrett (ed.), *Environmental Quality in a Growing Economy*. Baltimore, MD: Johns Hopkins University Press, pp. 3–14.

Dumay, J., Bernardi, C., Guthrie, J. and La Torre, M. (2017) Barriers to implementing the international integrated reporting framework: a contemporary academic perspective, *Meditari Accountancy Research*, 25(4): 461–480.

Eccles, R. and Krzus, M. (2010) *One Report: Integrated Reporting for a Sustainable Strategy*. Hoboken, NJ: Wiley.

Elkington, J. (1994) Towards the sustainable corporation: win-win-win business strategies for sustainable development, *California Business Review*, 36: 90–100.

Elkington, J. (1998) Accounting for the Triple Bottom Line, *Measuring Business Excellence*, 2(3): 18–22.

Elkington, J. (2018) 25 years ago I coined the phrase 'Triple Bottom Line'. Here's why it's time to rethink it. *Harvard Business Review*, June.

Esty, D.C. and Bell, M.L. (2018) Business leadership in global climate change responses, *American Journal of Public Health*, 108(2): 80–84.

Flower, J. (2015) The International Integrated Reporting Council: a story of failure, *Critical Perspectives on Accounting*, 27(1): 1–17.

Geddes, M. (1991) The social audit movement. In D.L. Owen (ed.), *Green Reporting*. London: Chapman, pp. 215–241.

Gray, R., Dillard, J. and Spence, C (2010) A brief re-evaluation of 'The Social Accounting Project': social accounting research as if the world matters. In S. Osborne and A. Ball (eds), *Social Accounting and Public Management*. New York, NY: Routledge.

HMSO (2013) *Foreign Involvement in Critical National Infrastructure: The Implications for National Security*, Cm8629. London: Her Majesty's Stationery Office (HMSO).

Melloni, G. (2015) Intellectual capital disclosure in integrated reporting: an impression management analysis, *Journal of Intellectual Capital*, 16: 661–680.

Milne, M.J. and Gray, R. (2013) W(hither) ecology? The Triple Bottom Line, the Global Reporting Initiative, and corporate sustainability reporting, *Journal of Business Ethics*, 118(1): 13–29.

Mook, L. (2013) *Accounting for Social Value*. Toronto: University of Toronto Press.

Nichols, J., Lawlor, E., Neitzert, E. and Goodspeed, T. (2009) *A Guide to Social Return on Investment*. London: Office of the Third Sector Cabinet Office.

Pun, N., Shen, Y., Guo, Y. and Lu, H. (2016) Apple, Foxconn, and Chinese workers' struggles from a global labor perspective, *Inter-Asia Cultural Studies*, 17(2): 166–185.

Romolini, A. and Gori, E. (2017) Exploring integrated reporting research: results and perspectives, *International Journal of Accounting and Financial Reporting*, 7(1): 3–61.

Scheyvens, R., Banks, G. and Hughes, E. (2016) The private sector and the SDGs: the need to move beyond 'business as usual', *Sustainable Development*, 24(6): 371–382.

Schiermeier, Q. (2015) The science behind the Volkswagen emissions scandal, *Nature*, September.

Schilit, H. and Perler, J. (2018) *Financial Shenanigans: How to Detect Accounting Gimmicks and Fraud in Financial Reporting*. New York, NY: McGraw-Hill.

Slaper, T.F. and Hall, T.J. (2011) The Triple Bottom Line: what is it and how does it work?, *Indiana Business Review*, 86(1): 4–8.

SROI Network (2012) *A Guide to Social Return on Investment.* London: SROI Network.

United Nations (2017) Resolution adopted by the General Assembly on 6 July 2017, Work of the Statistical Commission pertaining to the 2030 Agenda for Sustainable Development (A/RES/71/313).

Winrow, E. and Edwards, R. (2018) Effectiveness and stakeholder impact of the Sistema Cymru – Codi'r To music programme in north Wales: a social return on investment evaluation, *The Lancet*, 392(52): 593.

World Economic Forum and Deloitte (2020) Statement of intent to work together towards comprehensive corporate reporting, summary of alignment discussions among leading sustainability and integrated reporting organisations CDP, CDSB, GRI, IIRC and SASB, impact management project, New York, NY.

Yan, M. and Zhang, D. (2020) From corporate responsibility to corporate accountability, *Hastings Business Law Journal*, 16(1): 43–64.

Websites

Whalen, J. (2020) US charges China's Huawei with racketeering conspiracy to steal US trade secrets in new indictment, *The Washington Post*, 13 February: www.washingtonpost.com/technology/2020/02/13/us-charges-chinas-huawei-with-conspiracy-steal-us-trade-secrets-new-indictment/

CHAPTER 5

Alcaraz, J.M., Marcinkowska, M.W. and Thiruvattal, E. (2011) The UN Principles for Responsible Management Education: sharing (and evaluating) information on progress, *Journal of Global Responsibility*, 2(2): 155–169.

Aldersgate Group (2020) *Upskilling the UK Workforce for the 21st Century*. London: Aldersgate.

Armstrong, S.J. and Sadler-Smith, E. (2008) Learning on demand, at your own pace, in rapid bite-sized chunks: the future shape of management development? *Academy of Management Learning & Education*, 7(4): 571–586.

Bang, J.M. (2005) *Ecovillages: A Practical Guide to Sustainable Communities*. Edinburgh: Floris Books.

Barani, S., Alibeygi, A.H. and Papzan, A. (2018) A framework to identify and develop potential ecovillages: meta-analysis from the studies of world's ecovillages, *Sustainable Cities and Society*, 43: 275–289.

Bhutto, S.A. and Auranzeb, B. (2016) Effects of green human resource management on firm performance: an empirical study on Pakistani firms, *European Journal of Business and Management*, 8(6): 119–125.

Crawford-Lee, M. and Wall, T. (2018) Sustainability 2030: a policy perspective from the University Vocational Awards Council, *Higher Education, Skills and Work-Based Learning*, 8(3): 233–242.

Darnall, N. and Kim, Y. (2012) Which types of environmental management systems are related to greater environmental improvement? *Public Administration Review*, 72: 351–365.

Forray, J., Leigh, J. and Kenworthy, A.L. (2015) Special section cluster on responsible management education: nurturing an emerging PRME ethos, *Academic of Management Learning & Education*, 19(2): 293–296.

Hamid, U. and Johner, O. (2010) The United Nations global compact communication on progress policy: origins, trends and challenges. In A. Rasche and G. Kell (eds), *The United Nations Global Compact: Achievements, Trends and Challenges*. Cambridge: Cambridge University Press, pp. 265–280.

Jaeger, J. and Saha, D. (2020) *10 Charts Show the Economic Benefits of US Climate Action*. Washington DC: World Resources Institute.

Kompas, T., Keegan, M. and Witte, E. (2019) *Australia's Clean Economy Future: Costs and Benefits*. Melbourne: Melbourne Sustainable Society Institute.

Louw, J. (2015) 'Paradigm change' or no real change at all? A critical reading of the UN Principles for Responsible Management Education, *Journal of Management Education*, 39(2): 184–208.

Metcalf, L. and Benn, S. (2013) Leadership for sustainability: an evolution of leadership ability, *Journal of Business Ethics*, 112: 369–384.

Miller, D. and Xu, X. (2016) A fleeting glory: self-serving behavior among celebrated MBA CEO's, *Journal of Management Inquiry*, 25(3): 286–300.

Polman, P. and Bhattacharya, C.B. (2016) Engaging employees to create a sustainable business, *Stanford Social Innovation Review*, 14(4): 3.

Porter, M.E. and Kramer, M.R. (2006) Strategy and society: the link between competitive advantage and corporate social responsibility, *Harvard Business Review*, 84(12): 78–92.

Rajput, S. and Pachauri, V. (2018) A study of employees' perceptions towards green HRM initiatives, *International Journal of Academic Research and Development*, 3(2): 807–810.

Schaltegger, S., Ludeke-Freund, F. and Hansen, E.G. (2016) Business models for sustainability: a co-evolutionary analysis of sustainable entrepreneurship, innovation, and transformation, *Organization and Environment*, 29(3): 264–289.

Tourais, P.C. and Videira, N. (2016) Why, how and what do organizations achieve with the implementation of environmental management systems? – lessons from a comprehensive review on the eco-management and audit scheme, *Sustainability*, 8: 283.

Wall, T. (2017) A manifesto for higher education, skills and work-based learning: through the lens of the manifesto for work, *Higher Education Skills and Work-Based Learning*, 7(3): 304–314.

Websites

IEMA skills and training: www.iema.net/skills/training

KPMG (2016) KPMG in India's GRI Certified Training Course on sustainability reporting: https://assets.kpmg/content/dam/kpmg/pdf/2016/04/KPMG-GRI-Training%20Course-brochure.pdf

Times Higher Education World University Rankings 2020: www.timeshighereducation.com/impactrankings#!/page/0/length/25/sort_by/rank/sort_order/asc/cols/undefined

UK Parliament (2020) Can green jobs support Net Zero Britain ambitions while building back better from coronavirus, 17 November, London: https://committees.parliament.uk/committee/62/environmental-audit-committee/news/131696/can-green-jobs-support-net-zero-britain-ambitions-while-building-back-better-from-coronavirus/

CHAPTER 6

Belz, F. and Peattie, K. (2010) Sustainability marketing – an innovative conception of marketing, *Marketing Review St. Gallen*, 27 (50): 8–15.

Belz, F. and Peattie, K. (2012) *Sustainability Marketing: A Global Perspective*. Chichester: Wiley.

Haller, K., Lee, J. and Cheung, J. (2020) *Meet the 2020 Consumers Driving Change: Why Brands Must Deliver on Omnipresence, Agility and Sustainability*. Armonk, NY: IBM Institute for Business Value in association with the National Retail Federation.

Jang, S., Chung, J. and Rao, V. (2021) The importance of functional and emotional content in online consumer reviews of product sales: evidence from the mobile gaming market, *Journal of Business Research*, 130: 583–593.

Koenig-Lewis, N., Palmer, A., Dermody, J. and Urbye, A. (2014) Consumers' evaluations of ecological packaging – rational and emotional approaches, *Journal of Environmental Psychology*, 37: 94–105.

Kotler, P. (2011) Reinventing marketing to manage the environmental imperative, *Journal of Marketing*, 75 (July): 132–135.

Lim, W.M. (2016) A blueprint for sustainability marketing: defining its conceptual boundaries for progress, *Marketing Theory*, 16(2): 232–249.

Matthes, J., Wonneberger, A. and Schmuck, D. (2014) Consumers' green involvement and persuasive effects of emotional versus functional ads, *Journal of Business Research*, 67: 1885–1893.

McCarthy, E.J. (1960) *Basic Marketing: A Managerial Approach*. Homewood, IL: Irwin.

Rees, J.H., Klug, S. and Bamberg, S. (2014) Guilty conscience: motivating pro-environmental behavior by inducing negative moral emotions, *Climate Change*, 130(3): 439–452.

Schultz, D.E. and Block, M.P. (2015) Beyond brand loyalty: brand sustainability, *Journal of Marketing Communications*, 21(5): 340–355.

Sun, M. and Trudel, R. (2017) The effect of recycling versus trashing on consumption: theory and experimental evidence, *Journal of Marketing Research*, 54(2): 293–305.

Tukker, A. (2004) Product services for a resource-efficient and circular economy – a review, *Journal of Cleaner Production*, 97: 76–91.

Waseema, M. (2017) Enhancing destination competitiveness for a sustainable tourism industry: the case of Maldives, *OIDA International Journal of Sustainable Development*, 10(2): 11–24.

White, K., Habib, R. and Hardisty, D.J. (2019) How to SHIFT consumer behaviors to be more sustainable: a literature review and guiding framework, *Journal of Marketing*, 83(3): 22–49.

Website

Dekker, A (2018) The ultimate guide to emotional marketing: https://blog.hubspot.com/marketing/emotion-marketing

CHAPTER 7

Abbasi, M. and Nilson, F. (2012) Themes and challenges in making supply chains environmentally sustainable, *Supply Chain Management: An International Journal*, 17(5): 517–530.

Bhutta, M.F. (2017) Time for a global response to labour rights violations in the manufacture of health-care goods. *Bull World Health Organisation*, 95: 314.

Carter, C.R. and Jennings, M.M. (2011) Logistics social responsibility: An integrative framework, *Journal of Business Logistics*, 23(1): 145–180.

Carter, C.R. and Rogers, D.R. (2008) A framework of sustainable supply chain management: moving towards new theory, *International Journal of Physical Distribution & Logistics Management*, 38(5): 360–387.

Ekins, P., Domenech, T., Drummond, P., Bleischwitz, R., Hughes, N. and Lotti, L. (2019) The circular economy: what, why, how and where, background paper for an OECD/EC workshop within the workshop series 'Managing environmental and energy transitions for regions and cities', Paris.

Florida, R. (1996) Lean and green: the move to environmentally conscious manufacturing, *California Management Review*, 39(1): 80–105.

Hellweg, S. and Mila i Canals, L. (2016) Emerging approaches, challenges and opportunities in life cycle assessment, *Science*, 344(6188): 1109–1113.

Kloepffer, W. (2008) Life cycle sustainability assessment of products, *International Journal of Life Cycle Assessment*, 13: 89–95.

Muralikrishna, I.V. and Manickam, V. (2017) Life cycle assessment. In I.V. Muralikrishna and V. Manickam, *Environmental Management*. Oxford: Butterworth Heinemann, pp. 57–75.

New, S. (2015) McDonald's and the challenges of a modern supply chain. *Harvard Business Review Digital Articles*, 4 February.

Pagell, M. and Wu, Z. (2009) Building a more complete theory of sustainable supply chain management using case studies of ten exemplars, *Journal of Supply Chain Management*, 45(2): 37–56.

Porter, M.E. and Kramer, M.R. (2002) The competitive advantage of corporate philanthropy, *Harvard Business Review*, 80(12): 56–68.

Seuring, S. and Muller, M. (2008) From a literature review to a conceptual framework for sustainable supply chain management, *Journal of Cleaner Production*, 6(15): 1699–1710.

Slack, N. and Brandon-Jones, A. (2019) *Operations Management* (9th Edn). Harlow: Pearson.

Thomsen, C. (2013) Sustainability (World Commission on Environment and Development Definition). In S.O. Idowu, N. Capaldi, L. Zu and A.D. Gupta (eds), *Encyclopedia of Corporate Social Responsibility*. Berlin, Heidelberg: Springer.

Websites

Allen, A. (2017) Ford grows sustainable supply chain initiative: www.cips.org/supply-management/news/2017/april/ford-expands-sustainable-supply-chain-initiative/

BMA (2020) Fair medical trade: www.bma.org.uk/what-we-do/working-internationally/our-international-work/fair-medical-trade

Chartered Institute of Procurement and Supply: www.cips.org/knowledge/procurement-topics-and-skills/sustainability/

Coyle, F. (2018) The regulation and governance of medical devices in Scotland, Scottish Parliament Information Centre (SPICe) Briefing: https://digitalpublications.parliament.scot/ResearchBriefings/Report/2018/6/29/The-Regulation-and-Governance-of-Medical-Devices-in-Scotland

Dee, H. (2021) Medical and dental instrument manufacturing in the UK: https://my-ibis-world-com.gcu.idm.oclc.org/download/uk/en/industry/2140/7/0/pdf

EC (2015) Circular economy – overview: http://ec.europa/eurostat/web/circular-economy

Ellen MacArthur Foundation (2018) What is the circular economy?: www.ellenmacarthur-foundation.org/circular-economy/concept

First Research (2021) Medical equipment and supplies manufacturing industry profile: proquest.com/library/60b778338f08d85f0bd3b77b/?detoken=XOGhQoj5J8JpYtxoJe44

Ford (2019) Double shot of sustainability: Ford and McDonald's collaborate to convert coffee bean skin into car parts: https://media.ford.com/content/fordmedia/fna/us/en/news/2019/12/04/ford-mcdonalds-collaboration-convert-coffee-bean-waste-into-car-parts.html

Ford (2019) Creating a sustainable supply chain: strong relationships, shared commitment, and capacity building: http://ophelia.sdsu.edu:8080/ford/09-03-2012/microsites/sustainability-report-2011-12/supply-sustainable.html

Ford (2021) Leading a sustainable revolution: Ford and HP collaborate to transform 3D waste into auto parts, an industry first: https://media.ford.com/content/fordmedia/fna/us/en/news/2021/03/25/leading-a-sustainable-revolution.html

Genovese, D. (2019) Ford, McDonald's team up to turn coffee by-products into car parts: www.foxbusiness.com/markets/ford-mcdonalds-sustainability-coffee-beans

Grand Review Research (2021) Surgical equipment market size, share and trends analysis report by product (surgical sutures and staplers, electrosurgical devices), by application (plastic and reconstructive surgery, cardiovascular), and segment forecasts, 2021–2028: www.grandviewresearch.com/industry-analysis/surgical-equipment-market?utm_source=prnewswire&utm_medium=referral&utm_campaign=hc_04-feb-21&utm_term=surgical-equipment-market&utm_content=rd1

Josephs, J. (2021) Maersk: consumers can foot shipping's climate change bill. *BBC News*, 19 February: www.bbc.co.uk/news/business-56126559

KnowTheChain (2020) Company list: https://knowthechain.org/company-lists/

NHS National Services Scotland (2020) NHS National Services Scotland procurement strategy 2020 to 2025: www.nss.nhs.scot/media/1401/procurement-strategy-2020-to-2025.pdf

Trueba, M. Bhutta, M. and Shahvisi, A. (2020) Instruments of health and harm: how the procurement of healthcare goods contributes to global health inequality, *Journal of Medical Ethics*, 47(6): https://jme.bmj.com/content/47/6/423

Waste Framework Directive (Commission Decision EU 2019/1004): https://eur-lex.europa.eu/eli/dec_impl/2019/1004/oj

CHAPTER 8

Abad-Segura, E., Cortez-Garcia, J.F. and Belmonte-Urena, L.J. (2019) The sustainability approach to corporate social responsibility: a global analysis, *Sustainability*, 11: 1–22.

Aboka, Y.E., Cobbinna, S.J., Dzigbodi, D.A. (2018) Review of environmental and health impacts of mining in Ghana, *Journal of Health & Pollution*, 8(17): 43–52.

Ameen, K. (2020) Failure of ethical compliance: the case of Volkswagen, *International Journal of Science and Management Studies*, 3(1): 7–13.

Amos, J.G. (2018) Corporate social responsibility in the mining industry: an exploration of host communities' perceptions and expectations in a developing-country, *Corporate Governance International Journal of Business and Society*, 18(6): 177–1195.

Antonetti, P. and Maklan, S. (2014) Feelings that make a difference: how guilt and pride convince consumers of the effectiveness of sustainable consumption choices, *Journal of Business Ethics*, 124(1): 117–134.

Araya, J., Azocar, C. and Mayol, A. (2019) Exploring the daily life of mining communities: the case of Antofagasta, Chile, *Rural Society*, 28(3): 1037–1656.

Argenti, P.A. (2004) Collaborating with activists: how Starbucks works with NGOs, *California Management Review*, 17(1): 91–116.

Asongu, J.J. (2007) The legitimacy of strategic corporate social responsibility as a marketing tool, *Journal of Business and Public Policy*, 1(1): 1–12.

Audi, R. and Murphy, P.E. (2015) *The Many Faces of Integrity*. Cambridge: Cambridge University Press.

Bird, R., Hall, A.D. and Momente, F. (2007) What corporate social responsibility activities are valued by the market, *Journal of Business Ethics*, 76: 189–206.

Blowfield, M. and Murray, A. (2008) *Corporate Responsibility: A Critical Introduction*. Oxford: Oxford University Press.

Boatright, J. (2007) *Ethics and the Conduct of Business*. Englewood Cliffs, NJ: Pearson Prentice Hall Inc.

Brown, G. (1989) *Where There's Greed: Margaret Thatcher and the Betrayal of Britain's Future*. Edinburgh: Mainstream Publishing.

Carrigan, M. and Attalla, A. (2001) The myth of the ethical consumer: do ethics matter in purchase behaviour?, *Journal of Consumer Marketing*, 18(7): 560–578.

Carvalho, F.P. (2017) Mining industry and sustainable development: time for change. *Food and Energy Security*, 6(2): 61–77.

Combe, C. (2014) *Introduction to Management*. Oxford: Oxford University Press.

Deloitte (2019) *Value Beyond Compliance: A New Paradigm to Create Shared Value for Mines, Communities and Government*. Johannesburg: Deloitte.

Devinney, T.M., Auger, P. and Eckhardt, G.M. (2010) *The Myth of the Ethical Consumer*. Cambridge: Cambridge University Press.

Doane, D. (2005) Beyond corporate social responsibility: minnows, mammoths and markets, *Futures*, 37: 215–229.

Doh, J.P., Howton, S.D., Howton, S.W. and Siegel, D.S. (2010) Does the market respond to an endorsement of social responsibility? The role of institutions, information, and legitimacy, *Journal of Management*, 36(6): 1461–1485.

Entwistle, J.A., Hursthouse, A.S., Reis, P.A.M. and Stewart, A.G. (2019) Metalliferous mine dust: human health impacts and the potential determinants of disease in mining communities, *Human Health Effects of Environmental Pollution*, 5: 67–83.

Etzioni, A. (1964) *Modern Organizations*. Englewood Cliffs, NJ: Prentice Hall.

Fisher, C. and Lovell, A. (2006) *Business Ethics and Values: Individual, Corporate and International Perspectives*. Harlow: Pearson Education.

Friedman, M. (1962) *Capitalism and Freedom*. Chicago: University of Chicago Press.

Harrison, R., Newholm, T. and Shaw, D. (2005) *The Ethical Consumer*. London: Sage Publications.

Irina, N. and Stuckelberger, C. (2013) *Mining Ethics and Sustainability*. Geneva: Globethics.

Koehn, D. (2005) Integrity as a business asset, *Journal of Business Ethics*, 58: 125–136.

Lustgarten, A. (2012) *Run to Failure: BP and the Making of the Deepwater Horizon Disaster*. London: W.W. Norton & Co.

Meesters, M.E. and Behagel, J.H. (2017) The social licence to operate: ambiguities and the neutralization of harm in Mongolia, *Resources Policy*, 53: 274–282.

Mill, J.S. (1861) *Utilitarianism*. New York, NY: Dover Publications.

Miller, C. (2013) *Seeking the Greatest Good: The Conservation Legacy of Gifford Pinchot*. Pittsburgh, PA: University of Pittsburgh Press.

O'Connor, M.P. (1997) John Stuart Mill's utilitarianism and the social ethics of sustainable development, *European Journal of the History of Economic Thought*, 4(3): 478–506.

Oxfam (2014) *Even It Up: Time to End Extreme Inequality*. Cowley: Oxfam GB.

Patalidou, X., Zafeiriou, E., Giannarakis, G. and Sariannidis, N. (2020) The effects of corporate social responsibility performance on financial performance: the case of the food industry, *Benchmarking: An International Journal*, 27(10): 2701–2720.

Pinchot, G. (1998) *Breaking New Ground* (commemorative edition). New York, NY: Kogan Page.

Porter, M.E. and Kramer, M.R. (2006) Strategy and society: the link between competitive advantage and corporate social responsibility, *Harvard Business Review*, December: 78–92.

Rawls, J. (1971) *A Theory of Justice*. Cambridge, MA: Harvard University Press.

REFERENCES

Saeidi, S.P., Sofian, S., Saeidi, P. Saeidi, S.P. and Saeidi, S.A. (2015) How does corporate social responsibility contribute to firm financial performance? The mediating role of competitive advantage, reputation, and customer satisfaction, *Journal of Business Research*, 68(2): 341–350.

Schaltegger, S. and Burritt, R. (2015) Business cases and corporate engagement with sustainability: differentiating ethical motivations, *Journal of Business Ethics*, 147: 241–259.

Smith, A. (1776) *The Wealth of Nations* (ed. Andrew Skinner, 1974). Harmondsworth: Penguin.

Websites

INE (2017) Memoria Censo 2017 [Census Chile 2017], Government of Chile: www.censo2017.cl/memoria/

Perez-Rocha, M. and Moore, J. (2019) How mining companies use excessive legal powers to gamble with Latin American lives, foreign policy in focus: https://fpif.org/how-mining-companies-use-excessive-legal-powers-to-gamble-with-latin-american-lives/

CHAPTER 9

Adonis, J. (2006) *The 4 Key Elements of Employee Engagement*. Sydney: Adonis.

Bertels, S., Papania, L. and Papania, D. (2010) *Embedding Sustainability in Organisational Culture: A Systematic Review of the Body of Knowledge*. Vancouver: Simon Fraser University.

Burrell, G. and Morgan, G. (1979) *Sociological Paradigms and Organisational Analysis*. London: Heinemann.

Burton, E.L. (2015) The impact of risk aversion on economic development in Portugal, *Perspectives on Business and Economics*, 33(4): 27–34.

Combe, C.A. (2014) *Introduction to Management*. Oxford: Oxford University Press.

Deal, T. and Kennedy, A. (1982) *Corporate Cultures: The Rites and Rituals of Corporate Life*. Reading, MA: Addison-Wesley.

Farooq, O., Farooq, M. and Reynaud, E. (2019) Does employees' participation in decision making increase the level of corporate social responsibility and environmental sustainability? An investigation in South Asia, *Sustainability*, 11(2): 511.

Fietz, B. and Gunther, E. (2021) Changing organizational culture to establish sustainability, *Controlling & Management Review*, 3: 32–39.

Gerner, M. (2019) Assessing and managing sustainability in international perspective: corporate sustainability across culture – towards a strategic framework implementation approach, *International Journal of Corporate Social Responsibility*, 4(1): 1–34.

Global Action Plan: Our World, Our Planet (2020) *United in Compassion: Bringing Young People Together to Create a Better World*. London: Global Action Plan.

Handy, C. (1993) *Understanding Organisations* (4th edn). London: Penguin Books.

Kiesnere, A.L. and Baumgartner, R.J. (2019) Sustainability management in practice: organizational change for sustainability in smaller large-sized companies in Austria, *Sustainability*, 11(572): 1–40.

Millar, C., Hind, P. and Magala, S. (2012) Sustainability and the need for change: organisational change and transformational vision, *Journal of Organizational Change Management*, 25(4): 489–500.

Narayan, V. and Adams, C.A. (2017) Transformative change towards sustainability interaction between organisational discourse and organisational practices, *Accounting and Business Research*, 47(3): 344–368.

Ogbonna, E. (1992) Managing organisational culture: fantasy or reality? *Human Resource Management Journal*, 3(2): 42–54.

Oxenswardh, A. (2019) Knowledge sharing and sustainable development. In W. Leal Filho (ed.), *Encyclopedia of Sustainability in Higher Education*. Cham: Springer.

Peters, T.J. and Waterman, R.H. (1982) *In Search of Excellence*. New York: Harper & Row.

Schein, E.H. (1984) Coming to a new awareness of organizational culture, *Sloan Management Review*, Winter: 3–15.

Soderstrom, S.B. and Weber, K. (2019) Organizational structure from interaction: evidence from corporate sustainability efforts, *Administrative Science Quarterly*, 65(1): 226–271.

Websites

Tauranga Carbon Reduction Group: www.facebook.com/taurangacarbonreductiongroup/

CHAPTER 10

Adair, J. (1973) *Action-Centred Leadership*. New York: McGraw-Hill.

Chiu, C-Y., Balkundi, P. and Weinberg, F.J. (2017) When managers become leaders: the role of manager network centralities, social power, and followers' perception of leadership. *The Leadership Quarterly*, 28(2): 334–348.

Cole, M.S., Bruch, H. and Vogel, B. (2005) Development and validation of a measure of organizational energy. Proceedings of the 65th Annual Meeting of the Academy of Management, V1–V6.

Drath, W.H., McCauley, C.D., Palus, C.J., Van Velsor, E., O'Connor, P.M.G. and McGuire, J. (2008) Direction, alignment, commitment: toward a more integrative ontology of leadership, *The Leadership Quarterly,* 19(6): 635–653.

Fleishman, E.A., Zaccaro, S.J. and Mumford, M.D. (1991) Individual differences and leadership – II: an overview, *The Leadership Quarterly*, 3(1): 1–4.

Hackman, J.R. and Wageman, R. (2005) The theory of team coaching, *The Academy of Management Review*, 30(2): 269–287.

Hackman, J.R. and Walton, R.E. (1986) Leading Groups in Organizations. In P.S. Goodman & Associates (eds), *Designing Effective Work Groups*. San Francisco, CA: Jossey-Bass, pp. 72–1190.

Hersey, P. and Blanchard, K. (1977) *The Management of Organizational Behaviour*. Upper Saddle River, NJ: Prentice Hall.

Inceoğlu, I., Thomas, G., Chu, C., Plans, D. and Gerbasi, A. (2018) Leadership behavior and employee well-being: an integrated review and a future research agenda, *The Leadership Quarterly*, 29(1): 179–202.

Klein, K., Ziegert, J.C., Knight, A.P. and Xiao, Y. (2006) Dynamic delegation: shared, hierarchical and deindividualized leadership in extreme action teams, *Administrative Sciences Quarterly*, 51: 590–621.

Kotter, J.P. (1990) *A Force for Change: How Leadership Differs from Management*. New York, NY: The Free Press.

Lewin, K. (1947) *Field Theory in Social Science*. New York: Harper & Row.

Maslow, A.H. (1943) A theory of human motivation, *Psychological Review*, 50(4): 370–396.

McGrath, J.E. (1962) *Leadership Behavior: Requirements for Leadership Training*, Prepared for U.S. Civil Service Commission Office of Career Development, Washington, DC.

Visser, W. and Courtice, P. (2011) Sustainability leadership: linking theory and practice, SSRN Working Paper Series, 21, October 2011.

Zaccaro, S.J., Ritman, A.L. and Marks, M.A. (2001) Team leadership, *The Leadership Quarterly*, 12(4): 451–483.

WEBSITES

Greentown Labs: https://greentownlabs.com/insights-on-the-energy-transition-from-engie-north-america-ceo-gwenaelle-avice-huet/

INDEX